AAT
ASSESSMENT KIT

Intermediate Unit 5
Financial Records and Accounts

In this August 2000 edition

This Assessment Kit for *Unit 5 Financial Records and Accounts* covers both the Central and Devolved Assessments, it contains:

- Thorough reliable updating of material to 1 August 2000 taking into account changes in accounting standards and guidance
- Many additional assessment questions

FOR 2000 AND 2001 ASSESSMENTS

BPP Publishing
August 2000

First edition August 1999
Second edition August 2000

ISBN 0 7517 6237 7 (Previous edition 07517 6156 7)

British Library Cataloguing-in-Publication Data
A catalogue record for this book
is available from the British Library

Published by

BPP Publishing Limited
Aldine House, Aldine Place
London W12 8AW

www.bpp.com

Printed in England by WM Print
45-47 Frederick Street
WALSALL
West Midlands WS2 9NE

We are grateful to the Lead Body for Accounting for permission to reproduce
extracts from the Standards of Competence for Accounting and to the AAT for
permission to reproduce two of their simulations.

Page

INTRODUCTION

Questions   *Answers*

PART A: PRACTICE ACTIVITIES

PART B: DEVOLVED ASSESSMENTS

PRACTICE DEVOLVED ASSESSMENTS

TRIAL RUN DEVOLVED ASSESSMENT

AAT SAMPLE SIMULATION

PART C: CENTRAL ASSESSMENTS

PRACTICE CENTRAL ASSESSMENTS

TRIAL RUN CENTRAL ASSESSMENT (December 1999)

SAMPLE CENTRAL ASSESSMENT

ORDER FORM

REVIEW FORM AND FREE PRIZE DRAW

HOW TO USE THIS ASSESSMENT KIT

Aims of this Assessment Kit

> To provide the knowledge and practice to help you succeed in the devolved and central assessments for Intermediate Unit 5 *Financial Records and Accounts*.

To pass the devolved and central assessments you need a thorough understanding in all areas covered by the standards of competence.

> To tie in with the other components of the BPP Effective Study Package to ensure you have the best possible chance of success.

Interactive Text

This covers all you need to know for devolved and central assessments for Unit 5 *Financial Records and Accounts*. Icons clearly mark key areas of the texts. Numerous activities throughout the text help you practise what you have just learnt.

Assessment Kit

When you have understood and practised the material in the Interactive Text, you will have the knowledge and experience to tackle this Assessment Kit for Unit 5. In addition to practice activities this Kit contains four Devolved Assessments, a Trial run and the AAT's Sample Simulation. It also contains the AAT's Sample Central Assessment.

Recommended approach to this Assessment Kit

(a) To achieve competence in all units, you need to be able to do **everything** specified by the standards. Study the Interactive Text very carefully and do not skip any part of it.

(b) Learning is an **active** process. Do **all** the activities as you work through the Interactive Text so you can be sure you really understand what you have read.

(c) After you have covered the material in the Interactive Text, work through this **Assessment Kit**.

The Kit is divided into three sections:

(i) **Section A** contains a number of Practice Activities. These are short activities which are designed to reinforce your learning and consolidate the practice that you have had doing the activities in the Interactive Text. Try all the Practice Activities. Answers to Practice Activities are to be found at the end of this Section.

(ii) **Section B** contains a number of Practice Devolved Assessments, Trial Run Devolved Assessments and the AAT's Sample Simulation. The Practice Devolved Assessments are designed to test your competence in certain key areas of the Standards of Competence, but are not as comprehensive as the ones set by the AAT. They are a 'warm up' exercise, to develop your studies towards the level of full devolved assessment. Once you have tried the Practice Devolved Assessments, try the Trial Run Devolved Assessments and then try the AAT's Sample Simulation, which gives you the clearest idea of what a full assessment will be like.

(iii) **Section C** contains full central assessment standard questions which give you plenty of practice in the type of question that comes up in the central assessment. Many are taken from central assessments set by the AAT under the previous versions of the Standards. All have full answers with tutorial notes. Finally, we also include the AAT's December 1999 Central Assessment for the Unit with full answers provided by

BPP PUBLISHING

BPP - it is probably best to leave this until last and then attempt it as a 'mock' under 'exam conditions'. This will help you develop some key techniques in selecting questions and allocating time correctly. For guidance on this, please see Assessment Strategy on page (xiii).

This approach is only a suggestion. You or your college may well adapt it to suit your needs.

Remember this is a **practical** course.

(a) Try to relate the material to your experience in the workplace or any other work experience you may have had.

(b) Try to make as many links as you can to your study of the other Units at Intermediate level.

A **helpful tip**: photocopy the pages containing the blank proformas, especially the trial balance, this makes it easier to work on the assessments as you flick from page to page.

UNIT 5 STANDARDS OF COMPETENCE

The structure of the Standards for Unit 5

The Unit commences with a statement of the **knowledge and understanding** which underpin competence in the Unit's elements.

The Unit of Competence is then divided into **elements of competence** describing activities which the individual should be able to perform.

Each element includes:

- A set of **performance criteria** which define what constitutes competent performance

- A **range statement** which defines the situations, contexts, methods etc in which competence should be displayed

- **Evidence requirements**, which state that competence must be demonstrated consistently, over an appropriate time scale with evidence of performance being provided from the appropriate sources

- **Sources of evidence**, being suggestions of ways in which you can find evidence to demonstrate that competence.

The elements of competence for Unit 5: *Financial Records and Accounts* are set out below. Knowledge and understanding required for the Unit as a whole are listed first, followed by the performance criteria and range statements for each element. Performance criteria are cross-referenced below to chapters in the Unit 5 *Financial Records and Accounts* Interactive Text.

Unit 5:   Maintaining financial records and preparing accounts

What is the unit about?

This unit is concerned with the **collecting and recording of information for the purpose of preparing accounts and maintaining effective records.** It involves identifying the types of information that are required, recording it, making any appropriate calculations or adjustments and maintaining the appropriate records.

The unit requires you to have responsibility for collecting all the relevant information for preparing accounts and presenting it to your supervisor in the form of a trial balance or an extended trial balance. Also required are communication responsibilities relating to handling queries, making suggestions for improvements and maintaining confidentiality.

BPP PUBLISHING

Knowledge and understanding

The business environment

- Types and characteristics of different assets and key issues relating to the acquisition and disposal of capital assets (Element 5.1)

- Relevant legislation and regulations (Elements 5.1, 5.2, 5.3 & 5.4)

- Main requirements of relevant SSAPs (Elements 5.1, 5.2, 5.3 & 5.4)

- Methods of recording information for the organisational accounts of: sole traders; partnerships; manufacturing accounts; club accounts (Element 5.2)

- Understanding the structure of the organisational accounts of: sole traders; partnerships; manufacturing accounts; club accounts (Element 5.2)

- The need to present accounts in the correct form (Element 5.3)

- The importance of maintaining the confidentiality of business transactions (Elements 5.1, 5.2, 5.3 & 5.4)

Accounting techniques

- Methods of depreciation: straight line; reducing balance (Element 5.1)

- Accounting treatment of capital items sold, scrapped or otherwise retired from service (Element 5.1)

- Use of plant registers and similar subsidiary records (Element 5.1)

- Use of transfer journal (Elements 5.1, 5.2, 5.3 & 5.4)

- Methods of funding: part exchange deals (Element 5.1)

- Accounting treatment of accruals and prepayments (Elements 5.2, 5.3 & 5.4)

- Methods of analysing income and expenditure (Element 5.2)

- Methods of restructuring accounts from incomplete evidence (Element 5.3)

- Identification and correction of different types of error (Elements 5.3 & 5.4)

- Making and adjusting provisions (Elements 5.3 & 5.4)

Accounting principles and theory

- Basic accounting concepts and principles - matching of income and expenditure within an accounting period, historic cost, accruals, consistency, prudence, materiality (Elements 5.1, 5.2, 5.3 & 5.4)

- Principles of double entry accounting (Elements 5.1, 5.2, 5.3 & 5.4)

- Distinction between capital and revenue expenditure, what constitutes capital expenditure (Element 5.1)

- Function and form of accounts for income and expenditure (Element 5.2)

- Function and form of a trial balance, profit and loss account and balance sheet for sole traders, partnerships, manufacturing accounts and club accounts (Elements 5.3 & 5.4)

- Basic principles of stock valuation: cost or NRV; what is included in cost (Elements 5.3 & 5.4)

- Objectives of making provisions for depreciation and other purposes (Elements 5.3 & 5.4)

- Function and form of final accounts (Element 5.4)

The organisation

- Understanding of the ways the accounting systems of an organisation are affected by its organisational structure, its administrative systems and procedures and the nature of its business transactions (Elements 5.1, 5.2, 5.3 & 5.4)

Element 5.1 Maintain records relating to capital acquisition and disposal

Performance criteria	Chapters in the Text
1 Relevant details relating to capital expenditure are correctly entered in the appropriate records	5
2 The organisation's records agree with the physical presence of capital items	5
3 All acquisition and disposal costs and revenues are correctly identified and recorded in the appropriate records	5
4 Depreciation charges and other necessary entries and adjustments are correctly calculated and recorded in the appropriate records	5
5 The records clearly show the prior authority for capital expenditure and disposal and indicate the approved method of funding and disposal	5
6 Profit and loss on disposal is correctly calculated and recorded in the appropriate records	5
7 The organisation's policies and procedures relating to the maintenance of capital records are adhered to	5
8 Lack of agreement between physical items and records are identified and either resolved or referred to the appropriate person	5
9 When possible, suggestions for improvements in the way the organisation maintains its capital records are made to the appropriate person	5

Range statement

1 Methods of calculating depreciation: straight line; reducing balance	5
2 Records: asset register; ledger	5

Evidence requirements

- Competence must be demonstrated consistently, over an appropriate timescale with evidence of performance being provided of records being maintained.

Sources of evidence

(These are examples of sources of evidence, but candidates and assessors may be able to identify other, appropriate sources.)

- *Observed performance*, eg maintaining records of capital acquisition and disposal; calculating adjustments; calculating profit and loss on disposal; resolving discrepancies, unusual features or queries; making suggestions for improvements in the maintenance of capital records and accounts.

- *Work produced by the candidate,* eg a fixed asset register; a completed fixed asset reconciliation; a ledger; journals; invoices; minutes from meetings; cash books; disposals account or equivalent; correspondence relating to capital acquisition or disposal; authorisation for expenditure.

- *Authenticated testimonies from relevant witnesses*

- *Personal accounts of competence,* eg report of performance.

- *Other sources of evidence to prove competence of knowledge and understanding where it is not apparent from performance*, eg reports and working papers; performance in independent assessment; performance in simulation; responses to verbal questioning.

Element 5.2 Record income and expenditure

Performance criteria	Chapters in the Text
1 All income and expenditure is correctly identified and recorded in the appropriate records	2
2 Relevant accrued and prepaid income and expenditure is correctly identified and adjustments are made	8
3 The organisation's policies, regulations, procedures and timescales in relation to recording income and expenditure are observed	2
4 Incomplete data is identified and either resolved or referred to the appropriate person	10

Range statement

1 Records: day book; journal; ledger	1, 2, 7

Evidence requirements

- Competence must be demonstrated consistently, over an appropriate timescale with evidence of performance being provided from involvement with account records.

Sources of evidence

(These are examples of sources of evidence, but candidates and assessors may be able to identify other, appropriate sources.)

- *Observed performance*, eg recording income and expenditure; checking accounts; making adjustments; resolving incomplete data.

- *Work produced by the candidate,* eg nominal ledger listing; accruals and prepayments listings; petty cash book; journals for accruals and prepayments (reversibles) (recurring); invoices; minutes from meetings concerning incomplete data; cash books; disposals account or equivalent; correspondence relating to income and expenditure.

- *Authenticated testimonies from relevant witnesses.*

- *Personal accounts of competence,* eg report of performance.

- *Other sources of evidence to prove competence of knowledge and understanding where it is not apparent from performance*, eg reports and working papers; performance in independent assessment; performance in simulation; responses to verbal questioning.

Element 5.3 Collect and collate information for the preparation of final accounts

Performance criteria		Chapters in the Text
1	Relevant accounts and reconciliations are correctly prepared to allow the preparation of final accounts	7
2	All relevant information is correctly identified and recorded	6
3	Investigations into business transactions are conducted with tact and courtesy	6
4	The organisation's policies, regulations, procedures and timescales relating to preparing final accounts are observed	6
5	Discrepancies and unusual features are identified and either resolved or referred to the appropriate person	10
6	The trial balance is accurately prepared and, where necessary, a suspense account is opened and reconciled	2, 7

Range statement

1	Sources of information: ledger; bank reconciliation; creditors' reconciliation; debtors' reconciliation	6, 7
2	Discrepancies and unusual features: insufficient data has been provided; inconsistencies within the data	10

Evidence requirements

- Competence must be demonstrated consistently with evidence of performance being provided of collecting and collating information for sets of final accounts from different types of organisation.

Sources of evidence

(These are examples of sources of evidence, but candidates and assessors may be able to identify other, appropriate sources.)

- *Observed performance,* eg preparing accounts and reconciliations; investigating client's business transactions; preparing the trial balance; opening and reconciling a suspense account; resolving discrepancies or unusual features.

- *Work produced by the candidate,* eg control accounts/adjusted control accounts; bank reconciliations; trial balance; audit trail; suspense account; minutes from meetings; general ledger printout; copy of the extended trial balance; nominal ledger listing; correspondence relating to income and expenditure.

- *Authenticated testimonies from relevant witnesses.*

- *Personal accounts of competence,* eg report of performance.

- *Other sources of evidence to prove competence of knowledge and understanding where it is not apparent from performance,* eg reports and working papers; performance in independent assessment; performance in simulation; responses to verbal questioning.

Element 5.4 Prepare the extended trial balance

		Chapters in the Text
Performance criteria		
1	Totals from the general ledger or other records are correctly entered on the extended trial balance	12
2	Material errors disclosed by the trial balance are identified, traced and referred to the appropriate authority	12
3	Adjustments not dealt with in the ledger accounts are correctly entered on the extended trial balance	12
4	An agreed valuation of closing stock is correctly entered on the extended trial balance	9, 12
5	The organisation's policies, regulations, procedures and timescales in relation to preparing extended trial balances are observed	12
6	Discrepancies, unusual features or queries are identified and either resolved or referred to the appropriate person	12
7	The extended trial balance is accurately extended and totalled	12
Range statement		
1	Adjustments relating to: accruals; prepayments	12

Evidence requirements

- Competence must be demonstrated consistently, over an appropriate timescale with evidence of performance being provided from preparing an extended trial balance across the range.

Sources of evidence

(These are examples of sources of evidence, but candidates and assessors may be able to identify other, appropriate sources.)

- *Observed performance,* eg entering totals and adjustments on the extended trial balance; tracing and correcting material errors; resolving discrepancies, unusual features or queries; extending and totalling the trial balance.

- *Work produced by the candidate,* eg extended trial balance; ledger accounts; transfer journal.

- *Authenticated testimonies from relevant witnesses.*

- *Personal accounts of competence,* eg report of performance.

- *Other sources of evidence to prove competence of knowledge and understanding where it is not apparent from performance,* eg reports and working papers; performance in independent assessment; performance in simulation; responses to verbal questioning.

ASSESSMENT STRATEGY

This unit is assessed by both **central assessment** and by **devolved assessment**.

Central Assessment

A central assessment is a means of collecting evidence that you have the **essential knowledge and understanding** which underpins competence. It is also a means of collecting evidence across the **range of contexts** for the standards, and of your ability to **transfer skills**, knowledge and understanding to different situations. Thus, although central assessments contain practical tests linked to the performance criteria, they also focus on the underpinning knowledge and understanding. You should in addition expect each central assessment to contain tasks taken from across a broad range of the standards.

Section 1

This section will include one or more accounting exercises from the following:

- **Trial Balance**

  Example task: preparation of a trial balance from a list of balances given.

- **Extended Trial Balance**

  Example tasks: completion of the adjustments columns from information given. Extension of relevant figures into profit and loss and balance sheet columns.

  NOTE: exercises involving the extended trial balance will not necessarily include all of the columns. Tasks could, for example, be based entirely around the initial balances and the adjustments columns. In this case, the remaining columns would not be required for the assessment.

- **Identification and Correction of Errors**

  Example tasks: candidates given a number of transactions and entries made. Errors and correcting journal entries to be identified.

- **Suspense Accounts**

  Example tasks: suspense account required to balance a trial balance. Correcting entries to be identified to eliminate the suspense account balance.

- **Bank Reconciliation Statements**

  Example tasks: preparation of a statement to reconcile the opening balances and preparation of a further statement to reconcile the closing balances of a cash book and a bank statement.

- **Control Accounts**

  Example tasks: preparation of a debtors control account from information given and reconciliation with the total of the sales ledger balances.

  There will also be a number of short answer questions from across the range of the Standards for the unit.

Section 2

This section will comprise of one or more practical exercises concerned with the processing, restructuring and production of information for different types of organisations. Candidates will be expected to be able to produce:

- Manufacturing accounts from data given;

- Information from data given and / or incomplete records for sole traders, partnerships and clubs.

There will also be a number of short answer questions from across the range of the standards for the unit.

EXAMPLES. The processing, restructuring and production of information includes:

- calculation of opening and / or closing capital (accumulated fund for clubs);

- restructuring the cash and / or bank account;

- preparation of total debtors account and total creditors account to calculate, for example, sales and purchases;

- production of simple statements showing the calculation of gross profit and / or net profit and listing assets, liabilities and capital (or equivalent for clubs). These statements to summarise figures or to ascertain missing items of information;

- use of mark up and margin (the use of other accounting ratios is outside the scope of this unit);

- production of other statements and / or restructured ledger accounts. For example, to calculate expenses paid, expenses profit and loss figures, accruals and prepayments, profit or loss on the sale of an asset, provisions and subscriptions for the period.

Central Assessment Technique

Passing central assessments at this level is half about having the knowledge, and half about doing yourself full justice on the day. You must have the right **technique**.

The day of the central assessment

1 Set at least one **alarm** (or get an alarm call) for a morning central assessment

2 Have **something to eat** but beware of eating too much; you may feel sleepy if your system is digesting a large meal

3 Allow plenty of **time to get to where you are sitting the central assessment**; have your route worked out in advance and listen to news bulletins to check for potential travel problems

4 **Don't forget** pens, pencils, rulers, erasers

5 Put **new batteries** into your calculator and take a spare set (or a spare calculator)

6 **Avoid discussion** about the central assessment with other candidates outside the venue

Technique in the central assessment

1 *Read the instructions (the 'rubric') on the front of the paper carefully*

Check that the format of the paper hasn't changed. It is surprising how often assessors' reports remark on the number of students who attempt too few questions. Make sure that you are planning to answer the **right number of questions**.

2   *Select questions carefully*

Read through the paper once - don't forget that you are given 15 minutes' reading time - then quickly jot down key points against each question in a second read through. Select those questions where you could latch on to 'what the question is about' - but remember to check carefully that you have got the right end of the stick before putting pen to paper. Use your 15 minutes' reading time wisely.

3   *Plan your attack carefully*

Consider the **order** in which you are going to tackle questions. It is a good idea to start with your best question to boost your morale and get some easy marks 'in the bag'.

4   *Check the time allocation for each section of the paper*

Time allocations are given for each section of the paper. When the time for a section is up, you must go on to the next section. Going even one minute over the time allowed brings you a lot closer to failure.

5   *Read the question carefully and plan your answer*

Read through the question again very carefully when you come to answer it. Plan your answer to ensure that you **keep to the point**. Two minutes of planning plus eight minutes of writing is virtually certain to earn you more marks than ten minutes of writing.

6   *Produce relevant answers*

Particularly with written answers, make sure you **answer the question set**, and not the question you would have preferred to have been set.

7   *Gain the easy marks*

Include the obvious if it answers the question, and don't try to produce the perfect answer.

Don't get bogged down in small parts of questions. If you find a part of a question difficult, get on with the rest of the question. If you are having problems with something, the chances are that everyone else is too.

8   *Produce an answer in the correct format*

The assessor will state **in the requirements** the format in which the question should be answered, for example in a report or memorandum.

9   *Follow the assessor's instructions*

You will annoy the assessor if you ignore him or her. The **assessor will state** whether he or she wishes you to 'discuss', 'comment', 'evaluate' or 'recommend'.

10   *Lay out your numerical computations and use workings correctly*

Make sure the layout fits the **type of question** and is in a style the assessor likes.

Show all your **workings** clearly and explain what they mean. Cross reference them to your answer. This will help the assessor to follow your method (this is of particular importance where there may be several possible answers).

11   *Present a tidy paper*

You are a professional, and it should show in the **presentation of your work**. Students are penalised for poor presentation and so you should make sure that you write legibly, label diagrams clearly and lay out your work neatly. Markers of scripts

BPP PUBLISHING

each have hundreds of papers to mark; a badly written scrawl is unlikely to receive the same attention as a neat and well laid out paper.

12 *Stay until the end of the central assessment*

Use any spare time **checking and rechecking** your script.

13 *Don't worry if you feel you have performed badly in the central assessment*

It is more than likely that the other candidates will have found the assessment difficult too. Don't forget that there is a competitive element in these assessments. As soon as you get up to leave the venue, **forget** that central assessment and think about the next - or, if it is the last one, celebrate!

14 *Don't discuss a central assessment with other candidates*

This is particularly the case if you **still have other central assessments to sit**. Even if you have finished, you should put it out of your mind until the day of the results. Forget about assessments and relax!

Devolved Assessment

Devolved assessment is a means of collecting evidence of your ability to carry out **practical activities** and to **operate effectively in the conditions of the workplace** to the standards required. Evidence may be collected at your place of work or at an Approved Assessment Centre by means of simulations of workplace activity, or by a combination of these methods.

If the Approved Assessment Centre is a **workplace**, you may be observed carrying out accounting activities as part of your normal work routine. You should collect documentary evidence of the work you have done, or contributed to, in an **accounting portfolio**. Evidence collected in a portfolio can be assessed in addition to observed performance or where it is not possible to assess by observation.

Where the Approved Assessment Centre is a **college or training organisation**, devolved assessment will be by means of a combination of the following.

- Documentary evidence of activities carried out at the workplace, collected by you in an **accounting portfolio**.

- Realistic **simulations** of workplace activities. These simulations may take the form of case studies and in-tray exercises and involve the use of primary documents and reference sources.

- **Projects and assignments** designed to assess the Standards of Competence.

If you are unable to provide workplace evidence you will be able to complete the assessment requirements by the alternative methods listed above.

Possible assessment methods

Where possible, evidence should be collected in the workplace, but this may not be a practical prospect for you. Equally, where workplace evidence can be gathered it may not cover all elements. The AAT regards performance evidence from simulations, case studies, projects and assignments as an acceptable substitute for performance at work, provided that they are based on the Standards and, as far as possible, on workplace practice.

There are a number of methods of assessing accounting competence. The list below is not exhaustive, nor is it prescriptive. Some methods have limited applicability, but others are capable of being expanded to provide challenging tests of competence.

Assessment method	Suitable for assessing
Performance of an accounting task either in the workplace or by simulation: eg preparing and processing documents, posting entries, making adjustments, balancing, calculating, analysing information etc by manual or computerised processes	**Basic task competence.** Adding supplementary oral questioning may help to draw out underpinning knowledge and understanding and highlight your ability to deal with contingencies and unexpected occurrences
General case studies. These are broader than simulations. They include more background information about the system and business environment	Ability to **analyse a system** and suggest ways of modifying it. It could take the form of a written report, with or without the addition of oral or written questions
Accounting problems/cases: eg a list of balances that require adjustments and the preparation of final accounts	Understanding of the **general principles of accounting** as applied to a particular case or topic
Preparation of flowcharts/diagrams. To illustrate an actual (or simulated) accounting procedure	**Understanding of the logic** behind a procedure, of controls, and of relationships between departments and procedures. Questions on the flow chart or diagram can provide evidence of underpinning knowledge and understanding
Interpretation of accounting information from an actual or simulated situation. The assessment could include non-financial information and written or oral questioning	**Interpretative competence**
Preparation of written reports on an actual or simulated situation	**Written communication skills**
Analysis of critical incidents, problems encountered, achievements	Your ability to handle **contingencies**
Listing of likely errors eg preparing a list of the main types of errors likely to occur in an actual or simulated procedure	Appreciation of the range of **contingencies** likely to be encountered. Oral or written questioning would be a useful supplement to the list
Outlining the organisation's policies, guidelines and regulations	Performance criteria relating to these aspects of competence. It also provides evidence of competence in **researching information**
Objective tests and short-answer questions	**Specific knowledge**
In-tray exercises	Your **task-management ability** as well as technical competence
Supervisors' reports	**General job competence**, personal effectiveness, reliability, accuracy, and time management. Reports need to be related specifically to the Standards of Competence
Analysis of work logbooks/diaries	**Personal effectiveness**, time management etc. It may usefully be supplemented with oral questioning
Oral questioning	**Knowledge and understanding** across the range of competence including organisational procedures, methods of dealing with unusual cases, contingencies and so on. It is often used in conjunction with other methods.

Formal written answers to questions

Knowledge and understanding of the **general accounting environment** and its impact on particular units of competence.

Part A
Practice Activities

Country Crafts (December 1993)

The suggested time allocation for this extended trial balance exercise is 80 minutes.

Country Crafts Ltd is a small business started in 1989. It buys in craft items, for example, pottery, hand-made clothes and wooden toys from a large number of small craft producers, and then sells them to craft shops throughout the country.

The rented premises consist of a warehouse containing racks and bins to hold the craft products along with an adjoining office and garage. The company owns two delivery vans, used for both collections and deliveries, and two company cars.

The company was started by two friends, Sandip Patel and Abdul Mohim, who met on a small business training course in Leicester. Sandip has responsibility for buying and selling and has built up a network of small craftworkers who make stock for him. Abdul is responsible for the running of the warehouse and the office and the administration of the business.

In addition to the two owners, the business employs two drivers, a warehouseman, two accounts clerks and a secretary.

You are the senior of the two accounts clerks and you are responsible for the nominal ledger.

The company's accounts are currently operated using a manual system, but computerisation of the accounts should take place in the near future and some equipment has recently been purchased.

The sales ledger holds at present about 100 accounts; the company has no cash customers.

All purchases of craft products are on credit and the purchase ledger contains about 80 accounts.

There are very few cash transactions. Any that do occur, for example, window cleaning, office sundries and travel expenses, are dealt with by a simple petty cash system. A £50 float is maintained, expenditure is recorded in a simple petty cash book and at irregular intervals the expenditure is posted to the nominal ledger.

Depreciation policy

Rates:	Motor vehicles	25% pa	straight line
	Office furniture	10% pa	straight line
	Computer equipment	$33\frac{1}{3}$% pa	straight line

Depreciation is charged a full year in the year of purchase and is not charged for in the year of sale.

Zero scrap values are assumed.

Fixed asset information

Motor vehicles

Delivery vans	H247AFE	K174RFU
Date of purchase	9.8.90	12.8.92
Cost	£16,200	£19,800

Company cars	J168TFE	J169TFE
Date of purchase	11.9.91	11.9.91
Cost	£9,200	£9,200

Part A: Practice activities

Office furniture

All office furniture was purchased upon incorporation of the business on 1 September 1989.

Cost   £4,850

Computer equipment

Date of purchase   1 June 1993
Cost   £16,830

Mark-up policy

The company marks up all its products by 100% on cost.

Data

(a) Listed below is the company's trial balance at 31 December 1993.

COUNTRY CRAFTS LIMITED
TRIAL BALANCE AS AT 31 DECEMBER 1993

	Dr £	Cr £
Motor vans (cost)	36,000	
Motor cars (cost)	18,400	
Office furniture (cost)	4,850	
Computer equipment (cost)	16,830	
Motor vans (provision for dep'n)		17,100
Motor cars (provision for dep'n)		9,200
Office furniture (provision for dep'n)		1,940
Computer equipment (provision for dep'n)		
Stock	24,730	
Debtors control	144,280	
Bank		610
Cash	50	
Creditors control		113,660
Sales		282,490
Purchases	152,140	
Rent	12,480	
Heat and light	1,840	
Wages and salaries	75,400	
Office expenses	7,900	
Motor expenses	14,890	
Depreciation (motor vans)		
Depreciation (office furniture)		
Depreciation (computer equipment)		
Share capital		50,000
Profit and loss		35,850
VAT		12,640
Suspense	13,700	
	523,490	523,490

(b) Adjustments need to be made for the following.

(i) On 2 December 1993 a new delivery van, L673NFU, was purchased for £22,600. Van H247AFE was given in part exchange, the balance of £17,600 being paid for by cheque and debited to the suspense account.

(ii) On 4 December 1993, as a cost-saving measure, company car J168TFE was sold for £3,900 and the receipt credited to the suspense account.

(iii)   On 20 December 1993 the company had allowed a local organisation to use its car park and adjacent field for a Car Boot Sale. For this service the company was paid £250.00. This amount had been credited to the sales account.

(c)   The following additional matters need to be taken into account.

(i)   Depreciation for the year ended 31 December 1993 is to be provided for.

(ii)   On 15 December 1993 a rack full of china craft products fell in the warehouse. These products, valued at £2,300 at selling price, were so badly damaged that they had to be thrown away. The Raven Moon Insurance Company have agreed to compensate for the damage except for the first £200. A claim has been submitted, but so far no payment has been received.

(iii)   The stocktake on 30 December 1993 revealed stock at cost price of £31,640.

Two batches of stock, however, were of particular note.

(1)   A batch of Baby Beatrice mugs, value at selling price £320, were judged to be saleable for only £120.

(2)   A batch of Windsor Fire Damage plates, value at selling price £620, were judged to be saleable for only £350.

(iv)   Several small customers had been going out of business recently, probably because of the recession. The company's accountant had therefore judged it prudent to create a provision for doubtful debts representing 5% of the trade debtors figure at the year end.

(v)   Petty cash transactions for December were as follows.

December 3	Window cleaning	£10.00
December 8	Tea and coffee	£4.40
December 12	Xmas decorations	£28.60
December 20	Petty cash float replenished	£50.00

These transactions, including the withdrawal from the bank, have not yet been entered into the company's books.

(vi)   The electricity bill for the September, October, November quarter for £315 had been received on 16 December and entered into the purchase ledger. It is normal for the electricity bill for the December, January, February quarter to be double that for the previous quarter.

(vii)   The rent of £7,488 per annum is paid annually in advance on 1 September.

Task 1

Prepare journal entries for the transactions listed in (b) above. Narratives are required. Use the journal form on Page 6.

Task 2

Enter all the account balances, including those adjusted in Task 1, in the first two columns of the extended trial balance. Use the blank ETB on Page 7.

Task 3

Make appropriate entries in the adjustment columns of the extended trial balance.

BPP PUBLISHING

Task 4

Extend the figures into the extended trial balance columns for profit and loss account and balance sheet. Total all columns, transferring the balance of profit or loss as appropriate.

A suggested answer to this exercise is given on page 35.

Details	DR £	CR £
JOURNAL		

COUNTRY CRAFTS	Trial balance		Adjustments		Profit and Loss a/c		Balance Sheet	
Account	Debit £	Credit £	Debit £	Credit £	Debit £	Credit £	Debit £	Credit £
Motor vans (cost)								
Motor cars (costs)								
Office furniture (cost)								
Computer equipment (cost)								
Motor vans (prov for depreciation)								
Motor cars (prov for depreciation)								
Office furniture (prov for depreciation)								
Computer equipment (prov for depreciation)								
Stock								
Debtors control								
Bank								
Cash								
Creditors control								
Sales								
Purchases								
Rent								
Heat and light								
Wages and salaries								
Office expenses								
Motor expenses								
Depreciation (motor vans)								
Depreciation (motor cars)								
Depreciation (office furniture)								
Depreciation (computer equipment)								
Share capital								
Profit and loss								
VAT								
Subtotal								
Profit for the year								
TOTAL								

Part A: Practice activities

Futon Enterprises (June 1994)

The suggested time allocation for this extended trial balance exercise is 80 minutes.

Jason Sarmiento, trading as Futon Enterprises, is a sole trader assembling and selling futons. A futon is a Japanese-style bed, consisting of a slatted wooden frame and a mattress. Jason buys in the pre-cut timber and the mattresses and assembles the futons for sale through his retail shop in Lincoln and by mail order.

The assembly takes place in a small workshop to the rear of the shop and is carried out by a full-time assembler. The business also employs a driver, a secretary and you, the accounts clerk. Jason spends most of his time in the shop and dealing with the mail order side of the business.

The business accounts are currently operated using a manual system, though Jason is actively engaged in investigating computerised accounting systems.

A very simple sales ledger is operated and the purchase ledger contains about 20 accounts. There are few cash transactions. Any that do occur are handled through a traditional petty cash book. A £50 cash float is maintained and at weekly intervals the expenditure is posted to the nominal ledger and the float replenished.

Accounting policies

1 *Manufacturing*

Purchases of raw materials are posted to a materials account. The assembler's wages are posted to the production wages account. No separate production overheads account is maintained.

It has been agreed that finished goods stocks should be valued at a standard cost of production, calculated as follows per futon.

	£
Materials	36.00
Production wages	7.00
Overheads	5.00
	48.00

2 *Depreciation*

Rates:	Assembling machinery	10% per annum straight line
	Delivery van	30% per annum reducing balance
	Furniture and fittings	20% per annum straight line

Depreciation is charged a full year in the year of purchase and is not charged in the year of sale. Zero scrap values are assumed.

3 *Mark-up*

The company normally marks up all its products at 75% on standard production costs.

Fixed asset information

	Date of purchase	Cost £	£
Assembling machinery	1.6.90		3,650
Delivery van (see note (b)(i) below)	1.8.93		12,400
Furniture and fittings			
Shop fittings	1.6.90	7,200	
Office furniture	1.6.90	2,350	
Reception (materials only) (see note (b)(ii) below)	1.9.93	1,240	
			10,790

Data

(a)   Listed below is the company's trial balance at 31 May 1994.

FUTON ENTERPRISES
TRIAL BALANCE AS AT 31 MAY 1994

	Dr £	Cr £
Delivery vans (cost)	12,000	
Delivery vans (provision for depreciation)		7,884
Assembling machinery (cost)	3,650	
Assembling machinery (provision for depreciation)		1,095
Furniture and fittings (cost)	10,790	
Furniture and fittings (provision for depreciation)		5,730
Raw materials stock	1,320	
Finished goods stock	1,440	
Sales ledger total	1,860	
Bank		320
Cash	50	
Purchase ledger total		4,265
Sales		120,240
Materials	35,465	
Production wages	12,480	
Driver's wages	11,785	
Salaries	22,460	
Employer's national insurance	4,365	
Motor expenses	2,160	
Rent	3,930	
Sundry expenses	3,480	
VAT		1,220
Inland Revenue		1,365
Drawings	12,400	
Capital		7,516
Suspense	10,000	
	149,635	149,635

(b)   Adjustments need to be made for the following.

(i)   A new delivery van was purchased for £12,400 on 1 August 1993. The old delivery van, originally purchased for £12,000 on 1 August 1990, was given in part exchange; the balance of £10,000 was paid for by cheque and debited to Suspense Account.

(ii)   The reception area was re-built in the first week of September 1993. This work was carried out by the assembler as business was rather slack at that time. He spent the whole of the first week in September on this task; his pay is £12,480 per annum.

(iii)   Jason gave two futons as Christmas presents in December 1993. An account was opened in the sales ledger to record these transactions.

(c)   The following additional information needs to be taken into account.

(i)   Depreciation for the year ended 31 May 1994 is to be provided for.

(ii)   The stocktake at 31 May 1994 has revealed the following.

Stock of timber, mattresses and sundry materials = £1,526
23 fully completed futons were in stock

There was no work in progress.

(iii)   The electricity bill for £180 covering the February, March, April 1994 quarter had been received on 15 May and entered into the purchase ledger. Electricity usage is relatively even throughout the year. Electricity is included within sundry expenses.

(iv)   On 12 May the delivery van was involved in an accident, suffering minor damage. The repairs, costing £164, have been carried out and the cost included in motor expenses. A letter has been received today from the Mercury Insurance Company agreeing to compensate for all but the first £50 of the repair costs.

(v)   A customer, T Young, who bought two futons at the regular price in July 1993, has disappeared without paying. It has been decided to write off the amount owing.

(vi)   The rent of £3,144 per annum is paid annually in advance on 1 September.

Task 1

Prepare journal entries for the transactions listed in (b) above. Narratives are required. Use the blank journal form on Page 11.

Task 2

Enter all the account balances, including those adjusted in Task 1 above, in the first two columns of the extended trial balance. Use the blank ETB on Page 12.

Task 3

Make appropriate entries in the adjustments columns of the extended trial balance. Create additional accounts as required.

Task 4

Extend the figures into the extended trial balance columns for profit and loss account and balance sheet. Total all columns, transferring the balance of profit or loss as appropriate.

A suggested answer to this exercise is given on page 38.

JOURNAL		
Details	DR £	CR £

BPP
PUBLISHING

FUTON ENTERPRISES

Account	Trial balance		Adjustments		Profit and Loss a/c		Balance Sheet	
	Debit £	Credit £	Debit £	Credit £	Debit £	Credit £	Debit £	Credit £
Delivery vans (cost)								
Assembling machine (costs)								
Furniture and fittings (cost)								
Delivery vans (prov for depreciation)								
Assembling machine (prov for depreciation)								
Furniture and fittings (prov for depreciation)								
Stock : raw materials								
Stock : finished goods								
Sales ledger total								
Bank								
Cash								
Purchase ledger total								
Sales								
Materials								
Production wages								
Driver's wages								
Salaries								
Employer's NI								
Motor expenses								
Rent								
Sundry expenses								
VAT								
Inland Revenue								
Drawings								
Capital								
Depreciation: Delivery vans								
Depreciation: assembling machine								
Depreciation: furniture and fittings								
Subtotal								
Profit for the year								
TOTAL								

Kidditoys (December 1994)

The suggested time allocation for this extended trial balance exercise is 80 minutes.

Kidditoys is a retail shop which specialises in the sale of unusual toys, games and other baby products. The business was started in December 1987 and is owned and run by Sophie Stewart.

About half the sales of the business are cash sales through the shop, the remainder being on mail order. Mail order customers pay cash with order.

Sophie employs one sales assistant and one packing assistant.

Her present manual system of bookkeeping comprises a purchase ledger with approximately 30 active accounts, a nominal ledger and a petty cash book. A petty cash float of £50 is maintained for sundry expenses and is replenished as required. A further cash float of £50 is maintained in the sales till. All cash receipts are banked daily.

You are an accounting technician who is helping Sophie to prepare the business's accounts up to the trial balance stage.

Fixed asset information

	Date of purchase	*Cost* £	*Expected useful economic life* *(years)*
Motor van	07.08.93	12,640	5
Shop fittings	10.12.87	3,240	10
Office equipment	08.04.91	4,250	5

All fixed assets are depreciated on a straight line basis using the expected useful economic lives, above, and zero-estimated residual values.

Depreciation is charged a full year in the year of purchase and is not charged for in the year of sale.

Other information

Average mark up is 100%.

The VAT rate is 17.5%.

Data

(a) The following list of balances has been extracted from the nominal ledger at the business's year end, 30 November 1994.

	£
Sales	392,182
Sales returns	1,214
Purchases	208,217
Purchase returns	643
Stock	32,165
Wages	50,000
Rent	27,300
Rates	8,460
Light and heat	2,425
Office expenses	3,162
Selling expenses	14,112
Motor expenses	14,728
Sundry expenses	6,560
Motor vans (cost)	12,640
Motor vans (provision for depreciation) at 1.12.93	2,528
Shop fittings (cost)	3,240
Shop fittings (provision for depreciation) at 1.12.93	1,944
Office equipment (cost)	4,250
Office equipment (provision for depreciation) at 1.12.93	2,550
Cash	100
Bank current account (debit balance)	4,420
Bank investment account	68,340
Interest received	3,280
	£
Purchase ledger total	27,683
Capital	22,145
VAT (credit balance)	6,420
Suspense (see note (b)(ii))	1,958

(b) After extracting the balances listed in (a), the following six errors and omissions were discovered.

(i)   Credit purchases of £954 had been correctly posted to the purchases account, but had been debited in the supplier's account (T Ditton).

(ii) The shop had been entirely re-fitted during the year. The old fittings had been sold off to the local Boy Scouts for £50. This had been debited in the bank account, but had been credited in the suspense account.

The invoice for the new shop fittings, for £9,620, had been received from Kingston Displays Ltd on 15 November. This invoice had not yet been entered into the accounts. Sophie intended to pay the invoice in January after the Christmas sales period. The new shop fittings are expected to have a useful economic life of 10 years.

(iii) Sophie paid herself a 'wage' of £2,000 per calendar month which she debited to wages account.

(iv) During the year an invoice for £843 (for zero-rated supplies) had been received from a supplier (E Molesey). When payment was made, Sophie accidentally made out the cheque for £840. Sophie noticed this error and contacted E Molesey who told her to ignore such a small sum of money. No adjustment has yet been made for this discrepancy.

(v)   During the year Sophie gave away a number of toys from the shop as presents to relatives and friends. She kept a record of these, which came to £640 at selling price, including VAT, but has not so far entered the transactions into the accounts.

(vi) The company's current bank account statement arrived on 30 November 1994. This showed interest received for the month of November at £9. This has not yet been entered into the accounts.

(c) The following additional matters need to be taken into account.

(i) Depreciation for the year ended 30 November 1994 is to be provided for.

(ii) The stock in the shop at 30 November 1994 was valued at £42,120 at selling price.

(iii) Rent was £2,100 per month payable in advance. The rent for December 1994 had already been paid.

(iv) Business rates are paid half yearly on 1 May and 1 November. The business rates bill for the period 1 April 1994 - 31 March 1995 amounted to £6,240.

(v) The electricity bill for £318 covering the July, August and September quarter had been received on 15 October. This had been entered into the purchase ledger and duly paid. Electricity usage can be considered to be relatively even throughout the year.

Task 1

Prepare journal entries for the transactions listed in (b). Narratives are required. Use the journal voucher on the next two pages.

Task 2

Enter all the account balances, including those adjusted in Task 1 above, in the first two columns of the Extended Trial Balance shown on Page 18. Note that some of the balances have already been filled in for you. Create additional accounts as required.

Task 3

Make appropriate entries in the adjustments columns of the Extended Trial Balance. Create additional accounts as required.

Do not extend the figures in the extended trial balance into the profit and loss account and balance sheet columns.

Note. All final workings should be clearly shown in your finished answers.

A suggested answer to this exercise is given on page 40.

JOURNAL

Details	DR £	CR £

JOURNAL		
Details	DR £	CR £

BPP PUBLISHING

KIDDITOYS

Account	Trial balance		Adjustments	
	Debit £	Credit £	Debit £	Credit £
Sales				
Sales returns				
Purchases				
Purchase returns	32,165			
Stock				
Wages	27,300			
Rent	8,460			
Rates	2,425			
Light and heat	3,162			
Office expenses	14,112			
Selling expenses	14,728			
Motor expenses	6,560			
Sundry expenses	12,640			
Motor vans (cost)				
Shop fittings (cost)	4,250			
Office equipment (cost)				
Motor vans (prov for depreciation)				
Shop fittings (prov for depreciation)				
Office equipment (prov for depreciation)				
Cash	100			
Bank current account				
Bank investment account				
Interest received				
Capital				
VAT				
Subtotal				
Profit for the year				
TOTAL				

Country Crafts (December 1993)

The following short answer questions are mainly based on the scenario outlined in the extended trial balance exercise Country Crafts (Page 3). You may have to refer back to the information in that exercise in order to answer the questions.

The suggested time allocation for this set of short answer questions is 40 minutes.

1   The company had bought a small item of computer software, cost £32.50 earlier in the year. This had been treated as office equipment. Do you agree with this treatment? Give brief reasons.

2   If the company had depreciated its motor vehicles at 50% per annum on a reducing balance basis, what would have been the profit or loss on the company car sold on 4 December 1993?

3   If the organisation which had rented the car park and field for the car boot sale had rented the field for a similar event in January 1994 and had paid £250 in advance, how would that transaction be treated in the 1993 accounts? Briefly explain the effect in the 1994 accounts.

4   (a)   In manual accounts transposition errors can occur, for example, a credit purchase entered in the purchases a/c as £1,234, but entered in the supplier's account as £1,423. Can such errors occur in computerised accounting systems? Give reasons.

    (b)   In manual accounts, errors of principle can occur. For example, the purchase of a piece of office machinery might be posted to the office expenses a/c. Can such errors occur in computerised accounting systems? Give reasons.

5   You have heard a rumour that one of your customers, who owes you £1,640 is about to go out of business. Should this debt be treated as a bad debt, a doubtful debt or should the rumour be ignored? Give reasons.

6   Explain fully what the balance on VAT account represents.

7   If one of the company's vans had to have its engine replaced at a cost of £1,800, would this represent capital or revenue expenditure? Give brief reasons.

8   If the company decided it needed a china coffee set to use to entertain potential customers, and it took a suitable one from the stock in the warehouse, how would you record this in the books of the company?

A suggested answer to this exercise is given on page 43.

Futon Enterprises (June 1994)

The following short answer questions are mainly based on the scenario outlined in the extended trial balance exercise Futon Enterprises (Page 8). You may have to refer back to the information in that exercise in order to answer the questions.

The suggested time allocation for this set of short answer questions is 40 minutes.

1   Assume that two of the futons had been used as a shop window display and had faded somewhat. If it had been decided that the mattress required replacing at a cost of £18 each to make the futons saleable at a price of £50 each, how would this have affected the closing stock valuation?

    Give reasons for your answer.

2   What is the net book value of the assembling machinery at 31 May 1994? Is this the amount it is estimated would be realised if the machinery were disposed of at that date?

    Briefly justify your answer.

3   Give one reason why the company might have chosen reducing balance as the method for depreciating its delivery vans.

4   If the customer, T Young, whose amount owing in (c)(v) had been written off, subsequently paid later this year, how would you account for the payment?

5   Explain what the balance on Inland Revenue Account represents.

6   If the delivery van was refitted with wooden racks by the assembler in half an hour's spare time and using materials at a cost price of £24, would this be treated as capital or revenue expenditure?

     Give reasons.

7   An acquaintance wishes to use the shop to display and sell framed photographs. She will pay £40 per month for this service.

     (a)   How would you account for this transaction each month?

     (b)   If, at the end of the year, the acquaintance owed one month's rental, how would this be treated in the accounts?

8   The business maintains a traditional petty cash book. At the end of each week, the petty cash book is balanced, the totals of the analysis columns posted to the relevant accounts and the float of £50 replenished.

     (a)   Into which account would the total of the VAT analysis column be posted and would this be a debit or credit entry?

     (b)   What would the total of the VAT column represent?

     (c)   If the petty cash expenditure in one week had been £37, what would be the double entry to replenish the float?

A suggested answer to this exercise is given on page 43.

Kidditoys (December 1994)

The following short answer questions are mainly based on the scenario outlined in the extended trial balance exercise Kidditoys (Page 13). You may have to refer back to the information in that exercise in order to answer this question.

The suggested time allocation for this set of short answer questions is 40 minutes.

1   Give a reason why Sophie Stewart does not have any bad debts.

2   Explain in detail what the balance on her VAT a/c represents.

3   When cash sales are banked, which accounts would be debited and credited?

4   What is the net book value of the delivery van at 30 November 1994? What does this amount represent?

5   Assume that some of the shop's window display stock, comprising four dolls, had deteriorated. In their damaged state the dolls could be sold for only £5 each. Their original sales price was £16 each.

     (a)   How would this have affected the closing stock valuation at 30 November 1994?
     (b)   What would have been the effect on the company's profit?

6   Occasionally Kidditoys has to pay a special delivery charge on deliveries of toys it urgently requires. How should this delivery charge be dealt with in the accounts?

7   Sophie is considering sending a quantity of goods to John King on a sale or return basis. How should the transaction be dealt with when the goods are first delivered to John King?

Give reasons for your answer.

8   The company is considering buying some new software for the office word processor at a cost of £85. It is expected to be in use for five years. How would you deal with this transaction in the accounts?

Give detailed reasons for your answer.

9   If, in preparing the extended trial balance for Kidditoys, the business was found to be making a loss.

(a)   Would the loss appear in the debit or credit column of the profit and loss account balances?

(b)   How would the loss be dealt with in the balance sheet balances columns?

10   Using your figures from the extended trial balance in Part 1, complete the profit and loss a/c and balance sheet balances columns for stock, below.

Profit and Loss A/c		*Balance Sheet Balances*	
Dr	*Cr*	*Dr*	*Cr*

A suggested answer to this exercise is given on page 44.

BPP
PUBLISHING

Brian Hope (Sample)

The suggested time allocation for this incomplete records exercise is 60 minutes.

Data

You have been asked to help in preparing the accounts of Brian Hope. Brian started in business in 1991 doing repair and servicing of electrical equipment and he works in a rented workshop. So far he has not kept proper records of his transactions. His accounts to 31 December 1991 were prepared for him on the basis of enquiries and the closing position was then shown as follows.

	£	£
Bank balance	190	
Cash in hand	10	
Van	6,000	
Stock of materials	1,210	
Trade debtors and creditors	1,420	2,220
Vehicle repair bill owing		80
Insurance prepaid	340	
Rent prepaid	400	
Capital		7,270
	9,570	9,570

You have started by summarising the bank statements for the year ended 31 December 1992 as follows.

	£	£
Opening balance		260
Cash paid in		510
Receipts from debtors		21,120
		21,890
Payments to trade creditors (see (g) below)	3,930	
New vehicle (less trade-in)	3,600	
Vehicle running expenses	1,040	
Rent	2,640	
Insurance	960	
Other expenses	1,710	
Hope's drawings	8,000	
		21,880
Closing balance		10

You discover the following information regarding Hope's 1992 transactions in the year to 31 December 1992 and the closing position.

(a) He was paid in cash for some of the work done but cannot trace how much. However, you can find sufficient evidence to show that the debtors outstanding at the end of the year totalled £1,120 though £90 of this is probably irrecoverable. Hope does keep copies of all the invoices to his customers and these total £26,720 but he remembers allowing a customer £300 after a charge was disputed.

(b) Outstanding invoices from trade creditors at the end of the year totalled £2,460. Hope says that he is usually allowed a cash discount by one of the suppliers and the total discount for the year is estimated at £200.

(c) The rent was £200 per month until the end of August but was then increased to £240. Hope usually pays two months together in advance and has already paid (in December) for January and February 1993.

(d) At the end of the year £60 is outstanding for petrol and the insurance has been prepaid by £380.

(e) Hope changed the van at the end of December buying a new one for £8,000 with a trade-in allowance for the old one of £4,400. He thinks he agreed last year to a depreciation charge of 20% per annum on book value (but this would not apply in 1992 to the new vehicle just purchased).

(f) No adequate records of cash transactions have been kept but as indicated above it is known that customers often paid their accounts in cash and that Hope frequently withdrew cash for his own personal use. He estimates that payments for vehicle running costs of £500 have been made from cash and a similar amount for other expenses. There is no closing balance of cash.

(g) At the beginning of the year there were cheques to trade creditors unpresented at the bank totalling £70 and at the end of the year the unpresented cheques to trade creditors totalled £210.

Tasks

From the above information you are asked to draw up the ledger accounts on page 24 for each of the following showing the balances to be carried forward at the end of the year or the amounts to be transferred to the profit and loss account. (Dates need not be shown in the accounts.)

Trade debtors
Trade creditors
Rent
Vehicles
Vehicle running expenses
Insurance
Cash
Drawings

A suggested answer to this exercise is given on page 46.

TRADE DEBTORS			

VEHICLE RUNNING EXPENSES			

TRADE CREDITORS			

INSURANCE			

RENT			

CASH			

VEHICLES			

DRAWINGS			

Kuldipa Potiwal (December 1993)

The suggested time allocation for this incomplete records exercise is 60 minutes.

A friend of yours from Leicester, Kuldipa Potiwal, runs a small computer games retail and mail order business, but she does not keep proper accounting records. She has now been approached by the Inland Revenue for the details of the profit she has earned for the last year. She has provided you with the following bank account summary for the year ended 31 October 1993.

BANK ACCOUNT SUMMARY

	£
Balance at bank (1 November 1992)	
Bank overdraft	3,250
Receipts	
Cash paid in	56,000
Cheques from debtors	46,000
Investment income	1,500
Rent received	2,500
Payments	
Payments to trade creditors	78,000
Rent and rates	6,400
Postage and packing costs	2,200
Motor expenses	5,050
Administration expenses	4,600

Additional information was provided as follows.

(a) Kuldipa intends to sell all her computer games at cost plus 50%.

(b) Before paying cash receipts into the bank, Kuldipa used some of the cash received to make a number of payments.

Wages of shop assistant and driver	£350 per week
Drawings	£220 per week
Administration expenses	£750 per annum

All cash is paid into the bank daily.

(c) The investment income was interest on her private investment account.

(d) Other balances were as follows.

	31 October 1992	31 October 1993
	£	£
Delivery van (valuation)	17,500	12,500
Stock of games	12,200	13,750
Trade creditors	9,000	13,400
Trade debtors	6,000	7,200
Rates paid in advance	500	200
Rent receivable	-	250
Administration expenses owing	175	215

(e) During the year a vanload of games being delivered to credit customers was stolen. The van was recovered, undamaged, but the games have not been recovered. The insurance company has agreed to pay for 50% of the stolen games, but payment has not yet been received.

Kuldipa Potiwal calculated from the copy delivery notes that the selling price value of the games stolen was £6,000.

(f) At Christmas 1992 Kuldipa Potiwal gave games as presents to her young relatives. The selling price of these games was £480.00.

Task 1

Prepare a detailed calculation of the net profit of the business for the year ended 31 October 1993.

Task 2

Calculate the balance of Kuldipa's capital account at 31 October 1993.

A suggested answer to this exercise is given on page 47.

Fancy Flowers (June 1994)

The suggested time allocation for this incomplete records exercise is 60 minutes.

You belong to a badminton club at the local leisure centre and always have a drink with one of your friends, Sarah Harvey, in the coffee shop after a game. Sarah is the owner of a small florist's business and has been trading for a year as Fancy Flowers. She has never kept proper books of account and has asked you to calculate her profit for the first year of trading which ended on 31 May 1994.

On 31 May you carried out a stocktake which revealed the following situation.

	Cost £	Mark up %
Pot plants	280	100
Roses	240	75
Tulips	160	75
Sprays	340	100
Plant food	80	50
Vases	520	100

A quarter of the pot plants were rather withered and Sarah thought she would have to throw them away. She thought a further quarter would have to be sold at cost price.

The roses were of a very high quality and Sarah thought she could probably sell them at a mark-up of 100%.

One of the sprays, costing £80, had been prepared for a customer who had never collected. This would have to be thrown away.

A box of ten vases, selling price £6 per vase, was badly damaged and would have to be thrown away.

You also elicit the following information.

(a) All sales of the business are cash sales.

(b) A summary of the bank statements revealed the following.

	£
Cash paid into the bank	31,420
Cheque payments	
To plant and sundries wholesalers	24,180
Rent	5,000
Business rates	420
Advertising	385
Insurance	390
Electricity	780
Sundry expenses	560
Interest charged by bank	84

(c)   All the cash paid into the bank resulted from cash sales, except for an initial £5,000 invested by Sarah as start-up capital in the business.

(d)   Before paying the cash sales into the bank, Sarah withdrew cash for the following purposes.

	£
Wages for self	14,200
Sundry expenses	345

She also retained £60 change in a cash tin after paying the remaining cash into the bank.

(e)   From her file of purchase invoices, Sarah discovered that the following were unpaid.

	£
Purchase of cut flowers for May	850
Purchase of roses (28 May)	345
Electricity (quarter ended 30 April)	360
Advertising charges for May	45

(f)   She pays rent of £1,000 per quarter in advance.

(g)   She regularly takes home about £10 worth of flowers (at selling price) each week.

Task 1

Prepare a valuation of closing stock.

Task 2

Calculate the profit for the first year of trading for Fancy Flowers.

Task 3

Calculate the balance on capital account for Sarah at the end of the first year of trading.

Task 4

Comment briefly on the situation revealed. Show all your workings.

A suggested answer to this exercise is given on page 49.

Manuel

The suggested time allocation for this incomplete records exercise is 60 minutes.

Manuel has been required to write up the June accounts for the bar of a small hotel in Torquay while the usual bookkeeper, Polly, is on holiday. He finds bookkeeping very puzzling and has asked for your help. He provides you with the following information relating to transactions for the month.

(a)   Bar takings (cash): £200

(b)   Bar sales on credit to the Major, a valued customer: £100

(c)   Wages (cash) £50

(d)   Cash received from the Major for last month's bar bill: £80

(e)   Cash banked: £300

(f)   Wages (cheque): £40

(g)   Bank charges notified by bank: £35

(h)   Supplies purchased on credit from Torquay Wines: £500

(i) Payment to Torquay Wines by cheque of £300 less 5% discount for early payment

(j) Wine purchased on credit from Devon Wines, a local firm, on a sale or return basis: £175

(k) £100 worth of wine from Devon Wines sold at mark-up on cost of 20%, on credit to a Mr Twychin

(l) Wines returned to Devon Wines: £75

(m) Opening bank balance: £300, cash in till: £320

Task 1

Enter the above transactions into the following ledger accounts (shown below)

> Three column cash book
> Sales
> Purchases
> Major
> Wages
> Mr Twychin
> Bank charges
> Devon Wines
> Torquay wines

Task 2

Produce a partial trial balance as far as the information allows.

Note. There will be a difference on the trial balance.

CASH BOOK

DETAIL	DISCOUNT	CASH	BANK	DISCOUNT	CASH	BANK
	£	£	£	£	£	£

SALES

BPP PUBLISHING

PURCHASES							

MAJOR			

WAGES			

MR TWYCHIN			

BANK CHARGES			

DEVON WINES			

BPP PUBLISHING

TORQUAY WINES			

PARTIAL TRIAL BALANCE AS AT 30 JUNE

	Dr £	Cr £
Bank balance		
Cash in till		
Discounts		
Sales		
Purchases		
Major		
Wages		
Mr Twychin		
Bank charges		
Devon Wines		
Torquay Wines		
Difference		

A suggested answer to this exercise is given on page 51.

Answers to practice activities

SECTION 1

Country Crafts

Task 1

JOURNAL		
Details	DR £	CR £
Motor vans (cost) a/c	22,600	
Motor vans (cost) a/c		16,200
Motor vans (provision for dep'n) a/c	12,150	
(£16,200 × 25% × 3)		
Suspense a/c		17,600
Profit/loss on sale of fixed asset a/c		950
Being purchase of van L 673 NFU, transfer of provision for dep'n and sale of van H 247 AFE in part exchange		
Suspense a/c	3,900	
Motor cars (cost) a/c		9,200
Motor cars (provision for dep'n) a/c	4,600	
(£9,200 × 25% × 2)		
Profit/loss on sale of fixed asset a/c	700	
Being disposal of motor car J 168 TFE at a loss		
Sales	250	
Sundry income		250
Being transfer of sundry income into correct account		

Solutions to Tasks 2 to 4 are shown on the extended trial balance overleaf.

BPP PUBLISHING

COUNTRY CRAFTS

Account	Trial balance Debit £	Trial balance Credit £	Adjustments Debit £	Adjustments Credit £	Profit and Loss a/c Debit £	Profit and Loss a/c Credit £	Balance Sheet Debit £	Balance Sheet Credit £
Motor vans (cost)	42,400						42,400	
Motor cars (costs)	9,200						9,200	
Office furniture (cost)	4,850						4,850	
Computer equipment (cost)	16,830						16,830	
Motor vans (prov for depreciation)		4,950		10,600				15,550
Motor cars (prov for depreciation)		4,600		2,300				6,900
Office furniture (prov for depreciation)		1,940		485				2,425
Computer equipment (prov for depreciation)				5,610				5,610
Stock: opening	24,730				24,730			
Debtors control	144,280						144,280	
Bank		610		43				653
Cash	50		43				50	
Creditors control		113,660						113,660
Sales		282,240				282,240		
Purchases	152,140			1,150	150,990			
Rent	12,480			4,992	7,488			
Heat and light	1,840		210		2,050			
Wages and salaries	75,400				75,400			
Office expenses	7,900		43		7,943			
Motor expenses	14,890				14,890			
Depreciation (motor vans)			10,600		10,600			
Depreciation (motor cars)			2,300		2,300			
Depreciation (office furniture)			485		485			
Depreciation (computer equipment)			5,610		5,610			
Share capital		50,000						50,000
Profit and loss		35,850						35,850
VAT		12,640						12,640
Stock: closing (P&L)				31,600		31,600		
Stock: closing (B&S)			31,600				31,600	
Profit on sale of fixed asset		250				250		
Sundry income		250				250		
Insurance claim			950				950	
Stock loss			200		200			
Bad debt expense			7,214		7,214			
Provision for doubtful debts				7,214				7,214
Prepayments / accruals			4,992	210			4,992	210
Subtotal	506,990	506,990	64,247	64,247	309,900	314,340	255,152	250,712
Profit for the year					4,440			4,440
TOTAL	506,990	506,990	64,247	64,247	314,340	314,340	255,152	255,152

Workings

1   *Profit on sale of fixed asset account*

	£
Profit on van	950
Loss on car	700
Net profit	250

2   *Insurance claim*

Cost of damaged stock (mark-up 100%) = 50% × £2,300
= £1,150 (a credit to the purchases account)
Less £200 excess = £950

Note. £200 is a 'stock loss' not covered by insurance.

3   *Stock write-off*

Baby Beatrice mugs:	Cost 320/2 = £160
	NRV = £120

NRV below cost ∴ write-off necessary

Windsor fire damage plate:	Cost 620/2 = £310
	NRV = £350

∴ No write-off necessary, NRV above cost

Closing stock ∴ £31,640 – £(160 – 120) = £31,600.

4   *Bad debt expense/provision*

Provision required: 5% × £144,280 = £7,214

5   *Prepayments and accruals*

Rent: prepayment = 8/12 × £7,488 = £4,992

Electricity: bill for 3 months to February 1994 = 2 × £315 = £630
∴ Accrual for December = 1/3 × £630 = £210

Futon Enterprises

Details	DR £	CR £
JOURNAL		Page 20
(i) Delivery vans: cost	10,000	
Suspense account		10,000
Delivery vans: cost (£12,400 - £10,000)	2,400	
Van disposal account		2,400
Being correct treatment of cost of		
new van, clearing suspense account		
Van disposal	12,000	
Delivery van (cost)		12,000
Delivery van (provision for dep'n)	7,884	
Van disposal		7,884
Loss on sale of van	1,716*	
Van disposal		1,716
Being disposal of old van (in part exchange)		
(ii) Fixtures and fittings: cost	240	
Production wages		240
Being cost of rebuilding reception area		
in production wages (£12,480 ÷ 52 = £240)		
(iii) Sales	168	
Sales ledger balances		168
Being reversal of treatment of two futons		
given as presents (£48.00 × 2 × 175%)		
Drawings	96	
Materials		96
Being correct treatment of two futons		
given as presents (£48.00 × 2)		

Note. The credit entry to materials should be made to cost of sales. The alternative would be to post entries to materials, wages and overheads. However, overheads are split over several captions so this would be impractical.

	£
* Cost of van	12,000
Acc dep'n	7,884
NBV	4,116
Proceeds £(12,400 –10,000)	2,400
Loss on disposal	1,716

FUTON ENTERPRISES

Account	Trial balance Debit £	Trial balance Credit £	Adjustments Debit £	Adjustments Credit £	Profit and loss account Debit £	Profit and loss account Credit £	Balance sheet Debit £	Balance sheet Credit £
Delivery vans (cost)	12,400						12,400	
Assembling machine (costs)	3,650						3,650	
Furniture and fittings (cost)	11,030						11,030	
Delivery vans (prov for depreciation)				3,720				3,720
Assembling machine (prov for depreciation)		1,095		365				1,460
Furniture and fittings (prov for depreciation)		5,730		2,206				7,936
Stock : raw materials	1,320				1,320			
Stock : finished goods	1,440				1,440			
Stock : ledger total (1,860 - 168)	1,692			168			1,524	
Bank		320						320
Cash	50						50	
Purchase ledger total		4,265						4,265
Sales (120,240 - 168)		120,072				120,072		
Materials (35,465 - 96)	35,369				35,369			
Production wages (12,480-£240)	12,240				12,240			
Driver's wages	11,785				11,785			
Salaries	22,460				22,460			
Employer's NI	4,365				4,365			
Motor expenses	2,160			114	2,046			
Rent	3,930			786	3,144			
Sundry expenses	3,480		60		3,540			
VAT		1,220						1,220
Inland Revenue		1,365						1,365
Drawings (12,400 + 96)	12,496						12,496	
Capital		7,516						7,516
Depreciation: Delivery vans			3,720		3,720			
Depreciation: assembling machine			365		365			
Depreciation: furniture and fittings			2,206		2,206			
Loss on sale of van	1,716				1,716			
Closing stock (B/S): raw materials			1,526				1,526	
Closing stock (B/s): finished goods (£48 × 23)			1,104				1,104	
Closing stock (P&L): raw materials				1,526		1,526		
Closing stock (P&L): finished goods (£48 × 23)				1,104		1,104		
Insurance claim debtor			114				114	
Bad debts (48 × 1.75 × 2)			168		168			
Prepayments/accruals			786	60			786	60
Subtotal	141,583	141,583	10,049	10,049	105,884	122,702	44,680	27,862
Profit for the year					16,818			16,818
TOTAL	141,583	141,583	10,049	10,049	122,702	122,702	44,680	44,680

Kidditoys

Details	DR £	CR £
JOURNAL		Page 20
(i) DEBIT Suspense a/c	1,908	
CREDIT T. Ditton a/c (Purchase ledger)		1,908
Being correction of misposting		
(ii) DEBIT Suspense a/c	50	
DEBIT Provision for depreciation a/c (shop fittings)	1,944	
(W1)		
DEBIT Loss on sale of fixed assets a/c	1,246	
CREDIT Shop fittings (cost a/c)		3,240
Being disposal of shop fittings		
DEBIT Shop fittings (cost) a/c	9,620	
CREDIT Kingston Displays Ltd (Purchase ledger)		9,620
Being purchase of new shop fittings		
(iii) DEBIT Drawings a/c (12 × £2,000)	24,000	
CREDIT Wages a/c		24,000
Being correction of misposting		
(iv) DEBIT E. Molesey a/c (Purchase ledger)	3	
CREDIT Discount received a/c		3
Being discount received from E. Molesey after		
accidental underpayment		
(v) DEBIT Drawings a/c	640	
CREDIT Sales a/c		545
CREDIT VAT a/c		95
Being stock withdrawn for own use		
(vi) DEBIT Bank current a/c	9	
CREDIT Interest received a/c		9
Being posting of bank interest received credited on		
bank statement		

| KIDDITOYS | Trial balance | | Adjustments | |
Account	Debit	Credit	Debit	Credit
	£	£	£	£
Sales		392,727		
Sales returns	1,214			
Purchases	208,217			
Purchase returns		643		
Stock	32,165			
Wages	26,000			
Rent	27,300			2,100
Rates	8,460			2,080
Light and heat	2,425		212	
Office expenses	3,162			
Selling expenses	14,112			
Motor expenses	14,728			
Sundry expenses	6,560			
Motor vans (cost)	12,640			
Shop fittings (cost)	9,620			
Office equipment (cost)	4,250			
Motor vans (prov for depreciation)		2,528		2,528
Shop fittings (prov for depreciation)				962
Office equipment (prov for depreciation)		2,550		850
Cash	100			
Bank current account	4,429			
Bank investment account	68,340			
Interest received		3,289		
Capital		22,145		
VAT		6,515		
Purchase ledger total		29,588		
Loss on sale of fixed assets	1,246			
Kingston Displays Limited		9,620		
Drawings	24,640			
Discount received		3		
Depreciation (motor vans)			2,528	
Depreciation (shop fittings)			962	
Depreciation (office equipment)			850	
Stock (closing): P&L				21,060
Stock (closing): B/S			21,060	
Prepayments / accruals			4,180	212
Subtotal	469,608	469,608	29,792	29,792
Profit for the year				
TOTAL	469,608	469,608	29,792	29,792

Workings

1   *Accumulated depreciation on shop fittings disposed of*

   £324 × 6 years = £1,944

2   *Depreciation of fixed assets*

   Motor van: annual depreciation charge = $\dfrac{£12,640}{5}$ = £2,528

   ∴ Accumulated depreciation at 1.12.93 = £2,528

   Shop fittings: depreciation charge = $\dfrac{£9,620}{10}$ = £962

   Office equipment: annual depreciation charge = $\dfrac{£4,250}{5}$ = £850

   Accumulated depreciation as at 1.12.93 = £850 × 3 = £2,550

3   *Business rates prepayment*

   Prepayment = £6,240 × $\dfrac{4 \text{ months}}{12 \text{ months}}$ = £2,080

4   *Electricity accrual*

   Accrual = £318 × $\dfrac{2 \text{ months}}{3 \text{ months}}$ = £212

SECTION 2

Country Crafts

1 The computer software has been purchased for continuing use in the business, and in that sense, could be called a fixed asset. However, many small value assets are not recorded as assets but written off directly as an expense when purchased. The decision as to how to treat the item depends on materiality, that is whether or not the item has a significant effect on the financial statements. In this particular case the expenditure on software was not material, which suggests that the item should be treated as an expense.

2

	£
Cost 1991	9,200
Depreciation 1991: 50% × £9,200	4,600
Net book value	4,600
Depreciation 1992: 50% × £4,600	2,300
Net book value	2,300
Proceeds	3,900
Profit	1,600

3 A payment in advance is *deferred income*. It would be treated as a current liability in the 1993 accounts and as income in the 1994 accounts.

4 (a) An imbalance arising from a transposition error could not occur in a computerised accounting system, because the figure is entered only once and the computer carries out the double entry.

   (b) An error of principle could occur if a computerised accounting system is used. This is because the decision as to which account an item should be posted to rests with the person responsible, not with the computer.

5 It would be wrong to treat this as a bad debt since it is only a rumour, and a bad debt is a debt that has definitely gone bad. If the business is not already making a provision for doubtful debts, it should do so now, or should investigate whether the existing provision is adequate.

6 The balance on a VAT account represents the difference between output VAT (VAT collected from customers) and input VAT (VAT paid to suppliers). As the VAT account has a credit balance, the balance represents the excess of output tax over input tax.

7 The purpose of the expenditure was to maintain the existing capacity of the asset, rather than to improve it. This is therefore revenue expenditure.

8 The correct treatment would be:

   DEBIT   Office expenses
   CREDIT   Purchases

Futon Enterprises

1 *Stock valuation*

   Cost = £48.00 × 2 = £96.00

	£
NRV	
Selling price (£50.00 × 2)	100.00
Costs to complete (£18.00 × 2)	36.00
	64.00

BPP PUBLISHING

This stock would have been valued at £64.00, reducing the total stock value by £96.00 – £64.00 = £32.00. The stock should be valued at NRV because the prudence concept requires that losses should be recognised as soon as they are foreseen. The £32.00 is such a loss. In addition, SSAP 9 requires that stock be valued at the lower of cost and NRV.

2   The net book value of the assembling machinery at 31 May 1994 is £3,650 – £1,460 = £2,190. This does not mean that the business would obtain this amount if it sold the machinery at 31 May 1994, because the depreciation charged is not meant to reflect the market value of the asset. Rather, it is a measure of the wearing out of the asset through time and use; it is allocated to the accounting periods which are expected to benefit (ie make a profit) from the asset's use.

3   One reason for the choice of the reducing balance for vans is that motor vehicles lose a great deal of their value in the first year of use. This reflects the use made of the asset at its most efficient and it is a good example of 'matching' profits against costs.

4   The payment would have been accounted for as:

DEBIT	Bank	£168
CREDIT	Bad debt expense	£168

5   The balance on the Inland Revenue account represents the income tax owed on the profits of the business (probably just for the previous year) to the Inland Revenue, less any payments already made. Obviously, a tax charge is required for the current year and this would be accounted for as:

DEBIT	Profit and loss account
CREDIT	Inland Revenue account

6   Strictly speaking, the cost of refitting, including the assembler's wages, should be capitalised as an addition to delivery vans cost, because the refitting has added value to the van. However, the amount is immaterial to the results of the business; such small amounts are best treated as revenue expenditure in the profit and loss account.

7   (a)   The transaction should be treated on a monthly basis as:

DEBIT	Bank (or cash)	£40
CREDIT	Rental (or sundry) income	£40

    (b)   The outstanding £40 would be credited to the profit and loss account and shown as a sundry debtor in the balance sheet.

8   (a)   A debit entry in the VAT accounts.

    (b)   This represents the VAT on petty cash payments which the business can reclaim from HM Customs & Excise.

    (c)

DEBIT	Cash	£37
CREDIT	Bank	£37

Kidditoys

1   Sophie's customers either pay cash in the shop or send cash with their orders. Since, therefore, she has no debtors, Sophie will not have a problem with bad debts.

2   The credit balance on Sophie's VAT account is the amount by which VAT collected on sales exceeds VAT paid on purchases and expenses. The balance is owing to HM Customs & Excise.

3   DEBIT   Bank a/c
       CREDIT   Sales a/c
       CREDIT   VAT a/c

4   Net book value of van $= £12,640 \times \dfrac{3 \text{ years}}{5 \text{ years}} = £7,584$

This figure represents the cost of the van less accumulated depreciation to date. It is not an indication of the market value of the van.

5   (a)   The original sales price of each doll was £16, so the original cost must have been £8. Net realisable value at £5 is £3 lower, so the closing stock valuation will be reduced by £3 × 4 = £12.

      (b)   Profit would be reduced by £12.

6   DEBIT   Purchases
       CREDIT   Creditors

7   No transaction has yet taken place; the stock still belongs to Kidditoys. No entries should be made in the accounts until a sale is made by John King.

8   The accounting treatment of the £85 spent on software depends on whether the amount is regarded as material. If it is considered material it should be capitalised:

DEBIT	Office equipment (cost)	£85
CREDIT	Bank/creditors	£85

However if, as is more likely, the amount is not to be regarded as material, the amount would be written off to office expenses as follows.

DEBIT	Office expenses	£85
CREDIT	Bank/creditors	£85

9   (a)   It would appear in the credit column as a balancing figure because debits would exceed credits.

      (b)   It would appear in the debit column as a deduction from capital.

10

Profit and Loss A/c		Balance Sheet Balances	
Dr	*Cr*	*Dr*	*Cr*
32,165	21,060	21,060	

BPP PUBLISHING

SECTION 3

Brian Hope

Tutorial note. The three most difficult accounts to complete are trade debtors, cash and drawings. It is best to put in all the figures you know and complete the 'easier' accounts first. You should then be able to calculate, as a balancing figure, the amount for debtors who pay in cash. This will slot into the 'cash account', enabling you to calculate cash drawings as a balancing figure. The suggested time allocation for this incomplete records exercise is 1 hour.

TRADE DEBTORS

Balance b/f	1,420	Bank	21,120
		Allowance	300
Sales	26,720	Bad debt	90
		Balance c/f	1,030
		£(1120-90)	
		Cash	5,600
	28,140		28,140

VEHICLE RUNNING EXPENSES

		Balance b/f	80
Cash	500		
Bank	1,040	Profit & loss	1,520
Balance c/f	60		
	1,600		1,600

TRADE CREDITORS

Balance c/f	2,460	Balance b/f	2,220
Cash discount	200	Purchases	4,510
Bank *	4,070		
	6,730		6,730

* Payments to creditors: £(3,930 - 70 + 210) = £4,070

INSURANCE

Balance b/f	340		
		Profit & loss	920
Bank	960		
		Balance c/f	380
	1,300		1,300

RENT

Balance b/f	400		
		Balance c/f	480
Bank	2,640	Profit & loss	2,560
	3,040		3,040

CASH

Balance b/f	10	Bank	510
		Vehicle running costs	500
Debtors	5,600	Other expenses	500
		Drawings (bal)	4,100
	5,610		5,610

VEHICLES			
Balance b/f	6,000	Acc. dep'n	1,200
Bank	3,600	Profit & loss*	400
		Balance c/f	8,000
	9,600		9,600

DRAWINGS			
Bank	8,000	Capital	12,100
Cash	4,100		
	12,100		12,100

* £(6,000 - 1,200 - 4,000) = £400 loss

Kuldipa Potiwal

Task 1

CALCULATION OF NET PROFIT
FOR THE YEAR ENDED 31 OCTOBER 1993

	£	£
Sales (W1)		133,590
Opening stock	12,200	
Purchases (W2)	78,080	
Closing stock	(13,750)	
Cost of sales		76,530
Gross profit		57,060
Rent received (W3)		2,750
		59,810
Expenses		
Rent and rates (W3)	6,700	
Postage and packing	2,200	
Motor expenses	5,050	
Admin expenses (W3)	5,390	
Wages	18,200	
Stock loss (£6,000 × 100/150 × 50%)	2,000	
Depreciation £(17,500 – 12,500)	5,000	
		44,540
Net profit		15,270

Task 2

CALCULATION OF CAPITAL AS AT 31 OCTOBER 1993

	£
Opening capital (W4)	23,775
Profit	15,270
	39,045
Additional capital (investment income)	1,500
	40,545
Drawings (W5)	11,760
Closing capital	28,785

This figure can be confirmed by producing a balance sheet as at 31 October 1993, although this is not required by the question.

BPP
PUBLISHING

BALANCE SHEET AS AT 31 OCTOBER 1993

	£	£
Fixed assets		
Van		12,500
Current assets		
Stock	13,750	
Debtors	7,200	
Prepayments	200	
Insurance claim (50%)	2,000	
Rent receivable	250	
Bank	6,500	
	29,900	
Current liabilities		
Creditors	13,400	
Accruals	215	
	13,615	
		16,285
Net current assets		28,785
Closing capital		28,785

Workings

1 *Sales*

CASH BOOK

	Cash £	Bank £		Cash £	Bank £
Sales	86,390	Bankings	56,000	Bankings	56,000	Bal b/f 1.11.92	3,250
		Debtors	46,000	Wages (350 × 52)	18,200	Creditors	78,000
		Investment				Postage &	
		income	1,500	Drawings (220 × 52)	11,440	packing	2,200
		Rent	2,500	Admin exps	750	Rent & rates	6,400
						Motor exps	5,050
						Admin exps	4,600
						Bal c/f 31.10 93	6,500
	86,390		106,000		86,390		106,000

Note. As cash is banked daily, there will be no cash in hand b/fwd or c/fwd.

DEBTORS CONTROL A/C

		£			£
1.11.92	Balance b/fwd	6,000	31.10.92	Bank	46,000
	Sales (bal fig)	47,200		Balance c/fwd	7,200
		53,200			53,200

Total sales = £(86,390 + 47,200) = £133,590

2 *Purchases*

CREDITORS CONTROL A/C

		£			£
	Bank	78,000	1.11 92	Bal b/fwd	9,000
31.10.93	Bal c/fwd	13,400		Purchases (bal fig)	82,400
		91,400			91,400

	£
Purchases per CC a/c	82,400
Less stolen games £6,000 × 100/150	(4,000)
Less Christmas presents £480 × 100/150	(320)
	78,080

3   *Expenses*

Rent and rates:	£(6,400 + 500 − 200) = £6,700
Admin expenses:	£(750 + 4,600 − 175 + 215) = £5,390
Rent received:	£(2,500 + 250) = £2,750

4   *Opening capital*

	£	£
Assets		
Van	17,500	
Stock	12,200	
Debtors	6,000	
Prepayments	500	
		36,200
Liabilities		
Creditors	9,000	
Accruals	175	
Bank overdraft	3,250	
		12,425
Net assets = capital		23,775

5   *Drawings*

	£
Cash (W1)	11,440
Christmas presents* 480 × 100/150	320
	11,760

*Note. Drawings from stock are at cost price. Selling price inclusive of VAT may also be used.

Fancy Flowers

Task 1

Closing stock valuation

	Cost	Adjust	Total
	£	£	£
Pot plants	280	(70)	210
Roses	240		240
Tulips	160		160
Sprays	340	(80)	260
Plant food	80		80
Vases	520	(30)*	490
			1,440

*£6 × 100/200 × 10 = £30

Task 2

	£	£
Sales £(31,420 – 5,000 + 14,200 + 345 + 60)		41,025
Cost of sales		
Purchases £(24,180 + 850 + 345 – (£5* × 52))	25,115	
Closing stock (see *Task 1*)	(1,440)	
		23,675
Gross profit		17,350
Expenses		
Rent £(5,000 – 1,000)	4,000	
Rates	420	
Advertising £(385 + 45)	430	
Insurance	390	
Electricity £(780 + 360) + (1/3 × £360)	1,260	
Sundry expenses £(560 + 345)	905	
Interest	84	
		7,489
Profit		9,861

*£10 × 100%/200% = £5.

Note. It is not clear whether the flowers Sarah has taken have a mark-up of 100% or 75%.

Task 3

Capital account

	£
Balance at 1 June 1993	5,000
Add profit for year (see *Task 2*)	9,861
Less drawings: cash	(14,200)
goods	(260)
Balance at 31 May 1994	401

Task 4

The business is making a reasonable profit but Sarah is taking much more in wages for herself. As well as the profit for the year, she has also withdrawn a substantial part of her initial capital investment. It is unlikely that she will be able to continue drawing at this rate, particularly if the business requires more investment in future.

The gross profit figures shows a mark-up on cost of approximately 73%, or a gross profit percentage of 42%. the net profit percentage is 24%. These figures are quite healthy, although it might be wise to reduce stock write-offs in future (charge for special orders in advance?) and reduce the more discretionary expenses, such as advertising.

Manuel

Task 1

CASH BOOK

DETAIL	DISCOUNT	CASH	BANK	DISCOUNT	CASH	BANK
	£	£	£	£	£	£
Balance b/d		320	300			
Bar takings		200				
Major		80				
Bank			300		300	
Wages					50	40
Bank charges						35
Torquay Wines				15		285
Balance c/d					250	240
		600	600	15	600	600

BPP PUBLISHING

SALES

	£		£
		Cash	200
		Major	100
		Mr Twychin	120
Balance	420		
	420		420

PURCHASES

	£		£
Devon Wines	175	Devon Wines	75
Torquay Wines	500		
		Balance	600
	675		675

MAJOR

	£		£
Balance b/d	80	Cash	80
Sales	100		
		Balance c/d	100
	180		180

WAGES

	£		£
Cash	50		
Bank	40		
		Balance	90
	90		90

MR TWYCHIN

	£		£
Sales	120	Balance c/d	120
	120		120

BANK CHARGES

	£		£
Bank	35	Balance	35
	35		35

	£		£
DEVON WINES			
Purchases	75	Purchases	175
Balance c/d	100		
	175		175

	£		£
TORQUAY WINES			
Bank	285	Purchases	500
Discount	15		
Balance c/d	200		
	500		500

Task 2

PARTIAL TRIAL BALANCE AS AT 30 JUNE

	Dr	Cr
	£	£
Bank balance	240	
Cash in till	250	
Discounts		15
Sales		420
Purchases	600	
Major	100	
Wages	90	
Mr Twychin	120	
Bank charges	35	
Devon Wines		100
Torquay Wines		200
Difference (Note)		700
	1,435	1,435

Note. the £700 by which debits exceed credits corresponds to the opening balances as follows.

	£
Debtor (major)	80
Opening cash balance	320
Opening bank balance	300
	700

BPP PUBLISHING

Part B
Devolved Assessments

Practice Devolved Assessment 1: Reggie Stir

Practice devolved assessment
1 *Reggie Stir*

Performance criteria

The following performance criteria are covered in this Devolved Assessment.

Element 5.1: Maintain records and accounts relating to capital acquisition and disposal

1   Relevant details relating to capital expenditure are correctly entered in the appropriate records

3   All acquisition and disposal costs and revenues are correctly identified and recorded in the appropriate records

6   Profit or loss on disposal is correctly calculated and recorded in the appropriate records

7   The organisation's policies and procedures relating to the maintenance of capital records are adhered to

Notes on completing the Assessment

This Assessment is designed to test your ability to record capital transactions in the journal, the fixed assets register and the ledger.

You are provided with data (Page 62) which you must use to complete the tasks on Page 63.

You are allowed **two hours** to complete your work.

A high level of accuracy is required. Check your work carefully.

Correcting fluid should not be used. Errors should be crossed out neatly and clearly. You should write in ink and not in pencil.

A full suggested solution to this Assessment is provided on Page 167.

Do not turn to the suggested solution until you have completed all parts of the Assessment.

BPP PUBLISHING

PRACTICE DEVOLVED ASSESSMENT 1: REGGIE STIR

Data

Reggie Stir Ltd is a small company producing many different kinds of jugs. Skilled craftsmen make the jugs on a potter's wheel. They are then fired in a kiln and distributed by van to various gift shops.

You are Fletcher Clink, an accounting technician and your boss is Nick McKay, the financial controller. Mr McKay is concerned that the records relating to fixed assets should be kept up to date.

The company, which operates from rented premises, does not have a large number or turnover of fixed assets, the main ones being three potter's wheels, four kilns, one pugmill (a long tube for turning the clay), three delivery vans and various items of furniture, all of which were bought some time ago and are fully depreciated.

The firm keeps a manual fixed assets register, the relevant pages of which are reproduced below.

PLANT AND EQUIPMENT									
Ref	Description	Date of purchase	Cost £	Depreciation period	Accumulated depreciation 31 Dec 1994 £	Date of disposal	Net book value 31 Dec 1994 £	Sale/scrap proceeds £	Loss/ profit £
1/K	Kiln	1 Jan 1993	1200	6 years	400		800		
1/P	Pugmill	1 July 1994	300	4 years	75		225		
2/K	Kiln	1 Mar 1992	600	6 years	300		300		
3/K	Kiln	20 Aug 1991	750	6 years	500		250		
1/W	Wheel	31 Mar 1993	400	4 years	200		200		
2/W	Wheel	1 Feb 1992	400	4 years	300		100		
4/K	Kiln	1 Sep 1992	900	6 years	450		450		
3/W	Wheel	1 Mar 1994	420	4 years	105		315		
Totals			4970		2330		2640		

MOTOR VEHICLES									
Ref	Description	Date of purchase	Cost £	Depreciation type	Accumulated depreciation 31 Dec 1994 £	Date of disposal	Net book value 31 Dec 1994 £	Sale/scrap proceeds £	Loss/ profit £
1/V	Van reg G249 NPO	1 Feb 1990	4000	Reducing balance 25%	3051		949		
2/V	Van reg K697 JKL	1 June 1993	6000	Reducing balance 25%	2625		3375		
3/V	Van reg M894 TMG	30 Sep 1994	8000	Reducing balance 25%	2000		6000		
Totals			18000		7676		10324		

It is the firm's policy to charge a full year's depreciation in the year of purchase and none in the year of sale. Plant and equipment are depreciated on a straight line basis over the periods shown on the register. Motor vehicles are all depreciated at a rate of 25% using the reducing balance method.

During 1995 the following transactions in fixed assets took place.

(a) On 3 August an old kiln (ref. 1/K) was traded in at Cumere Oven Ltd and a new one (ref. 5/K) purchased for £1,600 from the same supplier. A trade-in allowance of £500 was given for the old kiln, the balance to be settled at a later date. An invoice (no. 35X42) was raised by the supplier for the amount in question.

(b)   On 5 September, a new potter's wheel (ref. 4/W) was purchased for £500 cash.

(c)   On 10 October the oldest delivery van (ref. 1/V) was traded in for a new one (ref. 4/V), registration N583 MNO, costing £9,000. The supplier, Van Guard Ltd, gave a trade-in allowance of £1,000 on the old van and raised an invoice (no. Z/2643) for the difference.

It is now 31 December 1995 and you have been asked to help prepare the year-end accounts.

Tasks

(a)   Record the above transactions and the year-end provisions for depreciation in:

   (i)   The journal
   (ii)   The ledger accounts
   (iii)   The fixed assets register

(b)   Produce an extract from the year-end balance sheet showing the following.

   (i)   Plant and equipment (cost)
   (ii)   Motor vehicles (cost)
   (iii)   Plant and equipment (provision for depreciation)
   (iv)   Motor vehicles (provision for depreciation)

All workings should be to the nearest £.

The relevant ledger accounts, journal pages and fixed assets register page are attached for you to complete.

Tutorial note. In practice you would post from the journal to the ledger accounts, but in this exercise you may find it helpful to do the opposite in order to calculate any profit or loss on disposal of fixed assets.

Date	Details	Folio Ref	£	£

JOURNAL   Page 50

Date	Details	Folio Ref	£	£

BPP PUBLISHING

LEDGER ACCOUNTS

PLANT AND EQUIPMENT

	£		£
Date		*Date*	
1995		*1995*	
1 Jan Balance b/f	4,970		

PLANT AND EQUIPMENT: PROVISION FOR DEPRECIATION

	£		£
		Date	
		1995	
		1 Jan Balance b/f	2,330

PLANT AND EQUIPMENT: DISPOSALS

	£		£

MOTOR VEHICLES

	£		£
Date			
1995			
1 Jan Balance b/f	18,000		

MOTOR VEHICLES: PROVISION FOR DEPRECIATION

	£		£
		Date	
		1995	
		1 Jan Balance b/f	7,676

MOTOR VEHICLES: DISPOSALS

	£		£

BPP PUBLISHING

PLANT AND EQUIPMENT

Ref	Description	Date of purchase	Cost £	Depreciation period	Accumulated depreciation 31 Dec 1995 £	Date of disposal	Net book value 31 Dec 1995 £	Sale/scrap proceeds £	Loss/ profit £
1/K	Kiln	1 Jan 1993	1200	6 years					
1/P	Pugmill	1 July 1994	300	4 years					
2/K	Kiln	1 Mar 1992	600	6 years					
3/K	Kiln	20 Aug 1991	750	6 years					
1/W	Wheel	31 Mar 1993	400	4 years					
2/W	Wheel	1 Feb 1992	400	4 years					
4/K	Kiln	1 Sep 1992	900	6 years					
3/W	Wheel	1 Mar 1994	420	4 years					
Totals									
Disposals									
Totals c/f									

MOTOR VEHICLES

Ref	Description	Date of purchase	Cost £	Depreciation type	Accumulated depreciation 31 Dec 1995 £	Date of disposal	Net book value 31 Dec 1995 £	Sale/scrap proceeds £	Loss/ profit £
1/V	Van reg G249 NPO	1 Feb 1990	4000	Reducing balance 25%					
2/V	Van reg K697 JKL	1 June 1993	6000	Reducing balance 25%					
3/V	Van reg M894 TMG	30 Sep 1994	8000	Reducing balance 25%					
Totals									
Disposals									
Totals c/f									

Practice Devolved Assessment 2: Booths

Practice devolved assessment
2 Booths

Performance criteria

The following performance criteria are covered in this Devolved Assessment.

Element 5.1: Maintain records and accounts relating to capital acquisition and disposal

1   Relevant details relating to capital expenditure are correctly entered in the appropriate records

Element 5.2: Record income and expenditure

1   All income and expenditure is correctly identified and recorded in the appropriate records

2   Relevant accruals and prepaid income and expenditure are correctly identified and adjustments are made

3   The organisation's policies, regulations, procedures and timescales are observed in relation to recording income and expenditure

Notes on completing the Assessment

This Assessment is designed to test your ability to post transactions correctly to the ledger accounts and the trial balance.

You are provided with data (Pages 72 to 81) which you must use to complete the tasks on Page 81.

You are allowed **two hours** to complete your work.

A high level of accuracy is required. Check your work carefully.

Correcting fluid should not be used. Errors should be crossed out neatly and clearly. You should write in ink and not in pencil.

A full suggested solution to this Assessment is provided on Page 175.

Do not turn to the suggested solution until you have completed all parts of the Assessment.

Data

You are acting as the temporary bookkeeper at Booths Ltd, a builder's merchant. The financial year end, 30 June 19X7, is approaching. During the day of 30 June 19X7, several primary documents are passed to you for posting to the ledger accounts.

All sales and all purchases are made on credit. All other expenses are paid *immediately* on receipt of a bill.

The ledger accounts appear as follows at the end of 29 June 19X7.

ADVERTISING					
19X7			19X7		
29 June Balance b/f	288	91			

ACCOUNTANCY FEES					
19X7			19X7		
29 June Balance b/f	1,500	00			

BANK ACCOUNT					
19X7			19X7		
29 June Balance b/f	19,330	65			

DOUBTFUL DEBT PROVISION					
19X7			19X7		
			29 June Balance b/f	1,242	94

ELECTRICITY					
19X7			19X7		
29 June Balance b/f	1,733	84			

FIXTURES AND FITTINGS					
19X7			19X7		
29 June Balance b/f	11,893	55			

GAS					
19X7			19X7		
29 June Balance b/f	1,161	20			

INSURANCE					
19X7			19X7		
29 June Balance b/f	658	38			

INTEREST					
19X7			19X7		
29 June Balance b/f	1,141	31			

BPP PUBLISHING

MAINTENANCE					
19X7			19X7		
29 June Balance b/f	3,807	43			

MOTOR EXPENSES					
19X7			19X7		
29 June Balance b/f	606	19			

MOTOR VEHICLES					
19X7			19X7		
29 June Balance b/f	43,675	07			

PROFIT AND LOSS ACCOUNT					
19X7			19X7		
			29 June Balance b/f	27,225	92

PURCHASES					
19X7			19X7		
29 June Balance b/f	76,648	31			

PURCHASE LEDGER CONTROL A/C

19X7			19X7		
			29 June Balance b/f	9,554	93

PRINT, POSTAGE & STATIONERY

19X7			19X7		
29 June Balance b/f	117	29			

RENT

19X7			19X7		
29 June Balance b/f	9,250	00			

SHARE CAPITAL

19X7			19X7		
			29 June Balance b/f	10,000	00

ACCUMULATED DEPRECIATION

19X7			19X7		
			29 June Balance b/f	27,241	12

BPP PUBLISHING

SALES

19X7			19X7		
			29 June Balance b/f	180,754	17

SALES LEDGER CONTROL A/C

19X7			19X7		
29 June Balance b/f	19,356	30			

SUNDRY EXPENSES

19X7			19X7		
29 June Balance b/f	1,427	70			

OPENING STOCK

19X7			19X7		
29 June Balance b/f	37,321	56			

TELEPHONE					
19X7			19X7		
29 June Balance b/f	3,879	09			

UNIFIED BUSINESS RATE					
19X7			19X7		
29 June Balance b/f	4,917	94			

VAT CONTROL A/C					
19X7			19X7		
			29 June Balance b/f	6,719	19

WAGES					
19X7			19X7		
29 June Balance b/f	21,575	63			

WATER RATES					
19X7			19X7		
29 June Balance b/f	2,447	92			

BPP PUBLISHING

The documents which have been passed to you are as follows:

BOOTHS LTD	62 Maple St NO7 3PN Tax point 30.06.X7 VAT No. 3171156327		
MP Price & Co A/C No. 01729		Q	£
Standard bricks		400	504.00
TOTAL			504.00
VAT 17.5%			88.20
			£592.20

BOOTHS LTD	62 Maple St NO7 3PN Tax point 30.06.X7 VAT No. 3171156327		
H Contractors A/C No. 02147		Q	£
Cement bags		10	67.00
Trowel		1	5.50
Spirit Level		1	17.95
TOTAL			90.45
VAT 17.5%			15.83
			£106.28

BOOTHS LTD	62 Maple St NO7 3PN Tax point 30.06.X7 VAT No. 3171156327		
NP Plumbers A/C No. 01227		Q	£
Piping: 1 metre length		40	210.00
Piping: 0.5 metre length		40	102.00
'A' type fittings		25	30.75
TOTAL			342.75
VAT 17.5%			59.98
			402.73

BOOTHS LTD	62 Maple St NO7 3PN Tax point 30.06.X7 VAT No. 3171156327		
CR Harris & Co A/C No. 03994		Q	£
Standard bricks		500	630.00
White bricks		50	100.00
TOTAL			730.00
VAT 17.5%			127.75
			857.75

LARKIN LUMBER LTD

The Mill
Park Lane
NO4 INQ

55321194   Tax point: 30 06 X7

To Booths Ltd

£

3" Timber   1,320.00
4" Timber   1,975.00
                                       3,295.00

VAT 17.5%   576.63
                                       3,871.63

30 days net   VAT No. 371 1942 678

Tax point	Inv. no.
3006X7	X371172L

PLUMBING SUPPLIES LTD
Unit 17 Park Estate No7 1ZR

To Booths Ltd

4cm piping   20m   486.23
6cm piping   30m   1.049.82

TOTAL   1,536.05
VAT   268.81
Amount due   1,804.86

VAT No. 442 1986 883   30 days net

Post Office Counters Ltd
Tax point: 30 06 X7

To Booths Ltd

Franking services
01 March 19X7 to 31 May 19X7

869   1st   208.56
942   2nd   169.56

                                378.12

HALFWAY INVESTMENTS LIMITED

To Booths Ltd   Tax point 29 June 19X7
                           VAT 497 3328 679

RENT

QUARTER TO
29 September 19X7   £2,312.50

WOODLEY GAZETTE
37 Half Lane
NO7 9RP

INV 21737
Tax point: 30/6/X7

VAT No. 113 4279 179

Booths Ltd Wednesday 5th June Half page ad.	33.50
VAT @ 17.5%	5.86
Total	39.36

007321

M Able & Co
Insurance Brokers
9 Green Lane
NO3 4PW

Tax point
30.06.19X7

To Booths Ltd
62 Maple St

Motor vehicle
insurance
per attatched   £1,437.50

Year to 31 May 19X8. Sorry
for the delay - you have
still been covered

Pratts Garage
114 Lark Road
NO1 1NR

S14117
Tax point: 30/6/X7

VAT No. 172 1173 499

BOOTHS LTD A/C 4173

Petrol and oil to 30 June 19X7	317.42
VAT @ 17.5%	55.55
	372.97

I134734

IRT DEALERS
4 The Forecourt

To: Booths Ltd
62 Maple St
NO7 3PN

VAT 147 3321 198
Tax point: 30/6/X7

Executive Car XZ3i Reg J172 BNC	12,600.00
Road Tax	100.00
Extras	542.75
	13,242.75
VAT £13,142.75 @ 17.5%	2,299.98
	15,542.73

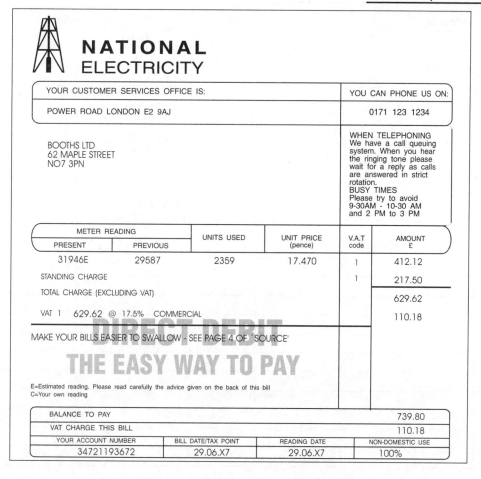

You have also received the following information.

(a) Bank interest of £67.48 has been charged on the company's bank account but has not yet been posted.

(b) The gross wages cost for June, paid on 30 June 19X7, amounted to £2,169.52.

Tasks

(a) Post the transactions shown above to the ledger accounts.

(b) Balance and close off the ledger accounts. You should balance off the revenue and expenditure accounts (as well as the asset and liability accounts), but there is no need to post the balances to the profit and loss account.

(c) Post the balances in the ledger accounts to the trial balance provided overleaf. Add up the trial balance to check that it balances. Investigate any discrepancies.

Note. For (a) to (c) ignore accruals and prepayments.

(d) Identify any accruals and prepayments which would require adjustment in the *extended* trial balance.

Folio	Account	Ref	Trial balance	
			Debit	Credit
			£	£
	TOTAL			

Practice Devolved Assessment 3: Lakeland Catering

Practice devolved assessment
3 Lakeland Catering

Performance criteria

The following performance criteria are covered in this Devolved Assessment.

Element 5.1: Maintain records and accounts relating to capital acquisition and disposal

1   Relevant details relating to capital expenditure are correctly entered in the appropriate records

4   Depreciation charges and other necessary entries and adjustments are correctly calculated and recorded in the appropriate records

Element 5.2: Record income and expenditure

4   Incomplete data is identified and either resolved or referred to the appropriate person

Element 5.4: Prepare the extended trial balance

1   Totals from the general ledger or other records are correctly entered on the ETB

2   Adjustments not dealt with in the ledger accounts are correctly entered on the ETB

4   An agreed valuation of closing work is correctly entered on the ETB

7   The ETB is accurately extended and totalled

Notes on completing the Assessment

This Assessment is designed to test your ability to record capital transactions, prepare accounts from incomplete records and prepare the extended trial balance.

You are provided with data (Pages 86 to 88) which you must use to complete the tasks on Pages 86 and 87.

You are allowed **four hours** in total to complete your work.

A high level of accuracy is required. Check your work carefully.

Correcting fluid should not be used. Errors should be crossed out neatly and clearly. You should write in ink and not in pencil.

A full suggested solution to this Assessment is provided on Page 185.

Do not turn to the suggested solution until you have completed all parts of the Assessment. determine

PRACTICE DEVOLVED ASSESSMENT 3: LAKELAND CATERING

Background information

Lakeland Catering is an organisation established by David Newsome in the early 1990s and which specialises in two main trading activities as follows:

1   Day to day catering operated through a shop and restaurant
2   Specialist catering for functions and banquets

The business which started in a small way has expanded quite rapidly and now employs 18 staff on either a full time or a part time basis.

David has been finding it increasingly difficult to find time to deal with the day to day paperwork and bookkeeping and has appointed you (Caroline Carter) to help him keep day to day control of the organisation's finances and produce some of the necessary financial year end figures for the organisation's accountant.

It is now 31 January 1997 and the firm's year end is 31 December.

In order to complete the tasks you will find attached the following items.

Shop and restaurant

1   Memorandum from David relating to the shop and restaurant

2   List of balances as at 1 January 1996

3   Cash book information for 1996

4   Statement of affairs proforma

5   Closing cash position proforma

6   Control account proformas

7   Trading and profit and loss account proforma

8   Balance sheet proforma

Specialist catering

1   Memorandum from David relating to vans

2   Depreciation methods memorandum proforma

3   Straight line depreciation calculation proforma

4   Reducing balance depreciation calculation proforma

5   Note from David relating to the extended trial balance as at 31 December 1996

6   Extended trial balance proforma

Tasks

Shop and restaurant

(a)   Prepare an opening statement of affairs as at 1 January 1996 clearly identifying the Capital account balance at 1 January 1996.

(b)   Calculate the cash position as at 31 December 1996.

(c)   Prepare the following control accounts.

   (i)   Trade debtors (credit sales only)
   (ii)   Trade creditors
   (iii)   Rent

     (iv)   Wages

     (v)   Electricity

(d)   Prepare the trading and profit and loss account for the period ended 31 December 1996.

(e)   Prepare the balance sheet as at 31 December 1996.

Specialist catering

(f)   Write a short note to David on the attached proforma, explaining the difference between straight line and reducing balance methods of depreciation.

(g)   Calculate the fixed asset records for the van using the proforma and the straight line method of depreciation.

(h)   Calculate the fixed asset records for the van using the proforma and, as an alternative, a reducing balance of 40% method of depreciation.

(i)   Extend the trial balance, calculate the profit or loss, and balance the extended trial balance.

MEMORANDUM

To: Caroline
From: David
Date: 31 January 1997

Shop and restaurant

As you are aware I have had some difficulty keeping up to date with all the necessary records and bookkeeping and so unfortunately I have not kept a complete set of records.

I have managed though to put together some information which I am enclosing as follows.

(a) Balances at 1 January 1996
(b) Cash book information for 1996.

Shop and restaurant

List of balances 1 January 1996

	£
Stock	6,000
Debtors	200
Creditors	1,100
Vehicle (NBV)	5,800
Restaurant fittings (NBV)	3,900
Rent owing	250
Wages owing	610
Electricity prepayment	150
Cash at bank	350

Cash book information for 1996

	£		£
Balance 1 January 1996	350	Payments to trade creditors	17,850
Receipts from debtors	4,910	Telephone	570
Cash sales	27,060	Restaurant maintenance	710
		Insurance	312
		Rent	745
		Wages	8,090
		Electricity	640

All cash and cheques had been banked.

The following needs to be taken into account.

(a) At 31 December 1996 £250 was owing for electricity and £60 rent was paid in advance.

(b) Fittings are depreciated at 20% and the vehicle at 30%, both on a reducing balance basis.

(c) Balances at 31 December 1996 were as follows:

	£
Debtors	615
Creditors	840
Stock	5,400

Shop and restaurant
For task (a)
Statement of affairs as at 1 January 1996

	£	£

Assets

Less: liabilities

BPP PUBLISHING

For task (b)

Closing cash position as at 31 December 1996

	£	£

Receipts

Payments

Closing cash book balance

For task (c)

Control accounts

Trade debtors

	£		£

Trade creditors

	£		£

Rent

	£		£

BPP
PUBLISHING

Wages

£

Electricity

£   £

For task (d)

Shop and restaurant
Trading and profit and loss account for the period ended 31 December 1996

£ £

For task (e)

Shop and restaurant
Balance sheet as at 31 December 1996

	£	£	£

MEMORANDUM

To: Caroline
From: David
Date: 31 January 1997

Specialist catering - vans

I have recently been reviewing the use of vans for our specialist catering division. I do not really understand depreciation but our accountant tells me that we should change our depreciation method from straight line to reducing balance, whatever that means.

The current van we use in the specialist catering division was bought on 1 January 1996 for £10,000 and it was estimated that it would have a useful life of six years, at the end of which it could be sold for £460. Depreciation was to be provided on a straight line basis.

The accountant informs me that the same van, if depreciated on a reducing balance basis would now have a different value in the business. This I do not understand.

For task (f)

MEMORANDUM

To: David
From: Caroline
Date: 31 January 1997

Depreciation methods

MEMORANDUM (cont'd)

MEMORANDUM (cont'd)

For task (g)

Van depreciation - straight line method

Depreciation charge $= \dfrac{10,000 - 460}{6} = 1,590$

		Depreciation charge for year £	*Book value* £
End of year	1		
	2		
	3		
	4		
	5		
	6		

For task (h)

Van depreciation - reducing balance method

Cost $= £10,000$

		Calculation of depreciation charge £	*Depreciation charge for year* £	*Book value* £
End of year	1			
	2			
	3			
	4			
	5			
	6			

BPP PUBLISHING

MEMORANDUM

To: Caroline
From: David
Date: 31 January 1997

Extended trial balance

Please can you complete the extended trial balance for the specialist catering division. I've made a start on it, but I know the following adjustments have still got to be put through.

(a) Vehicle depreciation   £1,590

(b) Fittings depreciation   £250

(c) Electricity owing   £100

(d) Rent prepayment   £250

(e) An invoice of £50 has been charged to insurance when it should have been charged to telephone.

(f) Closing stock at 31 December 1996 of £3,000.

LAKELAND CATERING - SPECIALIST CATERING DIVISION

Description	Trial balance Debit £	Trial balance Credit £	Adjustments Debit £	Adjustments Credit £	Profit and Loss a/c Debit £	Profit and Loss a/c Credit £	Balance Sheet Debit £	Balance Sheet Credit £
Sales		38,500						
Purchases	19,250							
Opening stock	4,000							
Wages	10,100							
Electricity	750							
P/L Depn								
- fittings								
- vehicles								
Telephone	600							
Insurance	450							
Rent	950							
Fixtures -								
cost	5,000							
depn		2,500						
Vehicle -								
cost	10,000							
dep'n								
Stock -								
bal sheet								
trading a/c								
Debtors	700							
Creditors		1,200						
Cash in hand	100							
Bank overdraft		1,400						
Capital		8,300						
Prepayments								
Accruals								
Net profit								
	51,900	51,900						

BPP PUBLISHING

Practice Devolved Assessment 4: Cut Price Electricals

Practice devolved assessment
4   Cut Price Electricals

Performance criteria

The following performance criteria are covered in this Devolved Assessment.

Element 5.1: Maintain records and accounts relating to capital acquisition and disposal

1   Relevant details relating to capital expenditure are correctly entered in the appropriate records

4   Depreciation charges and other necessary entries and adjustments are correctly calculated and recorded in the appropriate records

6   Profit or loss on disposal is correctly calculated and recorded in the accounts

Element 5.2: Record income and expenditure

4   Incomplete data is identified and either resolved or referred to the appropriate person

Element 5.4: Prepare the extended trial balance

1   Totals from the general ledger or other records are correctly entered on the ETB

3   Adjustments not dealt with in the ledger accounts are correctly entered on the ETB

4   An agreed valuation of closing work is correctly entered on the ETB

7   The ETB is accurately extended and totalled

Notes on completing the Assessment

This Assessment is designed to test your ability to record capital transactions, prepare accounts from incomplete records and prepare the extended trial balance.

You are provided with data (Pages 104 to 106) which you must use to complete the tasks on Pages 104 and 105.

You are allowed **four hours** in total to complete your work.

A high level of accuracy is required. Check your work carefully.

Correcting fluid should not be used. Errors should be crossed out neatly and clearly. You should write in ink and not in pencil.

A full suggested solution to this Assessment is provided on Page 193.

Do not turn to the suggested solution until you have completed all parts of the Assessment.

BPP
PUBLISHING

PRACTICE DEVOLVED ASSESSMENT 4: CUT PRICE ELECTRICALS

Background information

Cut Price Electricals is a medium sized organisation in the North of England specialising in two major areas of activity:

(a) Electrical products - wholesaling and retailing

(b) Electrical installation and contracting

The two aspects of the business are treated as separate for accounting purposes although both parts belong to the same business organisation.

The business was established in the mid 1980's by Ian McFarland who retired around 5 years ago leaving the day to day control of the business to his niece Karen Wiggans.

The business has been expanding rapidly over the last few years and Karen has increasingly needed to spend time away from the business attending trade fairs and negotiating contracts. In view of this, and given the significant amount of work which needs doing in establishing and maintaining the financial controls and systems within the organisation, she has recently appointed you (Peter Phillips) as an Accounting Technician to help her with the bookkeeping and the accounting.

It is now 30 November 1996 and the company's year end is 31 October.

Karen is extremely busy and has just left for a three week tour of major trade fairs in the South of England. She has had to leave you alone to put together some of the adjustments and records needed in preparing the accounts for the year ended 31 October 1996. You have been supplied with a certain amount of information which will help you with the more immediate tasks.

In order to complete the tasks, you will find attached the following items:

Retailing Division

(a) Memorandum from Karen Wiggans relating to the Retailing Division

(b) Proforma for opening capital statement

(c) Control account proformas

(d) Bank Reconciliation proforma

(e) Memorandum from Karen Wiggans relating to depreciation of vans

(f) Proforma for van depreciation and fixed asset disposal

Installation and contracting

(a) Memorandum from Karen Wiggans relating to the trial balance as at 31 October

(b) Extended trial balance proforma

Tasks

Retail Division

(a) Prepare a statement of opening capital for the Retail Division, as at 1 November 1995, in the form of a Trial Balance.

(b) Prepare the following control accounts

    (i)   Wages

    (ii)   Rent

    (iii)   Rates

    (iv)   Advertising

    (v)   Insurance

    (vi)   Debtors (trade) - not to include cash sales

    (vii) Creditors (trade) - not to include cash purchases

(c) Prepare a bank reconciliation statement for Mrs Wiggans.

(d) Complete the asset register for Van number 2.

(e) Complete the following accounts for the disposal of Van number 1.

    (i)   Van account

    (ii)   Van depreciation account

    (iii) Asset disposal account

Installation and Contracting Division

(f) Enter the balances as at 31 October 1996 onto the attached proforma.

(g) Make any adjustments necessary, following the memorandum from Karen Wiggans, onto the trial balance.

(h) Extend the trial balance, calculate the profit or loss, and balance the extended trial balance.

MEMORANDUM

To: Peter Phillips

From: Karen Wiggans

Date: 30/11/96

Retailing Division

Welcome to Cut Price Electricals!

I am sorry that I have to leave you alone so soon after joining Cut Price Electricals but as you know, I am on a three week tour of the major trade fairs in the South of England.

There are several urgent tasks which need doing in connection with our Retailing Division to help prepare the necessary books and records prior to completion of our annual accounts.

I have managed to gather some information which should help you with these tasks and this I set out below.

(a) The following balances are available

		1 November 1995 £'000	31 October 1996 £'000
Premises	- cost	100	100
	- depreciation	20	20
Fixtures	- cost	85	85
	- depreciation	15	15
Stock		36	46
Debtors (trade)		20	14
Creditors (trade)		16	27
Vans	- cost	20	20
	- depreciation	10	10
Wages in advance		2	5
Rent in advance		7	3
Rates in arrears		6	2
Insurance - in advance		6	-
Insurance - in arrears		-	3
Advertising - in arrears		5	8

(b)   A summary of the cash book shows the following for the year ended 31/10/96

	£'000
Receipts	
Cash in hand - 1/11/95	2
Debtors	212
Cash sales	37
Payments	
Bank overdraft - 1/11/95	7
Creditor payments (trade)	104
Cash purchases	12
Wages	79
Rent	17
Rates	14
Advertising	8
Insurance	16
Miscellaneous	24

All cash is banked at the earliest opportunity.

(c)   Mr Shah, our bank manager, has told me that we were significantly overdrawn on 31/10/96. I have looked at our cash book and checked it against the bank statement and the differences seem to be as follows.

(i)   Income not yet credited to bank statement but in cash book is £17,000.

(ii)   Cheques paid out of our cash book figures but not yet charged to our account:

101202	£900
101206	£1,100
101209	£650

There was no cash in hand at the year end because I ensured that it was all banked as soon as it was received.

For task (a)

Cut Price Electricals retail division opening capital statement as at 1 November 1995

	DR	CR
	£'000	£'000

BPP PUBLISHING

For task (b)

Control accounts - Retail division

Wages

£'000	£'000

Rent

£'000	£'000

Rates

£'000	£'000

For task (b) (continued)

Advertising

£'000		£'000

Insurance

£'000		£'000

Trade debtors

£'000		£'000

For task (b) (continued)

	Trade creditors	
£'000		£'000

For task (c)

Cut Price Electricals
Bank Reconciliation Statement

£

Balance as per bank statement

Unlodged credits

Uncleared cheques

Balance as per cash book

MEMORANDUM

To: Peter Phillips

From: Karen Wiggans

Date: 30/11/96

Depreciation of Vans

The Retailing Division has 2 vans, details of which are set out below.

Figures have been rounded and at the end of 1994/95, the NBV of both vans was £10,000. Depreciation needs adding for both vans for 1995/96. The depreciation rate for both vans will be 20% straight-line basis assuming no residual value.

You will not be aware that I have been considering selling van number 1 and the offer I received of £3,500 just before the year end I have now accepted. There was no estimated residual value for this van.

Retailing Division
Van Records

Van no	Purchased	Cost	Depreciation to 31/10/95	NBV
		£	£	£
1	1992/93	10,000	(6,000)	4,000
2	1993/94	10,000	(4,000)	6,000

For task (d)

Fixed asset register as at 31 October 1996
Van Number 2

Cost	Depreciation to 31/10/95	Depreciation for year ended 31/10/96	Net book value at 31/10/96
£	£	£	£

For task (e)

Van number 1

Van account

	£'000		£'000

Van depreciation account

	£'000		£'000

Asset disposal account

	£'000		£'000

MEMORANDUM

To: Peter Phillips

From: Karen Wiggans

Date: 30/11/96

Installation and Contracting

I have managed to obtain the attached list of balances for the Installation and Contracting Division as at 31/10/96. You will need to take account of the following adjustments.

(a)   Closing stock at 31/10/96 following the stocktaking was £14,000.

(b)   Depreciation needs providing as follows:

   (i)   Vans - straight line method at 30% with no estimated residual value
   (ii) Fixtures - straight line method at 4% with no estimated residual value

(c)   I would like to make a provision of £2,000 to cover possible bad debts.

(d)   Rent on the garage includes a payment for the next financial year of £1,000.

(e)   An invoice for £3,000 which has been charged to van expenses should have been charged to travel expenses.

(f)   There is an outstanding advertising invoice for £2,000 for the year to 31/10/96.

Installation and contracting
Balances as at 31 October 1996

	£'000
Sales	109
Purchases	64
Stock (1/11/95)	11
Wages	57
Van expenses	14
Travel expenses	3
Garage rent	6
Insurance	2
Tools allowance	5
Advertising	8
Miscellaneous expenses	4
Vans - cost	20
Vans - depreciation	12
Fixtures - cost	75
Fixtures - depreciation	60
Capital	100
Debtors	36
Creditors	21
Cash in hand	6
Bank overdraft	9

CUT PRICE ELECTRICALS - INSTALLATION AND CONTRACTING DIVISION

Description	Trial balance		Adjustments		Profit and Loss a/c		Balance Sheet	
	Debit £	Credit £	Debit £	Credit £	Debit £	Credit £	Debit £	Credit £

BPP
PUBLISHING

TRIAL RUN DEVOLVED ASSESSMENT

INTERMEDIATE STAGE - NVQ/SVQ3

Unit 5

Maintaining financial records

and

Preparing accounts

The purpose of this Trial Run Devolved Assessment is to give you an idea of what a Devolved Assessment could be like. It is not intended as a definitive guide to the tasks you may be required to perform.

The suggested time allowance for this Assessment is four hours. Extra time may be permitted in a real Devolved Assessment. Breaks in assessment may be allowed, but it must normally be completed in one day.

Calculators may be used but no reference material is permitted.

**DO NOT OPEN THIS PAPER UNTIL YOU ARE READY TO START
UNDER TIMED CONDITIONS**

INSTRUCTIONS

This Assessment is designed to test your ability to record capital transactions and prepare financial accounts.

Background information is provided on Page 119.

The tasks you are to perform are set out on Page 119.

You are provided with data on Pages 120 to 122 which you must use to complete the tasks.

Your answers should be set out in the answer booklet on Pages 123 to 128 using the documents provided. You may require additional answer pages.

You are allowed **four hours** to complete your work.

A high level of accuracy is required. Check your work carefully.

Correcting fluid may not be used. Errors should be crossed out neatly and clearly. You should write in black ink, not pencil.

You are advised to read the whole of the Assessment before commencing as all of the information may be of value and is not necessarily supplied in the sequence in which you might wish to deal with it.

A full suggested solution to this Assessment is provided on Pages 201 to 208.

BACKGROUND INFORMATION

Gordon Blur Ltd manufactures and trades in high quality kitchenware for sale to trade and retail customers. The company was established in 19X2 and operates from leasehold premises in Holloway, North London.

Gordon Blur is the managing director and the chief accountant is Kit Shenett. You are the accounts clerk. You have started the job only recently: the previous accounts clerk, Karen Taddup left suddenly having made a few errors and omissions.

The firm is rather old fashioned and still uses a manual accounting system and fixed assets register.

Kit Shenett has gone on holiday leaving you with a trial balance which needs adjusting, a fixed assets register which needs updating and a memo with various pieces of information.

TASKS TO BE COMPLETED

In the answer booklet on Pages 123 to 128 complete the tasks outlined below for the year ended 31 December 19X6. Data for this assessment is provided on Pages 120 to 122.

(a) Enter all the information relating to fixed assets in the ledger accounts given, the journal and the fixed assets register.

(b) Show the journal entries required for items (b) and (c) in the memorandum.

(c) Enter the opening trial balance on the attached proforma after making any adjustments in connection with fixed assets, including recording the profit or loss on the sale of the van.

(d) Make any other adjustments required arising from journal entries, accruals or prepayments on the ETB.

(e) Extend the trial balance, calculate the profit and balance the ETB.

DATA

In order to complete the tasks listed on the previous page you should find attached the following items.

(a) Memorandum from Kit Shenett with some information and helpful hints.
(b) Trial balance as at 31 December 19X6.
(c) Relevant pages of fixed asset register as at 31 December 19X5 (ie last year).

MEMORANDUM

To: Accounts Clerk
From: Kit Shenett
Date: 31 December 19X6

Please find attached a trial balance as at 31 December 19X6. Before the final accounts can be prepared there are several adjustments which need to be made. You will need to do these through the journal, and the extended trial balance (proformas attached).

(a) Could you update the fixed assets register? I always like to ensure that the fixed assets register is kept up to date. Your predecessor Karen didn't do this, omitting to record the fact that on 3 August 19X6 the old van (Reg F396 HJB) was traded in for a new one (K125 ATE) costing £12,000. We were given a trade in allowance of £2,000 on the old van, the balance to be paid later in 19X7 and to be included for now in sundry creditors.

No depreciation has been provided on fixed assets. Could you make the appropriate entries in the journal and adjust the trial balance for this and for the purchase and sale of the vans?

You may find it helpful to use the attached ledger accounts to calculate the profit or loss on disposal of the van. You will need to open an account to record this in the ETB.

Don't forget - plant and equipment is depreciated on the straight line basis over the periods shown in the fixed assets register. Leasehold property is amortised over the period of the lease and motor vehicles are depreciated using the reducing balance method at 25% per annum. We charge a full year's depreciation in the year of purchase and none in the year of sale.

(b) The suspense account balance consists of £4,770 which was money spent on repairs to the equipment. Karen was not very good at understanding the difference between capital and revenue expenditure, so she did not know where to put it. I take it you know where it should go!

(c) One of our customers, a Mr D Faults, has gone into liquidation owing us £200. We also need to increase the bad debts provision to 5% of net trade debtors.

(d) As you probably know, stock at 31.12.X6 is valued at £10,412.

(e) The audit fee of £1,500 needs to be accrued under accounting fees.

(f) We have paid some wages in advance to Luke Easword, amounting to £600.

(g) Our last electricity bill was dated 31 October and was for £300, the normal quarterly charge.

GORDON BLUR LIMITED
TRIAL BALANCE AS AT 31 DECEMBER 19X6

Folio		Dr £	Cr £
P110	Plant and equipment (cost)	55,330	
P120	Plant and equipment (provision for depreciation)		39,660
P130	Plant and equipment (depreciation expense)	-	
M110	Motor vehicles (cost)	25,500	
M120	Motor vehicles (provision for depreciation)		10,788
M130	Motor vehicles (depreciation expense)	-	
L110	Leasehold premises (cost)	100,000	
L120	Leasehold premises (accumulated amortisation)		8,000
L130	Leasehold premises (amortisation expense)	-	
C300	Sundry creditors		3,500
F100	Bank	6,132	
F200	Cash in hand	505	
A100	Accountancy fee	600	
B100	Bad debts provision		150
B200	Bad debts expense		
L300	Loan		10,000
R200	Repairs and maintenance	813	
M300	Motor expenses	1,506	
S100	Sales		205,806
D100	Trade debtors	50,287	
P100	Purchases	158,142	
C100	Trade creditors		65,416
E100	Electricity	900	
P300	Printing, postage, stationery	3,717	
P200	Profit and loss account		40,956
S200	Stock at 1.1.X6	9,125	
S300	Share capital		100,000
S400	Suspense account	4,770	
S500	Sundry expenses	6,428	
W100	Wages and salaries	60,521	
		484,276	484,276

FIXED ASSET REGISTER AS AT 31 DECEMBER 19X5

PLANT AND EQUIPMENT

Ref	Description	Date of purchase	Cost £	Depreciation period	Accumulated depreciation 31.12.X5 £	Date of disposal	Net book value 31.12.X5 £	Sale/scrap proceeds £	(Loss)/ profit £
P111	Cutter	1.3.X2	24,750	5 years	19,800		4,950		
P112	Moulding machine	2.5.X3	12,300	6 years	6,150		6,150		
P113	Assembler	6.6.X3	18,280	4 years	13,710		4,570		
Totals			55,330		39,660		15,670		

MOTOR VEHICLES

Ref	Description	Date of purchase	Cost £	Depreciation type	Accumulated depreciation 31.12.X5 £	Date of disposal	Net book value 31.12.X5 £	Sale/scrap proceeds £	(Loss)/ profit £
M111	Van reg G396 HJB	22.2.X2	6,500	Reducing balance 25%	4,444		2,056		
M112	Van reg H842 GSL	17.3.X4	8,500	Reducing balance 25%	3,719		4,781		
M113	Van reg J542 KLH	12.9.X5	10,500	Reducing balance 25%	2,625		7,875		
Totals			25,500		10,788		14,712		

LEASEHOLD PREMISES

Ref	Description	Date of purchase	Cost £	Term of lease	Accumulated amortisation 31.12.X5 £	Date of disposal	Net book value 31.12.X5 £	Disposal proceeds £	(Loss)/ profit £
L110	Leasehold property	1.1.X2	100,000	50 years	8,000		92,000		

TRIAL RUN DEVOLVED ASSESSMENT

Maintaining financial records

and

Preparing accounts

ANSWER BOOKLET

In this answer booklet you should find attached the following documents on which to complete the tasks.

(a) Partially completed fixed asset register as at 31 December 19X6 for updating
(b) Pages of the journal
(c) Extended trial balance proformas
(d) Ledger account proformas relating to fixed assets

FIXED ASSET REGISTER AS AT 31 DECEMBER 19X6

PLANT AND EQUIPMENT

Ref	Description	Date of purchase	Cost £	Depreciation period	Accumulated depreciation 31.12.X6 £	Date of disposal	Net book value 31.12.X6 £	Sale/scrap proceeds £	(Loss)/ profit £
P111	Cutter	1.3.X2	24,750	5 years					
P112	Moulding machine	2.5.X3	12,300	6 years					
P113	Assembler	6.6.X3	18,280	4 years					
Totals			55,330						

MOTOR VEHICLES

Ref	Description	Date of purchase	Cost £	Depreciation type	Accumulated depreciation 31.12.X6 £	Date of disposal	Net book value 31.12.X6 £	Sale/scrap proceeds £	(Loss)/ profit £
M111	Van reg G396 HJB	22.2.X2	6,500	Reducing balance 25%					
M112	Van reg H842 GSL	17.3.X4	8,500	Reducing balance 25%					
M113	Van reg J542 KLH	12.9.X5	10,500	Reducing balance 25%					
Totals									
Disposals									
Totals									

LEASEHOLD PREMISES

Ref	Description	Date of purchase	Cost £	Term of lease	Accumulated amortisation 31.12.X6 £	Net book value 31.12.X6 £	Disposal proceeds £	(Loss)/ profit £
L110	Leasehold property	1.1.X2	100,000	50 years				

BPP PUBLISHING

	JOURNAL			Page 20
Date	Details	Folio Ref	£	£

	JOURNAL		Page 21	
Date	Details	Folio Ref	£	£

BPP PUBLISHING

LEDGER ACCOUNTS

MOTOR VEHICLES

	£		£
Date			
19X6			
1 Jan Balance b/d	25,500		

MOTOR VEHICLES: PROVISION FOR DEPRECIATION

	£		£
		Date	
		19X6	
		1 Jan Balance b/d	10,788

MOTOR VEHICLES: DISPOSALS

	£		£

GORDON BLUR LIMITED

Folio	Account	Trial balance		Adjustments		Profit and Loss a/c		Balance Sheet	
		Debit £	Credit £	Debit £	Credit £	Debit £	Credit £	Debit £	Credit £
	Subtotal								
	Profit for the year								
	TOTAL								

AAT Sample Simulation

SAMPLE SIMULATION

INTERMEDIATE STAGE - NVQ/SVQ3

Unit 5

Maintaining Financial Records

and Preparing Accounts

(AAT Sample)

This Sample Simulation is the AAT's Sample Simulation for Unit 5. Its purpose is to give you an idea of what an AAT simulation looks like. It is not intended as a definitive guide to the tasks you may be required to perform.

The suggested time allowance for this Assessment is four hours. Up to 30 minutes extra time may be permitted in an AAT simulation. Breaks in assessment will be allowed in the AAT simulation, but it must normally be completed in one day.

Calculators may be used but no reference material is permitted.

**DO NOT OPEN THIS PAPER UNTIL YOU ARE READY TO START
UNDER TIMED CONDITIONS**

INSTRUCTIONS

This Simulation is designed to test your ability to maintain financial records and prepare accounts.

The situation is provided on Page 135.

The tasks you are to perform are set out on Page 136 and 137.

You are provided with data which you must use to complete the tasks.

Your answers should be set out in the answer booklet on Pages 145 to 165 using the documents provided.

You are allowed **four hours** to complete your work.

A high level of accuracy is required. Check your work carefully.

Correcting fluid may be used in moderation. Errors should be crossed out neatly and clearly. You should write in black ink, not pencil.

You are advised to read the whole of the Simulation before commencing as all of the information may be of value and is not necessarily supplied in the sequence in which you might wish to deal with it.

A full suggested solution to this Simulation is provided in this Kit on Pages 209 to 225.

THE SITUATION

Your name is Val Denning and you are an accounts assistant working for Branson & Co, a partnership business owned by two partners called Amy Brandreth and Sanjay Sondin. You report to the firm's Accountant, Jenny Holden.

Branson is a manufacturing business, purchasing raw materials and producing a finished product called a mendip. The manufacturing process is very simple, involving the assembly of just two bought-in parts and a small amount of finishing work. The firm's stocks consist of raw materials (the bought-in parts) and finished mendips; work in progress is negligible in value at any time.

Books and records

Branson maintains a full system of ledger accounts in manual format. Money coming in and going out is recorded in a manual cash book which serves both as a book of prime entry and a ledger account.

Branson also maintains a manual fixed assets register. This includes details of capital expenditure (but not revenue expenditure) incurred in acquiring or enhancing fixed assets, as well as details of depreciation and disposals.

Accounting policies and procedures

Branson is registered for VAT and all of its sales are standard-rated.

Branson classifies its fixed assets into three categories: company cars, plant and equipment, and other fixed assets. For each category the nominal (general) ledger includes accounts relating to cost, depreciation charge (ie the profit and loss expense), accumulated depreciation (ie the balance sheet provision), and disposals.

Company cars are depreciated at a rate of 45% per annum on the reducing balance. Plant and equipment and other fixed assets are depreciated at 25% per annum straight line, assuming nil residual value. In the year of an asset's acquisition a full year's depreciation is charged, regardless of the exact date of acquisition. In the year of an asset's disposal, no depreciation is charged. Company car running costs are recorded in the firm's accounts as an administration overhead. Branson is not able to recover input VAT on the purchase of company cars. Similarly, the firm is not required to account for output VAT when company cars are disposed of.

Authorisation for the acquisition and disposal of fixed assets, and for the method of finance, derives from the partners and is communicated to you by means of a memo from the firm's Accountant at the beginning of each month in which an acquisition or disposal is planned. In the month of March 1998 one acquisition and one disposal took place; these are referred to in the memo on Page 138.

The simulation

In this simulation you will be required to perform a number of tasks leading up to the preparation of an extended trial balance for the year ended 31 March 1998.

TASKS TO BE COMPLETED

In the answer booklet on Pages 145 to 165 complete the tasks outlined below. Data for this assessment is provided on Pages 138 to 143.

1   Refer to the memo on Page 138 and the supplier's invoice on Page 139. This refers to the purchase of a new company car and the trade-in of an existing company car. Record the acquisition and the trade-in in the fixed assets register (see Pages 147-149 in the answer booklet) and in the nominal (general) ledger (see Pages 150-152 in the answer booklet). You are reminded that Branson is *not* able to recover VAT on the acquisition of company cars.

2   By reference to the fixed assets register, calculate the depreciation for the year on each of the company cars and on each item of plant and equipment. You should record the relevant amounts in the fixed assets register and in the nominal (general) ledger. You should also calculate the depreciation for the year on 'other fixed assets' by reference to the relevant account in the nominal (general) ledger and record the amount in the nominal (general) ledger.

3   A member of staff has listed the company cars actually present on Branson's premises at close of business on 31 March 1998. His list is on Page 140. Compare this list with the details recorded in the fixed assets register and describe any discrepancies in a memo to the firm's Accountant. Use the memo form on Page 160 of the answer booklet.

4   The nominal (general) ledger already includes sales and purchases transactions up to 28 February 1998. The sales and purchases day books have been totalled for March 1998 and the totals are displayed on Page 140. Post these totals to the nominal (general) ledger. Note that the invoice from Task 1 was *not* included in the March totals because it was not received until April.

5   Refer to the business bank statement and the business cash book on Pages 141 and 142. Perform a bank reconciliation as at 31 March 1998. Set out your reconciliation on Page 161 of the answer booklet.

6   Post from the business cash book to the nominal (general) ledger for the month of March 1998.

7   Bring down a balance as at 1 April 1998 on each account in the nominal (general) ledger and enter the balances in the first two columns of the trial balance (see Page 162 of the answer booklet). The totals of the two columns will not be equal. You should establish why, and make the appropriate addition to the trial balance.

8   The debit entry in the suspense account (£750) represents a cheque made out on the business bank account earlier in the year. The payee is not known to you as a supplier or employee of Branson. Describe how you would ascertain the nature of this payment so that you can account for it correctly. Set out your answer on Page 163 of the answer booklet.

    (Note: once you have completed this task you should ask your assessor to explain what the payment represents. You will need this information to complete Task 9).

9   The credit entry on the suspense account is the proceeds on disposal of a fixed asset included in the category 'other fixed assets'. No other entries have been made in the nominal ledger in respect of this disposal. The asset originally cost £2,317.69, and its accumulated depreciation at 31 March 1997 was £946.23. Draft journal entries, dated 31 March 1998, to clear the balance on the suspense account. Set out your entries, with full narrative, on Page 164 of the answer booklet. (Note: you are *not* required to adjust the nominal (general) ledger accounts in the light of this transaction.)

10 Details of Branson's closing stocks are given on Page 143. Calculate the value of closing stock of raw materials and finished goods at 31 March 1998 for inclusion in the trial balance. Use the blank Page 165 of the answer booklet for your answer. Note that to calculate the value of finished goods stock you will need to prepare a manufacturing account for the year ended 31 March 1998.

11 On the trial balance, make appropriate adjustments in respect of the following matters.

(a) The journal entries prepared in Task 9

(b) Closing stock calculated in Task 10

(c) Accruals and prepayments. For details of these see Page 143.

12 Extend the trial balance. This includes totalling all columns of the trial balance and making entries to record the net profit or loss for the year ended 31 March 1998.

DATA

MEMO

To: Val Denning

From: Jenny Holden

Subject: Fixed asset acquisitions/disposals in March 1998

Date: 2 March 1998

Only one fixed asset acquisition is planned for the month of March. Our salesman, Andy Noble, will trade in his old car (registration M104PTY) and purchase a new one. The new one will be financed partly by the trade-in value (agreed at £1,850), and partly by cash.

SALES INVOICE

HYLEX MOTORS
BLANKTON

VAT registration: 318 1627 66

Extines Road, Blankton

Telephone: 01489 22514   Fax: 01489 56178

Date/tax point: 27 March 1998

Invoice to:

Branson & Co

Unit 6 Chalmers Industrial Estate

Blankton

BT3 4NY

Invoice number: 42176

Registration: R261 GHT   Registration date: 27/3/98   Stock number: Q4510

Chassis no: TWQQAW 66780   Engine no: ER43218   Sales person: M Easton

	£
Ford Mondeo	
List price	10,900.10
VAT at 17.5%	1,907.50
	12,807.50
Vehicle excise duty (12 months)140.00	
Total due	12,947.50
Less: part-exchange (M104 PTY)	1,850.00
Balance to pay	11,097.50

Terms: net, 30 days

Company cars on the premises, 31 March 1998

P321 HDR - in yard

N33 FGY - in yard

R261 GHT - in yard

Sales day book totals, March 1998

	£
Total value of invoices	36,514.59
Sales value	31,076.25
VAT	5,438.34

Purchases day book totals, March 1998

	£
Total value of invoices	9,133.18
Administration overheads	991.24
Factory overheads	1,451.09
Purchases	4,871.22
Selling and distribution overheads	524.87
VAT	1,294.76

Northern Bank plc

26 High Street, Blankton BT1 6FG

Account: Branson & Co

Account no: 28771243

STATEMENT

45-32-20

Statement no: 192

Details	Payments £	Receipts £	Date	Balance £
			1998	
Balance forward			1-Mar	1,912.90
19328	1,105.36		3-Mar	807.54
CC		4,227.18	4-Mar	5,034.72
19332	365.11		10-Mar	4,669.61
CC		4,265.77	11-Mar	8,935.38
19331	1,192.45		12-Mar	7,742.93
19333	2,651.08		16-Mar	5,091.85
CC		5,931.20	18-Mar	11,023.05
19335	299.52		23-Mar	10,723.53
19334	3,006.12		24-Mar	7,717,41
CC		3,773.81	25-Mar	11,491.22
19340	10,480.05		30-Mar	1,011.17
19336	2,561.29		31-Mar	1,550.12 O/D

Key S/O Standing order   DD Direct debit   CC Cash and/or cheques   CHGS Charges
BACS Bankers automated clearing services   O/D Overdrawn

CB122

RECEIPTS			PAYMENTS					
Total £	Sales ledger control £	Other £	Date 1998	Details	Cheque no	Total £	Purchases ledger control £	Other £
5,034.72			01-Mar	Balance b/f				
4,265.77	4,265.77		06-Mar	Cash and cheques banked				
5,931.20	5,931.20		13-Mar	Cash and cheques banked				
3,773.81	3,773.81		20-Mar	Cash and cheques banked				
6,071.88	6,071.88		27-Mar	Cash and cheques banked				
5,512.67	5,512.67		31-Mar	Cash and cheques banked				
			03-Mar	Hanway plc	19331	1,192.45	1,192.45	
			05-Mar	Peters Limited	19332	365.11	365.11	
			09-Mar	Wright & Parkin	19333	2,651.08	2,651.08	
			16-Mar	Westcott Limited	19334	3,006.12	3,006.12	
			17-Mar	Sidlow & Morris	19335	299.52	299.52	
			24-Mar	Harper John & Co	19336	2,561.29	2,561.29	
			24-Mar	Paul Darby plc	19337	278.01	278.01	
			27-Mar	Brandreth: drawings	19338	500.00		500.00
			27-Mar	Sondin: drawings	19339	450.00		450.00
			27-Mar	Wages and salaries (see analysis below)	19340	10,480.05		10,480.05
			31-Mar	Balance c/d		8,806.42		
30,590.05	25,555.33					30,590.05	10,353,58	11,430.05
8,806.42			01-Apr	Balance b/d				

Wages and salaries analysis

Direct labour		6,014.73
Admin overhead		1,105.69
Factory overhead		1,931.75
Sell and dist overhead		1,427.88
		10,480.05

Stock at 31 March 1998

Raw materials

	Cost	Net realisable value
	£	£
Material X	3,417.22	3,817.66
Material Y	5,441.08	4,719.33

Finished mendips

A total of 25,613 units were produced in the year ended 31 March 1998, of which 3,117 units remained in stock at the year end.

Accruals and prepayments at 31 March 1998

Branson & Co do not attempt to calculate accruals and prepayments for immaterial amounts, defined as being anything less than £200.

The only two items which may amount to more than this are included in administration overheads, as follows.

- Office rental of £3,250 was paid in December 1997 in respect of the six months ending 30 June 1998.

- Telephone and fax charges amount to about £630 per quarter. At 31 March 1998 these charges had already been paid for the quarter ended 31 January 1998, but the invoice for the subsequent quarter is not expected to arrive until May 1998.

SAMPLE SIMULATION

Maintaining Financial Records and Preparing Accounts

ANSWER BOOKLET

ANSWERS (Task 1,2, continued)

EXTRACTS FROM FIXED ASSETS REGISTER

Description/serial no	Location	Date acquired	Original cost £	Enhance-ments £	Total £	Deprecia-tion £	NBV £	Funding method £	Disposal proceeds £	Disposal date £
Plant and equipment										
Milling machine 45217809	Factory	20/6/94	3,456.08		3,456.08			Cash		
Year ended 31/3/95						864.02	2,592.06			
Year ended 31/3/96						864.02	1,728.04			
Year ended 31/3/97						864.02	864.02			
Lathe 299088071	Factory	12/6/95	4,008.24		4,008.24			Cash		
Year ended 31/3/96						1,002.06	3,006.18			
Year ended 31/3/97						1,002.06	2,004.12			
Drill assembly 51123412	Factory	12/2/96	582.44		582.44			Cash		
Year ended 31/3/96						145.61	436.83			
Year ended 31/3/97						145.61	291.22			
Punch drive 91775321	Factory	12/2/96	1,266.00		1,266.00			Cash plus trade-in		
Year ended 31/3/96						316.50	949.50			
Year ended 31/3/97						316.50	633.00			
Winding gear 53098871	Factory	13/3/96	1,082.68		1,082.68			Cash		
Year ended 31/3/96						270.67	812.01			
Year ended 31/3/97				341.79	1,153.80	384.60	769.20			

BPP PUBLISHING

ANSWERS (Tasks 1, 2, continued)

EXTRACTS FROM FIXED ASSETS REGISTER

Description/serial no	Location	Date acquired	Original cost £	Enhance-ments £	Total £	Deprecia-tion £	NBV £	Funding method	Disposal proceeds £	Disposal date £
Plant and equipment										
Tender press 44231809	Factory	8/8/96	4,256.04		4,256.04	1,064.01	3,192.03	Cash		

ANSWERS (Tasks 1, 2,) continued

EXTRACTS FROM FIXED ASSETS REGISTER

Description/serial no	Location	Date acquired	Original cost £	Enhance-ments £	Total £	Deprecia-tion £	NBV £	Funding method	Disposal proceeds £	Disposal date £
Company cars										
M412 RTW	Yard	25/8/94	8,923.71		8,923.71			Lease		
Year ended 31/3/95						4,015.67	4,908.04			
Year ended 31/3/96						2,208.62	2,699.42			
Year ended 31/3/97						1,214.74	1,484.68			
M104 PTY	Yard	15/3/95	8,643.00		8,643.00			Cash		
Year ended 31/3/95						3,889.35	4,753.65			
Year ended 31/3/96						2,139.14	2,614.51			
Year ended 31/3/97						1,176.53	1,437.98			
N33 FGY	Yard	18/9/96	10,065.34		10,065.34			Cash plus		
Year ended 31/3/96						4,529.40	5,535.94		trade-in	
Year ended 31/3/97						2,491.17	3,044.77			
P321 HDR	Yard	13/12/96	9,460.26		9,460.26			Cash		
Year ended 31/3/97						4,257.12	5,203.14			

149

BPP
PUBLISHING

ANSWERS (Tasks 1, 2, 4, 6, 7)

NOMINAL (GENERAL) LEDGER

Account Administration overheads					
Debit			Credit		
Date 1998	Details	Amount £	Date 1998	Details	Amount £
1 Mar	Balance b/f	15,071.23			

Account Brandreth capital account					
Debit			Credit		
Date 1998	Details	Amount £	Date 1998	Details	Amount £
			1 Mar	Balance b/f	17,063.24

Account Brandreth capital account					
Debit			Credit		
Date 1998	Details	Amount £	Date 1998	Details	Amount £
1 Mar	Balance b/f	11,056.73			

ANSWERS (Tasks 1, 2, 4, 6, 7 continued)

NOMINAL (GENERAL) LEDGER

Account Company cars: cost

Date 1998	Details	Amount £	Date 1998	Details	Amount £
1 Mar	Balance b/f	37,092.31			

Debit / Credit

Account Company cars: depreciation charge

Date 1998	Details	Amount £	Date 1998	Details	Amount £

Debit / Credit

Account Company cars: accumulated depreciation

Date 1998	Details	Amount £	Date 1998	Details	Amount £
			1 Apr	Balance b/f	25,921.74

Debit / Credit

BPP PUBLISHING

NOMINAL (GENERAL) LEDGER

Account Company cars: disposals

Date 1998	Details	Amount £	Date 1998	Details	Amount £

Debit — Credit

Account Direct labour costs

Debit — Credit

Date 1998	Details	Amount £	Date 1998	Details	Amount £
1 Mar	Balance b/f	60,012.64			

Account Factory overheads

Debit — Credit

Date 1998	Details	Amount £	Date 1998	Details	Amount £
1 Mar	Balance b/f	27,109.67			

ANSWERS (Tasks 1, 2, 4, 6, 7 continued)

NOMINAL (GENERAL) LEDGER

Account Other fixed assets: cost					
Debit			Credit		
Date 1998	Details	Amount £	Date 1998	Details	Amount £
1 Mar	Balance b/f	18,923.50			

Account Other fixed assets: depreciation charge					
Debit			Credit		
Date 1998	Details	Amount £	Date 1998	Details	Amount £

Account Other fixed assets: accumulated depreciation					
Debit			Credit		
Date 1997	Details	Amount £	Date 1997	Details	Amount £
			1 Apr	Balance b/f	6,224.12

ANSWERS (Tasks 1, 2, 4, 6, 7 continued)

NOMINAL (GENERAL) LEDGER

Account Other fixed assets: disposals

Date 1998	Details	Amount £	Date 1998	Details	Amount £

Debit — Credit

Account Plant and equipment: cost

Date 1998	Details	Amount £	Date 1998	Details	Amount £
1 Mar	Balance b/f	14,993.27			

Debit — Credit

Account Plant and equipment: depreciation charge

Date 1998	Details	Amount £	Date 1998	Details	Amount £

Debit — Credit

ANSWERS (Tasks 1, 2, 4, 6, 7 continued)

NOMINAL (GENERAL) LEDGER

Account Plant and equipment: accumulated depreciation

Debit			Credit		
Date 1997	Details	Amount £	Date 1997	Details	Amount £
			1 Apr	Balance b/f	7,239.68

Account Plant and equipment: disposals

Debit			Credit		
Date 1998	Details	Amount £	Date 1998	Details	Amount £

Account Purchases

Debit			Credit		
Date 1998	Details	Amount £	Date 1998	Details	Amount £
1 Mar	Balance b/f	54,231.89			

155

NOMINAL (GENERAL) LEDGER

Account Purchases ledger control

Debit				Credit	
Date 1998	Details	Amount £	Date 1998	Details	Amount £
			1 Mar	Balance b/f	18,457.20

Account Sales

Debit				Credit	
Date 1998	Details	Amount £	Date 1998	Details	Amount £
			1 Mar	Balance b/f	225,091.42

Account Sales ledger control

Debit				Credit	
Date 1998	Details	Amount £	Date 1998	Details	Amount £
1 Mar	Balance b/f	24,617.03			

ANSWERS (Tasks 1, 2, 4, 6, 7 continued)

NOMINAL (GENERAL) LEDGER

Account Selling and distribution overheads

Debit			Credit		
Date 1998	Details	Amount £	Date 1998	Details	Amount £
1 Mar	Balance b/f	14,303.12			

Account Sondin capital account

Debit			Credit		
Date 1998	Details	Amount £	Date 1998	Details	Amount £
			1 Mar	Balance b/f	8,703.28

Account Sondin current account

Debit			Credit		
Date 1998	Details	Amount £	Date 1998	Details	Amount £
1 Mar	Balance b/f	12,912.29			

BPP PUBLISHING

ANSWERS (Tasks 1, 2, 4, 6, 7 continued)

NOMINAL (GENERAL) LEDGER

Account Stock: raw materials

Debit			Credit		
Date 1997	Details	Amount £	Date 1998	Details	Amount £
1 Apr	Balance b/f	6,294.33			

Account Stock: finished goods

Debit			Credit		
Date 1997	Details	Amount £	Date 1998	Details	Amount £
1 Apr	Balance b/f	12,513.77			

Account Suspense

Debit			Credit		
Date 1998	Details	Amount £	Date 1998	Details	Amount £
26 Jan	Bank	750.00	24 Feb	Bank	1,124.55

ANSWERS (Tasks 1, 2, 4, 6, 7 continued)

NOMINAL (GENERAL) LEDGER

Account VAT					
Debit			Credit		
Date 1998	Details	Amount £	Date 1998	Details	Amount £
			1 Mar	Balance b/f	5,091.27

BPP PUBLISHING

MEMO

To:

From:

Subject:

Date:

ANSWERS (Task 5)

ANSWERS (Tasks 7, 11, 12)

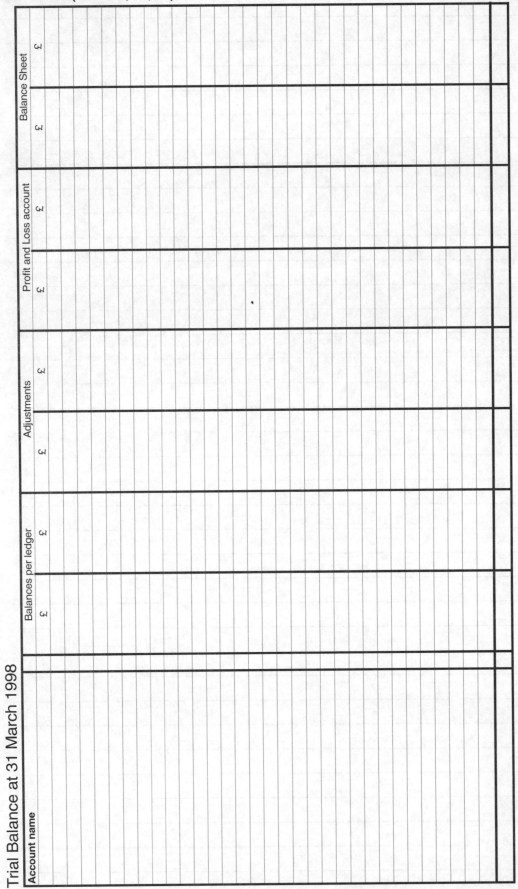

Trial Balance at 31 March 1998

ANSWERS (Tasks 8)

BPP
PUBLISHING

ANSWERS (Tasks 9)

JOURNAL

Date	Account names and narrative	Debit	Credit
1998		£	£

ANSWERS (Task 10)

Answers to Practice Devolved Assessment 1: Reggie Stir

SOLUTION TO PRACTICE DEVOLVED ASSESSMENT 1: REGGIE STIR

Tutorial note. When doing the journal entries you should not record the purchase of the potter's wheel. This is because the purchase was for *cash* and the journal only records *credit* purchases. The book of prime entry for cash purchases of fixed assets is the cash book.

Solution

(a)

	JOURNAL			Page 50
Date	Details	Folio Ref	£	£
3 August	Plant and equipment	P/E	1600	
	Plant and equipment disposals	P/D		500
	Cumere Oven Ltd	C/O		1100
	Being part exchange per agreement and invoice no 35X42			
3 August	Plant and equipment: disposals	NP/D	1200	
	Plant and equipment	P/E		1200
	Being transfer of plant (1/K) at cost to plant disposals a/c			
3 August	Plant and equipment: depreciation provision	PD/P	400	
	Plant and equipment: disposal	NP/D		400
	Being transfer of depreciation provision (1/K) to plant disposals a/c			
10 October	Motor vehicles	M/V	9000	
	Motor vehicles disposals	MV/D		1000
	Van Guard Ltd	V/G		8000
	Being part exchange per agreement and invoice no Z/2643			
10 October	Motor vehicles disposals	MV/D	4000	
	Motor vehicles	M/V		4000
	Being transfer of van 1/V at cost to disposals a/c			

BPP PUBLISHING

JOURNAL

Page 51

Date	Details	Folio Ref	£	£
10 October	Motor vehicles: depreciation provision	MV/DP	3051	
	Motor vehicles: disposals	MV/D		3051
	Being transfer of depreciation provision 1V to motor vehicles disposals a/c			
31 December	P & L a/c	P/L	300	
	Plant and equipment: disposals a/c	P/D		300
	Being loss on part exchange of kiln 1/K			
31 December	Motor vehicles: disposals	MV/D	51	
	P & L a/c	P/L		51
	Being profit on part exchange of van 1/V			
31 December	Plant and equipment: depreciation expense	P/DE	1147	
	Plant and equipment: depreciation provision	PD/P		1147
	Being year end provision for depreciation on plant			
31 December	Motor vehicles depreciation expense	MV/DE	4594	
	Motor vehicles depreciation provision	MV/DP		4594
	Being year end provision for depreciation on motor vehicles			

LEDGER ACCOUNTS

PLANT AND EQUIPMENT

Date		£	Date		£
1995			*1995*		
1 Jan	Balance b/f	4,970			
3 Aug	Creditors £(1,600 – 500)	1,100	3 Aug	Plant and equipment:	
3 Aug	Plant and equipment:			disposals	1,200
	disposals	500	31 Dec	Balance c/f	5,870
5 Sep	Bank	500			
		7,070			7,070

PLANT AND EQUIPMENT: PROVISION FOR DEPRECIATION

Date		£	Date		£
1995			*1995*		
3 Aug	Plant and equipment:		1 Jan	Balance b/f	2,330
	disposals	400	31 Dec	P & L a/c (W1)	1,147
31 Dec	Balance c/f	3,077			
		3,477			3,477

PLANT AND EQUIPMENT: DISPOSALS

Date		£	Date		£
1995			*1995*		
3 Aug	Plant and equipment	1,200	3 Aug	Depreciation	
				provision	400
			3 Aug	Plant and equipment	500
			31 Dec	P & L account	300
		1,200			1,200

MOTOR VEHICLES

Date		£	Date		£
1995			*1995*		
1 Jan	Balance b/f	18,000	10 Oct	Motor vehicles:	
10 Oct	Motor vehicles:			disposals	4,000
	disposals	1,000	31 Dec	Balance c/f	23,000
10 Oct	Creditors				
	£(9,000 – 1,000)	8,000			
		27,000			27,000

MOTOR VEHICLES: PROVISION FOR DEPRECIATION

Date		£	Date		£
1995			*1995*		
10 Oct	Motor vehicles:		1 Jan	Balance b/f	7,676
	disposals	3,051	31 Dec	P & L a/c (W2)	4,594
31 Dec	Balance c/f	9,219			
		12,270			12,270

MOTOR VEHICLES: DISPOSALS

Date		£	Date		£
1995			*1995*		
10 Oct	Motor vehicles	4,000	10 Oct	Depreciation provision	3,051
31 Dec	P & L account	51	10 Oct	Motor vehicles	1,000
		4,051			4,051

PLANT AND EQUIPMENT

Ref	Description	Date of purchase	Cost £	Depreciation period	Accumulated depreciation 31 Dec 1995 £	Date of disposal	Net book value 31 Dec 1995 £	Sale/scrap proceeds £	(Loss)/ profit £
1/K	Kiln	1 Jan 1993	1200	6 years	400	3 Aug 1995	800	500	(300)
1/P	Pugmill	1 July 1994	300	4 years	150		150		
2/K	Kiln	1 Mar 1992	600	6 years	400		200		
3/K	Kiln	20 Aug 1991	750	6 years	625		125		
1/W	Wheel	31 Mar 1993	400	4 years	300		100		
2/W	Wheel	1 Feb 1992	400	4 years	400		nil		
4/K	Kiln	1 Sep 1992	900	6 years	600		300		
3/W	Wheel	1 Mar 1994	420	4 years	210		210		
5/K	Kiln	3 Aug 1995	1600	6 years	267		1333		
4/W	Wheel	5 Sept 1995	500	4 years	125		375		
Totals			7070		3477		3593		
Disposals			1200		400		800	500	(300)
Totals c/f			5870		3077		2793		

MOTOR VEHICLES

Ref	Description	Date of purchase	Cost £	Depreciation type	Accumulated depreciation 31 Dec 1995 £	Date of disposal	Net book value 31 Dec 1995 £	Sale/scrap proceeds £	(Loss)/ profit £
1/V	Van reg D249 NPO	1 Feb 1990	4000	Reducing balance 25%	3051	10 Oct 1995	949	1000	51
2/V	Van reg K697 JKL	1 Jan 1993	6000	Reducing balance 25%	3469		2531		
3/V	Van reg J894 TMG	30 Sept 1994	8000	Reducing balance 25%	3500		4500		
4/V	Van reg N583 MNO	10 Oct 1995	9000	Reducing balance 25%	2250		6750		
Totals			27000		12270		14730		
Disposals			4000		3051		949	1000	51
Totals c/f			23000		9219		13781		

Workings

1 *Depreciation charge: plant and equipment*

	£
Kilns £(600 + 750 + 900 + 1,600) ÷ 6	642
Other £(300 + 400 + 400 + 420 + 500) ÷ 4	505
	1,147

Note. It should be assumed from the question that all kilns are depreciated over 6 years and all wheels over 4 years.

2 *Depreciation charge: motor vehicles*

	£	£
Van 2/V: NBV 1 January 1995	3,375	
Depreciation @ 25%		844
Van 3/V: NBV 1 January 1995	6,000	
Depreciation @ 25%		1,500
Van 4/V: depreciation (25% × £9,000)		2,250
Total charge to P & L		4,594

(b) REGGIE STIR LIMITED
     BALANCE SHEET EXTRACT AS AT 31 DECEMBER 1995

	Cost £	Accumulated depreciation £	NBV £
Fixed assets			
Plant and equipment	5,870	3,077	2,793
Motor vehicles	23,000	9,219	13,781
	28,870	12,296	16,574

Answers to Practice Devolved Assessment 2: Booths

SOLUTION TO PRACTICE DEVOLVED ASSESSMENT 2: BOOTHS

Tutorial note. You will realise from your earlier studies that the sales and purchase invoices shown in the question would normally be posted to the sales day book and purchases day book respectively. We have bypassed the day books in the example, for the sake of simplicity and because the main emphasis of the assignment is the posting of transactions to the correct ledger accounts.

Solution

(a) and (b)

The ledger accounts will appear as follows after the postings for 30 June 19X7 and after being balanced off.

ADVERTISING					
19X7			19X7		
29 June Balance b/f	288	91			
30 June Bank	33	50	30 June P+L account	322	41
	322	41		322	41

ACCOUNTANCY FEES					
19X7			19X7		
29 June Balance b/f	1,500	00	30 June P+L account	1,500	00

BANK ACCOUNT					
19X7			19X7		
29 June Balance b/f	19,330	65			
			30 June Woodley Gazette	39	36
			Electricity	739	80
			M Able & Co	1,437	50
			Interest bank	67	48
			Pratts Garage	372	97
			Post Office	378	12
			Halfway Investments	2,312	50
			Wages	2,169	52
30 June Balance c/f	3,729	33	Motor vehicles + road tax	15,542	73
	23,059	98		23,059	98

DOUBTFUL DEBT PROVISION					
19X7			19X7		
30 June Balance c/f	1,242	94	29 June Balance b/f	1,242	94

ELECTRICITY					
19X7			19X7		
29 June Balance b/f	1,733	84			
30 June Bank	629	62	30 June P+L account	2,363	46
	2,363	46		2,363	46

FIXTURES AND FITTINGS					
19X7			19X7		
29 June Balance b/f	11,893	55	30 June Balance c/f	11,893	55

GAS					
19X7			19X7		
29 June Balance b/f	1,161	20	30 June P+L account	1,161	20

INSURANCE					
19X7			19X7		
29 June Balance b/f	658	38			
30 June Bank	1,437	50	30 June P+L account	2,095	88
	2,095	88		2,095	88

INTEREST					
19X7			19X7		
29 June Balance b/f	1,141	31			
30 June Bank	67	48	30 June P+L account	1,208	79
	1,208	79		1,208	79

MAINTENANCE

19X7			19X7		
29 June Balance b/f	3,807	43	30 June P+L account	3,807	43

MOTOR EXPENSES

19X7			19X7		
29 June Balance b/f	606	19			
30 June Bank	317	42			
* Bank	100	00			
** Bank	1,437	50	30 June P+L account	2,461	11
	2,461	11		2,461	11

MOTOR VEHICLES

19X7			19X7		
29 June Balance b/f	43,675	07			
30 June Bank	15,442	73	30 June Balance c/f	59,117	80
	59,117	80		59,117	80

PROFIT AND LOSS ACCOUNT

19X7			19X7		
30 June Balance c/f	27,225	92	29 June Balance b/f	27,225	92

PURCHASES

19X7			19X7		
29 June Balance b/f	76,648	31			
30 June Larkin Lumber					
P/L Control a/c	3,295	00			
Plumbing supplies					
P/L Control a/c	1,536	05	30 June P+L account	81,479	36
	81,479	36		81,479	36

* A prepayment would not normally be required for such a small amount; in any case this would not be calculated until the ETB was prepared.

** This amount might have been posted to the insurance account, depending on company policy, but this is more appropriate.

PURCHASE LEDGER CONTROL A/C					
19X7			19X7		
			29 June Balance b/f	9,554	93
			30 June Larkin Lumber	3,871	63
30 June Balance c/f	15,231	42	Plumbing supplies	1,804	86
	15,231	42		15,231	42

PRINT, POSTAGE & STATIONERY					
19X7			19X7		
29 June Balance b/f	117	29			
30 June Bank	378	12	30 June P+L account	495	41
	495	41		495	41

RENT					
19X7			19X7		
29 June Balance b/f	9,250	00			
30 June Bank	2,312	50	30 June P+L account	11,562	50
	11,562	50		11,562	50

Note. The rent invoice just paid is for rent to 30 September 19X7. This would be adjusted as a prepayment on the *extended* trial balance.

SHARE CAPITAL					
19X7			19X7		
30 June Balance c/f	10,000	00	29 June Balance b/f	10,000	00

ACCUMULATED DEPRECIATION					
19X7			19X7		
30 June Balance c/f	27,241	12	29 June Balance b/f	27,241	12

SALES

19X7			19X7		
			29 June Balance b/f	180,754	17
			30 June Sales Ledger		
			Control a/c		
			MP Price & Co	504	00
			H Contractors	90	45
			NP Plumbers	342	75
30 June Balance c/f	182,421	37	CR Harris & Co	730	00
	182,421	37		182,421	37

SALES LEDGER CONTROL A/C

19X7			19X7		
29 June Balance b/f	19,356	30			
30 June Sales					
MP Price & Co	592	20			
H Contractors	106	28			
NP PLumbers	402	73			
CR Harris & Co	857	75	30 June Balance c/f	21,315	26
	21,315	26		21,315	26

SUNDRY EXPENSES

19X7			19X7		
29 June Balance b/f	1,427	70	30 June P+L account	1,427	70

OPENING STOCK

19X7			19X7		
29 June Balance b/f	37,321	56	30 June Balance c/f	37,321	56

TELEPHONE					
19X7			19X7		
29 June Balance b/f	3,879	09	30 June P & L account	3,879	09

UNIFORM BUSINESS RATE					
19X7			19X7		
29 June Balance b/f	4,917	94	30 June P & L account	4,917	94

VAT CONTROL A/C					
19X7			19X7		
30 June Bank	5	86	29 June Balance b/f	6,719	19
Bank	110	18	30 June Sales ledger	88	20
Bank	55	55	Sales ledger	15	83
Purchases ledger	576	63	Sales ledger	59	98
Purchases ledger	268	81	Sales ledger	127	75
Balance c/f	5,993	92			
	7,010	95		7,010	95

WAGES					
19X7			19X7		
29 June Balance b/f	21,575	63			
30 June Bank	2,169	52	30 June P & L account	23,745	15
	23,745	15		23,745	15

WATER RATES					
19X7			19X7		
29 June Balance b/f	2,447	92	30 June P & L account	2,447	92

(c) The balances on the ledger accounts, once extracted, will give the following trial balance.

FOLIO	DESCRIPTION	REF.	TRIAL BALANCE			
	Advertising		322	41		
	Accountancy fees		1,500	00		
	Bank				3,729	33
	Depreciation (accumulated)				27,241	12
	Doubtful debt provision				1,242	94
	Electricity		2,363	46		
	Fixtures and fittings		11,893	55		
	Gas		1,161	20		
	Insurance		658	38		
	Interest		1,208	79		
	Maintenance		3,807	43		
	Motor expenses		2,461	11		
	Motor vehicles		59,117	80		
	Profit and loss account				27,225	92
	Purchases		81,479	36		
	Purchase ledger control a/c				15,231	42
	Print, post and stationery		495	41		
	Rent		11,562	50		
	Share capital				10,000	00
	Sales				182,421	37
	Sales ledger control a/c		21,315	26		
	Sundry expenses		1,427	70		
	Stock 1.1 X4		37,321	56		
	Telephone		3,879	09		
	Unified Business Rate		4,917	94		
	VAT				5,993	92
	Wages		23,745	15		
	Water rates		2,447	92		
	TOTAL		273,086	02	273,086	02

BPP
PUBLISHING

(d) The following accruals and prepayments should be identified.

Accruals

Franking services: £378.12 × 1/3 = £126.04

Prepayments

Rent: quarter to 30 September 19X7: £2,312.50

Motor insurance: £1,437.50 × 11/12 = £1,317.71

Answers to Practice Devolved Assessment 3: Lakeland Catering

SOLUTION TO PRACTICE DEVOLVED ASSESSMENT 3: LAKELAND CATERING

Shop and restaurant
Task (a)

Statement of affairs as at 1 January 1996

	£	£
Assets		
Vehicle	5,800	
Restaurant fittings	3,900	
Stock	6,000	
Debtors	200	
Bank	350	
Prepayment	150	
		16,400
Less: liabilities		
Creditors	(1,100)	
Accruals – rent	(250)	
– wages	(610)	
		(1,960)
Capital (as at 1 January 1996)		14,440

Task (b)

Closing cash position as at 31 December 1996

	£	£
Receipts		
Opening balance	350	
Sales	31,970	
		32,320
Payments		(28,917)
Closing cash book balance		3,403

Task (c)

Control accounts

Trade debtors

	£		£
b/f 1 January 1996	200	Cash/bank	4,910
P&L	5,325	c/f 31 December 1996	615
	5,525		5,525
b/f 1 January 1997	615		

Trade creditors

	£		£
Cash/bank	17,850	b/f 1 January 1996	1,100
c/f 31 December 1996	840	P&L	17,590
	18,690		18,690
		b/f 1 January 1997	840

Rent

	£		£
Cash/bank	745	b/f 1 January 1996	250
		P&L	435
		c/f 31 December 1996	60
	745		745
b/f 1 January 1997	60		

Wages

	£		£
Cash/bank	8,090	b/f 1 January 1996	610
		P&L	7,480
	8,090		8,090

Electricity

	£		£
b/f 1 January 1996	150	P&L	1,040
Cash/bank	640		
c/f 31 December 1996	250		
	1,040		1,040
		b/f 1 January 1997	250

Task (d)

Shop and restaurant

Trading and profit and loss account for the period ended 31 December 1996

	£	£
Sales		32,385
Opening stock	6,000	
Add: purchases	17,590	
	23,590	
Less: closing stock	(5,400)	
Cost of goods sold		(18,190)
Gross profit		14,195
Less: rent	435	
wages	7,480	
electricity	1,040	
depreciation — fittings	780	
— vehicle	1,740	
telephone	570	
restaurant maintenance	710	
insurance	312	
		(13,067)
Net profit		1,128

Task (e)

Shop and restaurant

Balance sheet as at 31 December 1996

	b/f £	Depn £	NBV £
Fixed assets			
Fittings	3,900	(780)	3,120
Van	5,800	(1,740)	4,060
	9,700	(2,520)	7,180
Current assets			
Stock	5,400		
Debtors	615		
Rent prepayment	60		
Cash	3,403		
		9,478	
Less: current liabilities			
Creditors	840		
Accrual - electricity	250		
		(1,090)	
			8,388
			15,568
Financed by			
Capital as at 1 January 1996			14,440
Net profit			1,128
			15,568

Task (f)

MEMORANDUM

To: David
From: Caroline
Date: 31 January 1997

Depreciation methods

Straight line depreciation is obtained by calculating a fixed annual sum by which an asset will be depreciated. So, for example, if an asset was purchased for £10,000 and is to be depreciated over four years and have an expected selling price at the end of four years of £4,100 then the annual depreciation charge per annum will be £1,475.

The reducing balance method of depreciation means that the depreciation charged against profits reduces year on year. The main justification for using this method is that each year, as the machine wears out, more and more will be spent on repairing and maintaining it. The reducing balance method is expressed as a percentage of the book value so, for example, if we use a reducing balance percentage of 20% for the previous example the figures would be as follows.

Cost £10,000

End of year	Calculation	Depreciation	Book value
1	£10,000 × 20%	£2,000	£8,000
2	£8,000 × 20%	£1,600	£6,400

etc.

Task (g)

Van depreciation - straight line method

$$\text{Depreciation charge} = \frac{10,000 - 460}{6} = 1,590$$

		Depreciation charge for year £	Book value £
End of year	1	1,590	8,410
	2	1,590	6,820
	3	1,590	5,230
	4	1,590	3,640
	5	1,590	2,050
	6	1,590	460

Task (h)

Van depreciation - reducing balance method

Cost = £10,000

		Calculation of depreciation charge £	Depreciation charge for year £	Book value £
End of year	1	10,000 × 40%	4,000	6,000
	2	6,000 × 40%	2,400	3,600
	3	3,600 × 40%	1,440	2,160
	4	2,160 × 40%	864	1,296
	5	1,296 × 40%	518	778
	6	778 × 40%	311	467

LAKELAND CATERING - SPECIALIST CATERING DIVISION

Description	Trial balance Debit £	Trial balance Credit £	Adjustments Debit £	Adjustments Credit £	Profit and Loss a/c Debit £	Profit and Loss a/c Credit £	Balance Sheet Debit £	Balance Sheet Credit £
Sales		38,500				38,500		
Purchases	19,250				19,250			
Opening stock	4,000				4,000			
Wages	10,100				10,100			
Electricity	750		100		850			
P/L Depn								
- fittings			250		250			
- vehicles			1,590		1,590			
Telephone	600		50		650			
Insurance	450			50	400			
Rent	950			250	700			
Fixtures -								
cost	5,000						5,000	
depn		2,500		250				2,750
Vehicle -								
cost	10,000						10,000	
depn				1,590				1,590
Stock -								
bal sheet			3,000				3,000	
trading a/c				3,000		3,000		
Debtors	700						700	
Creditors		1,200						1,200
Cash in hand	100						100	
Bank overdraft		1,400						1,400
Capital		8,300						8,300
Prepayments			250				250	
Accruals				100				100
Net profit					3,710			3,710
TOTALS	51,900	51,900	5,240	5,240	41,500	41,500	19,050	19,050

Answers to Practice Devolved Assessment 4: Cut Price Electricals

SOLUTION TO PRACTICE DEVOLVED ASSESSMENT 4: CUT PRICE ELECTRICALS

Task (a)

*Cut Price Electricals retail division opening capital statement
as at 1 November 1995*

	DR £'000	CR £'000
Premises - cost	100	
Premises - depreciation		20
Fixtures - cost	85	
Fixtures - depreciation		15
Vans - cost	20	
Vans - depreciation		10
Stock	36	
Debtors	20	
Creditors		16
Wages - in advance	2	
Rent - in advance	7	
Rates - in arrears		6
Advertising - in arrears		5
Insurance - in advance	6	
Cash in hand	2	
Bank overdraft		7
Capital as at 1/11/95 (balancing item)		199
	278	278

Task (b)

Control accounts - Retail Division

Wages

	£'000		£'000
b/f 1/11/95	2	P&L	76
Cash/bank	79	c/f 31/10/96	5
	81		81
b/f 1/11/96	5		

Rent

	£'000		£'000
b/f 1/11/95	7	P&L	21
Cash/bank	17	c/f 31/10/96	3
	24		24
b/f 1/11/96	3		

Rates

	£'000		£'000
Cash/bank	14	b/f 1/11/95	6
c/f 31/10/96	2	P&L	10
	16		16
		b/f 1/11/96	2

Advertising

	£'000		£'000
Cash/bank	8	b/f 1/11/95	5
c/f 31/10/96	8	P&L	11
	16		16
		b/f 1/11/96	8

Insurance

	£'000		£'000
b/f 1/11/95	6	P&L	25
Cash/bank	16		
c/f 31/10/96	3		
	25		25
		b/f 1/11/96	3

Trade debtors

	£'000		£'000
b/f 1/11/95	20	Cash/bank	212
P&L	206	c/f 31/10/96	14
	226		226
b/f 1/11/96	14		

Trade creditors

	£'000		£'000
Cash/bank	104	b/f 1/11/95	16
c/f 31/10/96	27	P&L	115
	131		131
		b/f 1/11/96	27

Task (c)

Cut Price Electricals
Bank Reconciliation Statement

	£
Balance as per bank statement	(44,350)
Unlodged credits	17,000
Uncleared cheques	(2,650)
Balance as per cash book	(30,000)

Tasks (d) and (e)

Fixed asset register as at 31 October 1996
Van number 2

Cost	Depreciation to 31/10/95	Depreciation for year ended 31/10/96	Net book value at 31/10/96
£10,000	£4,000	£2,000	£4,000

BPP PUBLISHING

Van number 1

Van account

	£'000		£'000
b/f 1/11/95	10	Asset disposal	10

Van depreciation account

	£'000		£'000
Asset disposal	8	b/f 1/11/95	6
	8	Charge for year	2
			8

Asset disposal account

	£'000		£'000
Van	10.0	Depreciation account	8.0
Profit on disposal to P&L	1.5	Cash/bank	3.5
	11.5		11.5

CUT PRICE ELECTRICALS - INSTALLATION AND CONTRACTING DIVISION

Description	Trial balance Debit £'000	Trial balance Credit £'000	Adjustments Debit £'000	Adjustments Credit £'000	Profit and Loss a/c Debit £'000	Profit and Loss a/c Credit £'000	Balance Sheet Debit £'000	Balance Sheet Credit £'000
Sales		109				109		
Purchases	64				64			
Stock	11				11			
Wages	57				57			
Van expenses	14			3	11			
Travel expenses	3		3		6			
Garage rent	6			1	5			
Insurance	2				2			
Tools allowance	5				5			
Advertising	8		2		10			
Misc - expenses	4				4			
Vans - cost	20						20	
Vans - depn		12		6				18
Fixtures - cost	75						75	
Fixtures - depn		60		3				63
Capital		100						100
Debtors	36						36	
Creditors		21						21
Cash in hand	6						6	
Bank overdraft		9						9
Stock - B sheet			14				14	
- Trading a/c				14		14		
P/L Depn - Vans			6		6			
Fixtures			3		3			
Bad debt provsn								
- B sheet				2				2
- P/L a/c			2		2			
Prepayments / accruals			1	2			1	2
Net loss						63	63	
	311	311	31	31	186	186	215	215

ANSWERS TO TRIAL RUN
DEVOLVED ASSESSMENT

PLANT AND EQUIPMENT

Ref	Description	Date of purchase	Cost £	Depreciation period	Accumulated depreciation 31.12.X6 £	Date of disposal	Net book value 31.12.X6 £	Sale/scrap proceeds £	(Loss)/ profit £
P111	Cutter	1.3.X2	24,750	5 years	24,750		- - - - -		
P112	Moulding machine	2.5.X3	12,300	6 years	8,200		4,100		
P113	Assembler	6.6.X3	18,280	4 years	18,280		- - - - -		
Totals			55,330		51,230		4,100		

MOTOR VEHICLES

Ref	Description	Date of purchase	Cost £	Depreciation type	Accumulated depreciation 31.12.X6 £	Date of disposal	Net book value 31.12.X6 £	Sale/scrap proceeds £	(Loss)/ profit £
M111	Van reg F396 HJB	22.2.X2	6,500	Reducing balance 25%	4,444	3.8.X6	2,056	2,000	56
M112	Van reg H842 GSL	17.3.X4	8,500	Reducing balance 25%	4,914		3,586		
M113	Van reg J542 KLH	12.9.X5	10,500	Reducing balance 25%	4,594		5,906		
M114	Van reg K125 ATE	3.8.X6	12,000	Reducing balance 25%	3,000		9,000		
Totals			37,500		16,952		20,548		
Disposals			6,500		4,444		2,056	2,000	56
Totals c/f			31,000		12,508		18,492		

LEASEHOLD PREMISES

Ref	Description	Date of purchase	Cost £	Term of lease	Accumulated amortisation 31.12.X6 £	Date of disposal	Net book value 31.12.X6 £	Disposal proceeds £	(Loss)/ profit £
L110	Leasehold property	1.1.X2	100,000	50 years	10,000		90,000		

LEDGER ACCOUNTS

MOTOR VEHICLES

Date 19X6		£	Date 19X6		£
1 Jan	Balance b/d	25,500	3 Aug	Motor vehicles: disposals	6,500
3 Aug	Motor vehicles: disposals	2,000	31 Dec	Balance c/d	31,000
3 Aug	Sundry creditors	10,000			
		37,500			37,500

MOTOR VEHICLES: PROVISION FOR DEPRECIATION

Date 19X6		£	Date 19X6		£
3 Aug	Motor vehicles: disposals	4,444	1 Jan	Balance b/d	10,788
31 Dec	Balance c/d	12,508	31 Dec	Motor vehicles: depreciation (W1)	6,164
		16,952			16,952

MOTOR VEHICLES: DISPOSALS

Date 19X6		£	Date 19X6		£
3 Aug	Motor vehicles	6,500	3 Aug	Motor vehicles	2,000
			3 Aug	Provision for depreciation	4,444
			31 Dec	Profit and loss	56
		6,500			6,500

JOURNAL

Page 20

Date	Details	Folio Ref	£	£
3 August	Motor vehicles	M110	12,000	
	Motor vehicles disposals	M150		2,000
	Sundry creditors	L300		10,000
	Being purchase of van K125 ATE by part exchange			
3 August	Motor vehicles disposals	M150	6,500	
	Motor vehicles	M110		6,500
	Being transfer of van F396 HJB at cost to disposals a/c			
3 August	Motor vehicles depreciation provision	M120	4,444	
	Motor vehicles disposals	M150		4,444
	Being transfer of depreciation provision to motor vehicles a/c			
	Profit and loss a/c			
31 December	Profit and loss a/c	P200	56	
	Motor vehicles disposals a/c	M150		56
	Being loss on part exchange of van F306 HJB			
31 December	Motor vehicles depreciation	M130(W1)	6,164	
	Motor vehicles depreciation provision	M120		6,164
	Being year end provision for depreciation on motor vehicles			
31 December	Plant and equipment depreciation	P130(W3)	11,570	
	Plant and equipment depreciation provision	P120		11,570
	Being year end provision for depreciation on plant and equipment			

BPP PUBLISHING

JOURNAL

Date	Details	Folio Ref	£	£
	Leasehold premises amortisation	L130(W2)	2,000	
	Leasehold premises accumluated amortisation	L120		2,000
	Being year end amortisation on leasehold premises			
31 December	Repairs and maintenance	R200	4,770	
	Suspense a/c	S400		4,770
	Being elimination of suspense a/c balance and correct classification of expense			
31 December	Bad debt expense a/c	B200	200	
	Trade debtors	D100		200
	Being bad debt written off			
31 December	Bad debt expense a/c	B200	2,354	
	Bad debt provision	B100		2,354
	Being bad debt provision			

Folio	Account	Trial balance Debit £	Trial balance Credit £	Adjustments Debit £	Adjustments Credit £	Profit and Loss a/c Debit £	Profit and Loss a/c Credit £	Balance Sheet Debit £	Balance Sheet Credit £
P110	Plant & Equipment: cost	55,330						55,330	
P120	Plant & Equipment: dep'n provision		51,230						51,230
P130	Plant & Equipment: dep'n expense	11,570				11,570			
M110	Motor vehicles: cost	31,000						31,000	
M120	Motor vehicles: dep'n provision		12,508						12,508
M130	Motor vehicles: dep'n expense	6,164				6,164			
L110	Leasehold premises: cost	100,000						100,000	
L120	Leasehold premises: acc amortis'n		10,000						10,000
L130	Leasehold premises: amortis'n exp	2,000				2,000			
C300	Sundry creditors		13,500						13,500
F100	Bank	6,132						6,132	
F200	Cash in hand	505						505	
A100	Accountancy fee	600		1,500		2,100			
B100	Bad debts provision		150		2,354				2,504
B200	Bad debts expense			2,554		2,554			
L300	Loan		10,000						10,000
R200	Repairs and maintenance	813		4,770		5,583			
M300	Motor expenses	1,506				1,506			
S100	Sales		205,806				205,806		
D100	Trade debtors	50,287			200			50,087	
P100	Purchases	158,142				158,142			
C100	Trade creditors		65,416						65,416
E100	Electricity	900		200		1,100			
P300	Printing, postage, stationery	3,717				3,717			
P200	Profit and loss account		40,956						40,956
S200	Stock at 1.1.X6	9,125				9,125			
S300	Share capital		100,000						100,000
S400	Suspense account	4,770			4,770				
S500	Sundry expenses	6,428				6,428			
W100	Wages and salaries	60,521			600	59,921			
M400	Loss on sales of van	56				56			
S200P	Stock at 31.12.X6 (B/S)			10,412				10,412	
S200B	Stock at 31.12.X6 (P&L)				10,412		10,412		
	Prepayments / accruals			600	1,700			600	1,700
	SUB-TOTAL	509,566	509,566	20,036	20,036	269,966	216,218	254,066	307,814
	Profit for the year						53,748	53,748	
	TOTAL	509,566	509,566	20,036	20,036	269,966	269,966	307,814	307,814

Workings

1   *Depreciation expense: motor vehicles*

Ref		£
M112	£4,781 × 25%	1,195
M113	£7,875 × 25%	1,969
M114	£12,000 × 25%	3,000
	Total	6,164

2   *Depreciation expense: premises*

$$\frac{£100,000}{50} = £2,000$$

3   *Depreciation expense: plant and equipment*

Ref		£
P111	£24,750 ÷ 5	4,950
P112	£12,300 ÷ 6	2,050
P113	£18,280 ÷ 4	4,570
		11,570

4   *Bad debts provision*

	£
Trade debtors per trial balance	50,287
Less bad debt written off	200
	50,087

	£
Provision required (£50,087 × 5%)	2,504
Provision b/d	150
Increase required	2,354

Total bad debt expense £(200 + 2,354) = £2,554

ANSWERS TO SAMPLE SIMULATION

**DO NOT TURN THIS PAGE UNTIL YOU HAVE
COMPLETED THE SAMPLE SIMULATION**

ANSWERS TO SAMPLE SIMULATION: BRANSON & CO

EXTRACTS FROM FIXED ASSETS REGISTER

Tasks 1 and 2

Description/ serial no	*Location*	*Date acquired*	*Original cost £*	*Enhance- ments £*	*Total £*	*Dep'n £*	*NBV £*	*Funding method*	*Disposal proceeds £*	*Disposal date*
Plant and equipment										
Milling machine										
45217809	Factory	20.6.94	3,456.08		3,456.08			Cash		
Y/e 31.3.95						864.02	2,592.06			
Y/e 31.3.96						864.02	1,728.04			
Y/e 31.3.97						864.02	864.02			
Y/e 31.3.98						864.02	0.00			
Lathe 299088071	Factory	12.6.95	4,008.24		4,008.24			Cash		
Y/e 31.3.96						1,002.06	3,006.18			
Y/e 31.3.97						1,002.06	2,004.12			
Y/e 31.3.98						1,002.06	1,002.06			
Drill assembly										
51123412	Factory	12.2.96	582.44		582.44			Cash		
Y/e 31.3.96						145.61	436.83			
Y/e 31.3.97						145.61	291.22			
Y/e 31.3.98						145.61	145.61			
Punch drive										
91775321	Factory	12.2.96	1,266.00		1,266.00			Cash plus		
Y/e 31.3.96						316.50	949.50	trade-in		
Y/e 31.3.97						316.50	633.00			
Y/e 31.3.98						316.50	316.50			
Winding gear										
53098871	Factory	13.3.96	1,082.68		1,082.68			Cash		
Y/e 31.3.96						270.67	812.01			
Y/e 31.3.97				341.79	1,153.80	356.12	797.68			
Y/e 31.3.98						356.12	441.56			
Tender press										
44231809	Factory	8.8.96	4,256.04		4,256.04			Cash		
Y/e 31.3.97						1,064.01	3,192.03			
Y/e 31.3.98						1,064.01	2,128.02			

BPP PUBLISHING

Description/ serial no	Location	Date acquired	Original cost £	Enhance- ments £	Total £	Dep'n £	NBV £	Funding method	Disposal proceeds £	Disposal date
Company cars										
M412 RTW	Yard	25.8.94	8,923.71		8,923.71			Lease		
Y/e 31.3.95						4,015.67	4,908.04			
Y/e 31.3.96						2,208.62	2,699.42			
Y/e 31.3.97						1,214.74	1,484.68			
Y/e 31.3.98						668.11	816.57			
M104 PTY	Yard	15.3.95	8,643.00		8,643.00			Cash		
Y/e 31.3.95						3,889.35	4,753.65			
Y/e 31.3.96						2,139.14	2,614.51			
Y/e 31.3.97						1,176.53	1,437.98			
Y/e 31.3.98									1,850.00	
N33 FGY	Yard	18.9.95	10,065.34		10,065.34			Cash plus		
Y/e 31.3.96						4,529.40	5,535.94	trade-in		
Y/e 31.3.97						2,491.17	3,044.77			
Y/e 31.3.98						1,370.15	1,674.62			
P321 HDR	Yard	13.12.96	9,460.26		9,460.26			Cash		
Y/e 31.3.97						4,257.12	5,203.14			
Y/e 31.3.98						2,341.41	2,861.73			
R261 GHT	Yard	27.3.98	12,807.50		12,807.50			Cash plus		
Y/e 31.3.98						5,763.38	7,044.12	trade-in		

Tasks 1, 2, 4, 6, 7

NOMINAL (GENERAL) LEDGER

Account	Administration overheads				
Debit			Credit		
Date 1998	*Details*	*Amount* £	*Date* 1998	*Details*	*Amount* £
1 Mar	Balance b/f	15,071.23			
27 Mar	P/L control	140.00			
31 Mar	P/L control	991.24			
31 Mar	Bank	1,105.69	31 Mar	Balance c/d	17,308.16
		17,308.16			17,308.16
1 Apr	Balance b/d	17,308.16			

Account Debit	Brandreth capital account		Credit		
Date 1998	*Details*	*Amount* £	*Date* 1998	*Details*	*Amount* £
			1 Mar	Balance b/f	17,063.24

Account Debit	Brandreth current account		Credit		
Date 1998	*Details*	*Amount* £	*Date* 1998	*Details*	*Amount* £
1 Mar	Balance b/f	11,056.73			
31 Mar	Bank	500.00	31 Mar	Balance c/d	11,556.73
		11,556.73			11,556.73
1 Apr	Balance b/d	11,556.73			

BPP PUBLISHING

Account Company cars: cost

Debit					Credit

Date 1998	Details	Amount £	Date 1998	Details	Amount £
1 Mar	Balance b/f	37,092.31	27 Mar	Disposal a/c	8,643.00
27 Mar	P/L control.	12,807.50	31 Mar	Balance c/d	41,256.81
		49,899.81			49,899.81
1 Apr	Balance b/d	41,256.81			

Account Company cars: depreciation charge

Debit					Credit

Date 1998	Details	Amount £	Date 1998	Details	Amount £
31 Mar	Accumulated depreciation	10,143.05			

Account Company cars: accumulated depreciation

Debit					Credit

Date 1997	Details	Amount £	Date 1997	Details	Amount £
			1 Apr	Balance b/f	25,921.74
1998			1998		
27 Mar	Disposal a/c	7,205.02	31 Mar	Change for year	10,143.05
31 Mar	Balance c/d	28,859.77			
		36,064.79			36,064.79
			1 Apr	Balance b/d	28,859.77

Tasks 1, 2, 4, 6, 7 (continued)

Account Debit	Company cars: disposals		**Credit**		
Date 1998	*Details*	*Amount* £	*Date* 1998	*Details*	*Amount* £
27 Mar	Cost	8,643.00	27 Mar	Accumulated depreciation	7,205.02
			27 Mar	Purchases ledger	
31 Mar	Balance c/d	412.02		control account	1,850.00
		9,055.02			9,055.02
			1 Apr	Balance b/d	412.02

Account Debit	Direct labour costs		**Credit**		
Date 1998	*Details*	*Amount* £	*Date* 1998	*Details*	*Amount* £
1 Mar	Balance b/f	60,012.64			
31 Mar	Bank	6,014.73	31 Mar	Balance c/d	66,027.37
		66,027.37			66,027.37
1 Apr	Balance b/d	66,027.37			

Account Debit	Factory overheads		**Credit**		
Date 1998	*Details*	*Amount* £	*Date* 1998	*Details*	*Amount* £
1 Mar	Balance b/f	27,109.67			
31 Mar	P/L control	1,451.09			
31 Mar	Bank	1,931.75	31 Mar	Balance c/d	30,492.51
		30,492.51			30,492.51
1 Apr	Balance b/d	30,492.51			

Account Debit	Other fixed assets: cost		Credit		
Date 1998	*Details*	*Amount* £	*Date* 1998	*Details*	*Amount* £
1 Mar	Balance b/f	18,923.50			

Account Debit	Other fixed assets: depreciation charge		Credit		
Date 1998	*Details*	*Amount* £	*Date* 1998	*Details*	*Amount* £
31 Mar	Accumulated depreciation	4,730.88			

Account Debit	Other fixed assets: accumulated depreciation		Credit		
Date 1997	*Details*	*Amount* £	*Date* 1997	*Details*	*Amount* £
			1 Apr	Balance b/f	6,224.12
1998			1998		
			31 Mar	Charge for year	4,730.88
31 Mar	Balance c/d	10,955.00			
		10,955.00			10,955.00
			1 Apr	Balance b/d	10,955.00

Tasks 1, 2, 4, 6, 7 (continued)

Account	Other fixed assets: disposals					
Debit			Credit		
Date 1998	Details	Amount £	Date 1998	Details	Amount £

Account	Plant and equipment: cost				
Debit			Credit		
Date 1998	Details	Amount £	Date 1998	Details	Amount £
1 Mar	Balance b/f	14,993.27			

Account	Plant and equipment: depreciation charge				
Debit			Credit		
Date 1998	Details	Amount £	Date 1998	Details	Amount £
31 Mar	Accumulated depreciation	3,776.80			

Tasks 1, 2, 4, 6, 7 (continued)

Account Debit	Plant and equipment: accumulated depreciation		Credit		
Date 1997	*Details*	*Amount* £	*Date* 1997	*Details*	*Amount* £
			1 Apr	Balance b/f	7,239.68
1998 31 Mar	Balance c/d	11,016.48 11,016.48	1998 31 Mar	Charge for year	3,776.80 11,016.48
			1 Apr	Balance b/d	11,016.48

Account Debit	Plant and equipment: disposals		Credit		
Date 1998	*Details*	*Amount* £	*Date* 1998	*Details*	*Amount* £

Account Debit	Purchases		Credit		
Date 1998	*Details*	*Amount* £	*Date* 1998	*Details*	*Amount* £
1 Mar 31 Mar	Balance b/f P/L control	54,231.89 4,871.22 59,103.11	31 Mar	Balance c/d	59,103.11 59,103.11
1 Apr	Balance b/d	59,103.11			

Tasks 1, 2, 4, 6, 7 (continued)

Account Purchases ledger control Debit			Credit		
Date 1998	*Details*	*Amount* £	*Date* 1998	*Details*	*Amount* £
27 Mar	Car disposal a/c	1,850.00	1 Mar	Balance b/f	18,457.20
31 Mar	Bank	10,353.58	27 Mar	Purchase of new car	12,947.50
			31 Mar	Purchase invoices	9,133.18
31 Mar	Balance c/d	28,334.30			40,537.88
		40,537.88			
			1 Apr	Balance b/d	28,334.30

Account Sales Debit			Credit		
Date 1998	*Details*	*Amount* £	*Date* 1998	*Details*	*Amount* £
			1 Mar	Balance b/f	225,091.42
31 Mar	Balance c/d	256,167.67	31 Mar	S/L control	31,076.25
		256,167.67			256,167.67
			1 Apr	Balance b/d	256,167.67

Account Sales ledger control Debit			Credit		
Date 1998	*Details*	*Amount* £	*Date* 1998	*Details*	*Amount* £
1 Mar	Balance b/f	24,617.03	31 Mar	Bank	25,555.33
31 Mar	Sales invoices	36,514.59	31 Mar	Balance c/d	35,576.29
		61,131.62			61,131.62
1 Apr	Balance b/d	35,576.29			

Tasks 1, 2, 4, 6, 7 (continued)

Account Debit	Selling and distribution overheads		Credit		
Date 1998	*Details*	*Amount* £	*Date* 1998	*Details*	*Amount* £
1 Mar	Balance b/f	14,303.12			
31 Mar	P/L control	524.87			
31 Mar	Bank	1,427.88	31 Mar	Balance c/d	16,255.87
		16,255.87			16,255.87
1 Apr	Balance b/d	16,255.87			

Account Debit	Sondin capital account		Credit		
Date 1998	*Details*	*Amount* £	*Date* 1998	*Details*	*Amount* £
			1 Mar	Balance b/f	8,703.28

Account Debit	Sondin current account		Credit		
Date 1998	*Details*	*Amount* £	*Date* 1998	*Details*	*Amount* £
1 Mar	Balance b/f	12,912.29			
31 Mar	Bank	450.00	31 Mar	Balance c/d	13,362.29
		13,362.29			13,362.29
1 Apr	Balance b/d	13,362.29			

Tasks 1, 2, 4, 6, 7 *(continued)*

Account	Stock: raw materials				
Debit			Credit		
Date 1997	*Details*	*Amount* £	*Date* 1997	*Details*	*Amount* £
1 Apr	Balance b/f	6,294.33			

Account	Stock: finished goods				
Debit			Credit		
Date 1997	*Details*	*Amount* £	*Date* 1997	*Details*	*Amount* £
1 Apr	Balance b/f	12,513.77			

Account	Suspense				
Debit			Credit		
Date 1998	*Details*	*Amount* £	*Date* 1998	*Details*	*Amount* £
26 Jan	Bank	750.00	24 Feb	Bank	1,124.55
31 Mar	Balance c/d	374.55			
		1,124.55			1,124.55
			1 Apr	Balance b/d	374.55

BPP PUBLISHING

Tasks 1, 2, 4, 6, 7 (continued)

Account	VAT					
Debit					Credit	
Date	*Details*	*Amount*	*Date*	*Details*		*Amount*
1998		£	1998			£
31 Mar	P/L control	1,294.76	1 Mar	Balance b/f		5,091.27
31 Mar	Balance c/d	9,234.85	31 Mar	S/L control		5,438.34
		10,529.61				10,529.61
			1 Apr	Balance b/d		9,234.85

Task 3

MEMORANDUM

To: Jenny Holden, Accountant

From: Val Denning, Accounts Assistant

Subject: Check on company cars at 31 March 1998

Date: 20 April 1998

I have compared the schedule of company cars actually on the premises at 31 March with the details in the fixed assets register. The only discrepancy is that the car M412 RTW was not on the premises, though listed in the register. I suggest that we check physical existence of this car at another time.

Task 5

Bank reconciliation as at 31 March 1998

	£	£
Balance per bank statement		(1,550.12) O/D
Outstanding lodgements		
27 March	6,071.88	
31 March	5,512.67	
		11,584.55
		10,034.43
Unpresented cheques		
19337	278.01	
19338	500.00	
19339	450.00	
		(1,228.01)
Balance per cash book		8,806.42

Extended trial balance at 31 March 1998

Account name	Balances per ledger £	£	Adjustments £	£	Profit and loss account £	£	Balance sheet £	£
Administration overheads	17,308.16		420.00	1,625.00	16,103.16			
Brandreth capital account		17,063.24						17,063.24
Brandreth current account	11,556.73		750.00				12,306.73	
Company cars: cost	41,256.81						41,256.81	
Company cars: depreciation charge	10,143.05				10,143.05			
Company cars: accum depreciation		28,859.77						28,859.77
Company cars: disposals		412.02				412.02		
Direct labour costs	66,027.37				66,027.37			
Factory overheads	30,492.51				30,492.51			
Other fixed assets: cost	18,923.50			2,317.69			16,605.81	
Other fixed assets: depreciation charge	4,730.88				4,730.88			
Other fixed assets: accum depreciation		10,955.00	946.23					10,008.77
Other fixed assets: profit/loss on disposal			246.91		246.91			
Plant and equipment: cost	14,993.27						14,993.27	
Plant and equipment: depreciation charge	3,776.80				3,776.80			
Plant and equipment: accum depreciation		11,016.48						11,016.48
Purchases	59,103.11				59,103.11			
Purchases ledger control		28,334.30						28,334.30
Sales		256,167.67				256,167.67		
Sales ledger control	35,576.29						35,576.29	
Selling & distribution overheads	16,255.87				16,255.87			
Sondin: capital account		8,703.28						8,703.28
Sondin: current account	13,362.29						13,362.29	
Stock: raw materials	6,294.33		8,136.55	8,136.55	6,294.33	8,136.55	8,136.55	
Stock: finished goods	12,513.77		18,714.47	18,714.47	12,513.77	18,714.47	18,714.47	
Suspense		374.55	1,124.55	750.00				
VAT		9,234.85						9,234.85
Bank balance	8,806.42						8,806.42	
Accruals and prepayments			1,625.00	420.00			1,625.00	420.00
Net profit for the year					57,742.95			57,742.95
Total	371,121.16	371,121.16	31,963.71	31,963.71	283,430.71	283,430.71	171,383.64	171,383.64

Task 8

This cheque probably represents payment of a personal expense incurred by one or other of the partners. If so it will need to be treated as drawings.

To establish that this is so I will first ask Jenny Holden, the Accountant, whether she knows about the payment. If she does not, it may then be necessary for either she or I to inquire tactfully of the partners themselves.

Task 9

Journal

Date 1998	Account names and narrative	Debit £	Credit £
31 March	Brandreth: current account	750.00	
	suspense		750.00
	Being cash paid for personal expenses, classified as drawings		
31 March	Other fixed assets: accumulated depreciation	946.23	
	Other fixed assets: loss on disposal	246.91	
	Suspense account	1,124.55	
	Other fixed assets: cost		2,317.69
		2,317.69	2,317.69
	Being disposal of fixed asset, removed from suspense account		

Task 10

Valuation of raw materials stock (lower of cost and net realisable value)

	£
Material X	3,417.22
Material Y	4,719.33
Total	8,136.55

Manufacturing account for the year ended 31 March 1998

	£
Raw materials	
Opening stock	6,294.33
Purchases	59,103.11
	65,397.44
Closing stock	(8,136.55)
	57,260.89
Direct labour	66,027.37
Prime cost	123,288.26
Factory overheads	30,492.51
Factory cost of finished goods produced	153,780.77

The cost of 25,613 units is £153,780.77, a unit cost of production of £6.004.

The value of closing stock (3,117 units) is therefore £18,714.47.

Part C
Central Assessments

Practice Central Assessments

Practice Central Assessment 1: Highbury Discs

PRACTICE CENTRAL ASSESSMENT 1: HIGHBURY DISCS (JUNE 1995)

SECTION 1

The suggested time allocation for this extended trial balance exercise is 80 minutes.

You have been working for some months now as an accounting technician with Highbury Discs. The business specialises in recording and distributing compact discs of choral and organ music. Recordings are made on location and artists are paid a fixed fee plus a royalty based on the number of discs sold. Royalties are calculated and paid quarterly in arrears. The owners of the recording location are paid a fee for the hire of the location.

Anthony Sedgewick, the proprietor of Highbury Discs, uses only a minimum of high quality recording equipment, believing that a wise choice of recording venue and the optimal placing of a single microphone are the dominant factors in producing a good recording. All production work is subcontracted to independent operators. This approach has resulted in a number of recordings which have been highly praised in the specialist hi-fi press. The business sells to a number of UK stores, one of which acts as an agent for overseas sales.

The business rents a unit on an industrial estate. The premises are used for administration, distribution and the storage of recording equipment and stocks of compact discs.

The financial year for the business ended on 31 May 1995.

The following alphabetical list of balances has been taken from the business ledger as at 31 May 1995.

	£
Artists' fees and royalties	41,120
Bank and cash	1,420
Capital	26,449
Drawings	14,500
Employer's national insurance	3,619
Equipment (cost)	38,200
Equipment (provision for depreciation)	19,100
Loan	10,000
Loan interest	1,350
Mastering and production costs	143,400
Motor expenses	6,330
Motor vehicles (cost)	29,800
Motor vehicles (provision for depreciation)	17,880
Recording costs	12,550
Rent	13,000
Sales	307,800
Stocks of compact discs	22,500
Sundry creditors	4,080
Sundry debtors	12,500
Sundry expenses	1,270
VAT (amount owing)	3,250
Wages and salaries	47,000

Task 1

Enter the above balances into the first two columns of the extended trial balance provided on Page 234 and total the columns. The list of balances is provided on the left of the trial balance columns to help you.

HIGHBURY DISCS

Account	Trial balance Debit £	Trial balance Credit £	Adjustments Debit £	Adjustments Credit £	Profit and Loss a/c Debit £	Profit and Loss a/c Credit £	Balance Sheet Debit £	Balance Sheet Credit £
Artists' fees and royalties	41,120		4752		45 872			
Bank and cash	1,420			220			1 200	
Capital		26,449						26 449
Drawings	14,500		2110				16 610	
Employer's NI	3,619				3 619			
Equipment (cost)	38,200						38 200	
Motor vehicles (cost)	29,800						29 800	
Equipment (prov for depreciation)		19,100		9550				28 650
Motor vehicles (prov for depreciation)		17,880		3576				21 456
Loan		10,000						10 000
Loan interest	1,350		150		1 500			
Mastering and production costs	143,400				143 400			
Motor expenses	6,330			2110	4 220			
Recording costs	12,550				12 550			
Rent	13,000			1000	12 000			
Sales		307,800				307 800		
Stocks of compact discs	22,500				22 500			
Sundry creditors		4,080		4452				8832
Sundry debtors	12,500		220				12 720	
Sundry expenses	1,270				1 270			
VAT (amount owing)		3,250						3 250
Wages and salaries	47,000				47 000			
PREPAYMENTS / ACCRUALS			1 000	150			1 000	150
DEPRECIATION			13 126		13 126			
CLOSING STOCK B/S			27 700				27 700	
" " P&L				27 700		27 700		
	777,118							
Subtotal	388 559	388 559	49 058	49 058	307 057	335 500	127 230	98 787
Profit for the year					28 443			28 443
TOTAL	388 559	388 559	49 058	49 058	335 500	335 500	127 230	127 230

Task 2

The policy of the business is to provide for depreciation as follows.

Motor vehicles	30% per annum, reducing balance method, full year basis
Equipment	25% per annum, straight line method, full year basis

Depreciation for the year ended 31 May 1995 has not been recorded in the accounts.

Calculate the depreciation charge for the year ended 31 May 1995 and complete the following table.

	Depreciation charge for the year ended 31 May 1995 £
Motor vehicles	3576
Equipment	9550
TOTAL	13 126

Task 3

Stocks of compact discs are valued at cost. Cost includes a share of the recording, mastering and production costs as well as any direct overheads attributable to that recording. Stocks as at 31 May 1995 have not been recorded in the accounting system. The following is an extract of the stock sheets as at 31 May 1995 along with Anthony Sedgewick's comments.

STOCK SHEETS

Title	*Number of discs in stock*	*Total cost* £	*Total price to retailers* £	*Total recom- mended retail price* £	*Comments*
Total b/f from previous pages	4,500	18,000	27,600	39,800	No problems with any of these. We'll be able to make a profit on all of these discs.
Bambino choir of Prague	1,000	3,500	8,500	12,000	This batch of CDs arrived too late for the 1994 Christmas season. We're keeping them for the 1995 Christmas season. I think they will sell very well then.
The Joyful Singers sing Wesley	400	2,000	3,600	4,800	We just cannot get rid of these. We'll have to reduce the price to retailers to £3 a disc and recommend that retailers sell them for £5.50 a disc.
Bach at St Thomas's	2,000	7,000	14,000	20,000	This has not sold at all well. We're going to withdraw these discs and repackage them as 'The King of Instruments' and sell them to a chain store for £4 a disc. The repackaging will cost £1.50 per disc.
TOTAL	7,900	30,500	53,700	76,600	

Complete the following table to calculate the value of closing stock for incorporation into the accounts.

Stock sheets		Value £
Total b/f from previous pages		18 000
Bambino choir of Prague		3 500
The Joyful Singers sing Wesley		1 200
Bach at St Thomas's	?	5 000
VALUE OF STOCK as at 31 May 1995		27 700

Task 4

The following additional information was discovered after the list of balances was extracted from the ledger.

(a) Royalties due to artists for the quarter ended 31 May 1995 have just been calculated at £4,500, but these have not yet been recorded in the accounts. It has also been discovered that there has been an error in the calculation of the royalties due to Arnold Willis-Brown for the quarter ended 31 December 1994. Mr Willis-Brown had been paid a £1 royalty based on sales of 28 discs. In actual fact the number of discs sold had been 280. Anthony Sedgewick has decided that the next cheque to be sent to Mr Willis-Brown should be adjusted to correct the error.

(b) A cheque for £220 received from 'The CD Shop', a credit customer, which had been correctly recorded in the accounts, has just been returned by the bank marked 'refer to drawer'. This has not yet been recorded in the accounts.

(c) Anthony Sedgewick has estimated that one third of motor expenses have been for private use.

Prepare journal entries to record the above information in the accounts. Dates are not required, but you should include narratives. Use the blank journal on Page 237.

Task 5

The following additional information is available from the business records.

(a) The loan was taken out on 1 June 1994, bears interest at 15% per annum, and is repayable in full on 31 May 1996.

(b) The rent on the business premises is fixed at £1,000 per month from 1 June 1993 to 31 May 1998.

Incorporate the following into the adjustments columns of the extended trial balance on Page 234.

(a) Any adjustments arising from the above additional information.

(b) The depreciation charge for the year and the value of closing stock you calculated as Tasks 2 and 3.

(c) Any adjustments resulting from the journal entries you prepared as Task 4.

Task 6

Extend the figures into the extended trial balance columns for the profit and loss account and the balance sheet. Total all columns, transferring the balance of profit or loss as appropriate.

JOURNAL		
Details	DR £	CR £
ROYALTIES	4 752	
SUNDRY CREDITORS		4 752
DEBTORS	220	
BANK		220
DRAWINGS	2110	
MOTOR EXPS		2110

BPP PUBLISHING

SECTION 2

The following short answer questions are mainly based on the scenario outlined in Section 1. You may have to refer back to the information in that exercise in order to answer the questions.

The suggested time allocation for this set of short answer questions is 40 minutes.

1   The list of account balances on Page 234 includes an amount of £3,250 as VAT (amount owing). Explain fully what this balance represents. To whom is the amount payable?

2   Included in 'Equipment' are several high quality microphones. Apart from wear and tear through usage, there could be other factors causing these microphones to depreciate. Identify and explain one such factor.

3   Highbury Discs uses DAT (digital to analogue) tapes to record performances. These are purchased wholesale for £8 each. They can be used over a number of years to make and archive recordings. The policy of the business is to charge the cost of the tapes as an expense in the year in which they are purchased. Justify this treatment.

4   Suppose that the value of this year's closing stock had been mistakenly overestimated by £1,000 and that the error had not been detected. What would the effect be:

(a)   On this year's profit?

(b)   On next year's profit?

5   Highbury Discs values its stock of compact discs at the end of each financial year so that the costs incurred in producing those discs are not charged until discs are sold. Name the fundamental accounting concept of which this is an example.

6   Anthony Sedgewick has asked you to write him a memorandum explaining the rules you have used to calculate the value of closing stock in Section 1, Task 3. He would like you to refer to any relevant SSAPs and/or FRSs and illustrate the rules by demonstrating how you have calculated the value of the stocks of the three compact discs referred to in the stock sheets given for Task 3. Prepare a suitable memorandum in reply to Anthony Sedgewick.

SECTION 3

The suggested time allocation for this exercise is 60 minutes.

You have been asked to help in preparing the accounts of Lynda Booth who has been trading as a painter and decorator for some years from a rented garage and workshop. Lynda is an excellent painter and decorator but does not have the expertise to maintain a double entry set of records. Your supervisor prepared Lynda's accounts last year and has provided you with a set of working accounts consisting of all accounts with start of year balances. The balances have been entered in the accounts.

You have already spent some time analysing the statements for Lynda's business bank account for the year ended 31 May 1995 and have the following summary.

	£	£
Opening balance		323
Payments in		
Lottery winnings (see note (a), page 239)	10,000	
Cash takings paid in	2,770	
Receipts from trade debtors	43,210	
		55,980
		56,303

	£	£
Payments out		
Payments to trade creditors	30,060	
Withdrawn for personal use	12,000	
Purchase of new van	4,800	
Rent and insurance	5,330	
Motor expenses	3,400	
		55,590
		713

Your analysis of the other business documentation kept by Lynda gives you the following additional information as at 31 May 1995.

(a) Invoices for work done for customers during the year ended 31 May 1995 totalled £52,000 (of which £2,000 was unpaid as at 31 May 1995).

(b) Unpaid invoices for raw materials purchased from suppliers totalled £4,230.

(c) Insurance was prepaid by £200.

(d) Motor expenses were accrued by £209.

Your supervisor has supplied you with the following notes which were made during a meeting with Lynda Booth.

(a)	Lynda was a winner in the National Lottery earlier this year. She was not a jackpot winner and certainly did not win enough to retire. She paid some of her winnings into the business bank account to help with a temporary cash flow problem. *CAP INTRODUCED ?*
(b)	Lynda thinks that £480 of the amount collectable from customers as at 31 May 1995 will not be recovered because one of her customers has gone into bankruptcy. *BAD DEBT*
(c)	Lynda buys all her supplies from one supplier who offers 10% discount for prompt settlement. Lynda has been able to take advantage of that discount on all payments made during the year. *+ MATS*
(d)	Some customers paid in cash during the year but Lynda has not kept any records. We've estimated that about £600 was paid for motor expenses from these cash receipts. There was £34 in the business safe as at 31 May 1995.
(e)	Lynda bought the additional motor van on 1 February 1995 because she thought the price was particularly good. She has used both vans in the business herself but feels that this van will be particularly useful next summer when she expects she will have to employ an assistant. We have agreed that the vans should be written off equally on a month for month basis over an expected life of four years. This is what we did with the first van which was purchased on 1 June 1993.
(f)	There were materials costing £1,600 unused in the workshop at 31 May 1995. *STOCKS*

Task 1

From the above information reconstruct the ledger accounts provided for the year ended 31 May 1995 on Pages 241 to 243, showing the balances to be carried forward at the end of the year and/or the amounts to be transferred to the profit and loss account for the year ended 31 May 1995.

Notes

(a) Dates are not required.

(b) The following accounts are not supplied and need not be shown.

> Capital
> Work done/sales
> Bad debts
> Discounts received/allowed

A SUGGESTED ANSWER TO THIS PRACTICE CENTRAL ASSESSMENT IS GIVEN ON PAGE 365.

BANK				
	£			**£**
Balance b/f	323	PAYMENTS		55 590
RECEIPTS	55980	BAL C/FWD		713
	56 303			56 303
BAL B/FWD	713			

CASH				
	£			**£**
Balance b/f	25	BANK		2770
DEBTORS	8340	MOTOR EXPS		600
		BAL C/FWD		34
		DRAWINGS		4961
	8365			8365
BAL B/FWD	34			

MOTOR EXPENSES				
	£			**£**
BANK	3400	Balance b/f		174
CASH	600	TO P & L A/c		4035
ACCRUAL C/FWD	209			
	4209			4209
		BAL B/FWD		209

BPP PUBLISHING

MOTOR VAN(S)			
	£	DEPRECIATION	£
Balance b/f	7,500		2 500
BANK	4 800	"	400
		BAL c/fwd	9 400
	12 300		12 300
BAL B/fwd	9 400		

RENT AND INSURANCE			
	£		£
Balance (insurance) b/f	180	Balance (rent) b/f	250
BANK	5330	To P & L A/c	5060
		INS PREPAID c/fwd	200
	5510		5510
BAL B/fwd	200		

MATERIALS USED			
	£		£
Balance b/f	1,530	To P & L A/c	33910
TRADE CREDITORS	33 980	BAL c/fwd	1600
	33 510		33 510
Bal B/fwd	1600		

TRADE CREDITORS

	£		£
PAYMENTS (BANK)	30 060	Balance b/f	3,650
DISCOUNTS RECEIVED	3340	PURCHASES	33980
BAL c/fwd	4230		
	37630		37630
		BAL B/fwd	4230 ✓

TRADE DEBTORS

	£		£
Balance b/f	1,550	RECEIPTS (BANK)	43210
WORK DONE (SALES)	52 000	BAD DEBTS	480
		CASH (RECEIPTS)	8 340
BAL c/fwd		BAL c/fwd	1520
	53 550		53 550 ✓
BAL B/fwd	1520		

DRAWINGS

	£		£
BANK	12 000	CAPITAL	16 961
CASH	4961		
	16 961		16 961

Practice Central Assessment 2: Jason Brown

246

PRACTICE CENTRAL ASSESSMENT 2: JASON BROWN (DECEMBER 1995)

SECTION 1

The suggested time allocation for this extended trial balance exercise is 80 minutes.

Jason Brown is a sole trader who operates out of a warehouse in Nottingham. He buys and sells a range of office furniture and equipment and trades under the name J B Office Supplies. Most of his sales are made on credit to businesses in the Midlands area of England, although occasionally customers will call at his premises to make purchases for cash.

You are employed by Jason to assist with the bookkeeping. This is currently a manual system and consists of a general ledger, where double entry takes place, a sales ledger and a purchases ledger. The individual accounts of debtors and creditors are therefore regarded as memoranda accounts. Day books are used and totals from the columns of these are transferred periodically into the general ledger.

The following balances were extracted from the general ledger at the end of the financial year on 31 October 1995.

	£
Purchases	170,240
Sales	246,412
Purchases returns	480
Sales returns	670
Stock at 1 November 1994	54,200
Salaries	30,120
Rent	2,200
Insurance	360
Delivery vans at cost	12,800
Provision for depreciation - delivery vans	3,520
Equipment at cost	22,800
Provision for depreciation - equipment	5,760
Bad debts	2,700
Provision for doubtful debts	1,980
Debtors control account	41,600
Creditors control account	33,643
Drawings	10,522
Capital	83,171
Bank overdraft	348
Cash	568
VAT (credit balance)	2,246
Bank interest received	1,200
Bank deposit account	30,000
Suspense account	?

Task 1

Enter the above balances into the first two columns of the extended trial balance provided on Page 248. Total the two columns whilst at the same time entering an appropriate balance for the suspense account to ensure that the two totals agree.

31/OCT/95

JASON BROWN

Account	Trial balance Debit £	Trial balance Credit £	Adjustments Debit £	Adjustments Credit £	Profit and Loss a/c Debit £	Profit and Loss a/c Credit £	Balance Sheet Debit £	Balance Sheet Credit £
Purchases	170 240				170 240			
Sales		246 412				246 412		
Purchases returns		480				480		
Sales returns	670				670			
Opening Stock	54 200				54 200			
Salaries	30 120				30 120			
Rent	2 700		200		2 400			
Insurance	360			130	230			
Delivery vans (cost)	21 808						12 800	
Equipment (cost)	22 800						22 800	
Delivery vans (prov for depn)		3 520		1 856				5 376
Equipment (prov for depn)		5 760		2 280				8 040
Bad debts	2 700		2 460		5 160			
Provision for bad debts		1 980	23					1 957
Debtors control account	41 600			2 460			39 140	
Creditors control account		33 643		1 266				34 903
Drawings	10 522		1 260				10 522	
Capital		83 171						83 171
Bank overdraft		348					912	
Cash	898						862	
VAT		2 246						2 246
Bank interest received		1 200		600		1 800		
Bank deposit account	30 000						30 000	
Suspense account		20						20
Depreciation			4 136		4 136			
Bank interest owing			600				600	
Closing stock (P&L)				58 194		58 194		
Closing stock (B/S)			58 194				58 194	
Provision for bad debts (adjustment)				23		23		
Prepayments / accruals			130	200			130	
Subtotal	378 780	378 780	67 003	67 003	267 156	306 909	175 666	135 913
Profit for the year					39 753			39 753
TOTAL	378 780	378 780	67 003	67 003	306 909	306 909	175 666	175 666

Task 2

Unfortunately the errors causing the need for the suspense account cannot immediately be found and Jason is anxious that a draft extended trial balance should be produced as quickly as possible.

Make appropriate entries in the adjustment columns of the extended trial balance to take account of the following.

(a) Depreciation is to be provided as follows.

Delivery vans: 20% per annum reducing balance method
Equipment: 10% per annum straight line method

(b) The £30,000 in the bank deposit account was invested on 1 November 1994 at a fixed rate of interest of 6% per annum. A cheque for £300 interest was received by J B Office Supplies on 2 January 1995 and a further cheque for £900 on 3 July 1995.

(c) It is thought highly unlikely that £2,460 owed by M C Miller will be recovered and towards the end of October the decision was made for the debt to be written off. To date no entries have been passed. The provision on remaining debtors should be adjusted to a figure of 5%.

(d) Closing stock has been valued at cost at £58,394. However, this figure includes four office chairs, cost price £230 each, which have been damaged in storage. It has been estimated that if a total of £40 was spent on repairing the worst of the damage then they could be sold for £190 each.

4 × 230 = 920
4 × 190 = 760
− 40
720

(e) J B Office Supplies had sent a cheque for £1,260 to Metalux Imports, a supplier on 15 October 1995. Unfortunately the cheque had not been signed and was returned in the post on 30 October. No entries have been passed.

(f) Insurance is paid annually in advance on 1 April. The premium for the period 1 May 1995 to 30 April 1996 was £260.

(g) The rent on the property used by J B Office Supplies was set on 1 January 1994 at £200 per month payable in arrears. The next rent review has been scheduled to take place on 1 January 1996.

Task 3

Extend the figures into the extended trial balance columns for profit and loss and balance sheet. Total all of these columns, transferring the balance of the profit or loss as appropriate.

Task 4

Subsequent to the completion of the extended trial balance a further search for the errors which necessitated the opening of the suspense account takes place. The following are found.

(a) A cheque for £60 received from Pauline Ransome, a credit customer, had been entered in the bank account but not in the appropriate control account.

(b) Discounts allowed totalling £125 had been credited to discounts received.

(c) Credit purchases totalling £15,840 had been transferred from the day book into the purchases account at £15,480.

(d) In totalling the columns of the sales day book, the 'net' column had been undercast by £570.

Prepare journal entries to record the correction of these errors. Dates and narratives are not required. Use the blank journal on Page 250.

JOURNAL		
Details	DR £	CR £
SUSPENSE A/c	60	
DEBTORS CONTROL		60
DISCOUNTS ALLOWED	125	
" RECEIVED	125	
SUSPENSE A/c		250
PURCHASES	360	
SUSPENSE A/c		360
SUSPENSE A/c	570	
SALES		570

SECTION 2

The following short answer questions are mainly based on the scenario outlined in Section 1. You may have to refer back to the information in that exercise in order to answer the questions.

The suggested time allocation for this set of short answer questions is 45 minutes.

1   The delivery vans figures of £12,800 shown in the trial balance is made up from two vehicles, one costing £6,000 bought on 1 November 1993 and one costing £6,800 bought on 1 November 1994. If the first van was now to be sold on 1 May 1996 for £3,200, then assuming that depreciation is calculated on a monthly basis: ye 94   NBV = 4800
                                                                                                ye 95   ..   3840

   (a)   What would be the book value of the van at the date of sale?   3496
   (b)   Show the disposals account as it would appear in the ledger on 31 October 1996.

MOTOR VANS DISPOSAL ACCOUNT			
	£		£
MOTOR VEHICLES COST	6000	DEP'N TO DATE	2504
		BANK	3200
		To P-e-L a/c	296
	6 000		6000

2   Jason Brown intends to launch a new computer consultancy service during 1997. He is confident that this will bring about a substantial increase in business for his financial year ended 31 October 1997. A major advertising campaign has been planned for September and October 1996. What is the argument for including the cost of the campaign in the calculation of profit for the year end 31 October 1997? Make reference in your answer to the accounting concept or concepts that relate to this matter.

3   In Task 4 of Section 1 the following errors, amongst others, were identified.

   (a)   Discounts allowed totalling £125 had been credited to discounts received.

   (b)   Credit purchases totalling £15,840 had been transferred from the day book into the purchases account as £15,480.

   In correcting each error, would the reported profit be increased or decreased and by what amount?

                                                        250 +
                                                        360
                                                        610

4 Included in Jason Brown's stock are some standard office swivel chairs. At the beginning of October ten chairs each costing £30 were in stock. Stock movements during the month were as follows.

Stock at	1/10/95	10 at £30
Purchases	10/10/95	12 at £32
Sales	13/10/95	2
Sales	18/10/95	4
Purchases	23/10/95	10 at £31
Sales	30/10/95	6

Chairs are sold at £50 each.

Stock is valued on a FIFO basis.

Calculate the value of the following.

(a) Sales for October. $12 \times 50 = 600$

(b) Cost of goods sold for October. $(10 \times 30) + (2 \times 32) = 364$

(c) Closing stock at the end of October. $(10 \times 31) + (10 \times 32) = 630$

5 'Capital expenditure is expenditure on fixed assets which appear in the balance sheet. The cost of a fixed asset does not therefore affect the calculation of profit.' State whether or not you agree with the above statement and briefly explain the reason for your answer.

6 The total sales figure to be used in the calculation of profit is £246,412.

(a) Does this figure include or exclude VAT?

(b) Briefly explain the reason for your answer.

7 You have received the following note from Jason Brown.

'Thank you for producing the extended trial balance showing key figures for the year. I am concerned about the profitability of the business for next year and I am considering the following changes to improve the profit figure.

(a) Running down the stock levels at the end of the financial year. This can be achieved by reducing purchases and a smaller purchases figure will increase profit.

(b) Writing off M C Millar's debt this year significantly reduce the profit. If towards the end of next year any large bad debts are identified we should delay writing them off until the following year.

(c) We should calculate depreciation on all fixed assets using both the straight line and reducing balance methods. Each year we can then use the method which gives us the highest profit.'

Prepare a memorandum to Jason Brown covering each of the points he has raised.

8 Some days after preparing the extended trial balance it was discovered that a credit sale for £96.20 had, in error, not been entered into the account of John Pearce Furniture in the sales ledger. Jason Brown is concerned about the control of errors and had contacted you for an explanation.

Write a note to Jason in the form of a memorandum, explaining why the error would not have been detected by drawing up a trial balance and how the existence of such an error would normally be detected by checking the total of the balances in the sales ledger.

SECTION 3

The suggested time allocation for this exercise is 55 minutes.

Jason's younger sister Natasha had originally intended joining him in the business as his assistant. However, when she inherited some money an opportunity arose to set up on her own buying and selling stationery and eventually she decided to go ahead with this venture. During October 1995 she purchased premises costing £74,400, fixtures and fittings at £28,800 and stock at £15,613. The stock was partly bought with her own funds and partly on credit. Her supplier, Carlton Office Supplies Ltd, offered her £10,000 credit and at this point she made full use of the facility. At the end of the month she borrowed £48,000 by way of a loan from the bank at an interest rate of 10% per annum. After these transactions had taken place she had £1,220 of surplus funds remaining and on 1 November, the date the business opened, this sum was paid into a business bank account.

All of Natasha's sales were for cash and all were at a mark up of 25% on cost. Unfortunately Natasha did not appreciate the importance of recording sales despite the fact that she had bought a computer on 1 November with the intention of using it to record business transactions. It is estimated that the computer will be used for three years after which time it will have a residual value of £250. Depreciation should be calculated on a monthly basis for the computer and for other fixed assets. (Any depreciation for October should, however, be ignored.)

During November, Natasha took out from the takings any money she needed for her own use but, again, without recording the sums involved. The following amounts were also paid out of the cash and the remainder of the takings were then deposited in the bank.

Postages   £43
Cash purchases   £187
Sundry expenses   £52

Apart from the cash purchases, all other purchases of stock during November were made on credit from Carlton Office Supplies Ltd. Natasha's summarised business bank account for the period appeared as follows.

	Discount £	Bank £		Discount £	Bank £
Balance b/d		1,220	Purchase of the computer		1,402
Takings		30,408	Carlton Office Supplies	200	9,800
			Sundry expenses		61
			Insurance		384
			Carlton Office Supplies	250	12,250
			Balance c/d		7,731
		31,628		450	31,628

The insurance payment covered the period 1 November 1995 to 31 October 1996. On 30 November an invoice received from Carlton Office Supplies Ltd for £8,600 was still outstanding and this sum was therefore owed to the company. On the same date Natasha's stock was valued at £11,475. This, however, included £275 for a new electronic diary supplied for trial purposes on a sale or return basis. The £275 had not been included in any of the invoices received.

Depreciation is to be calculated at 2% per annum on cost for the premises and at 10% per annum on cost for the fixtures and fittings.

Tasks

Jason has asked you to help his sister by producing some figures for her business.

1   Calculate Natasha's original capital sum introduced into the business.

2   Draw up the account for Carlton Office Supplies Ltd showing clearly the total purchases made on credit from the company during October and November.

3   Calculate the value of the total purchases made up to the end of November, including the purchase of the initial stock.

4   Prepare a draft statement calculating the net profit for the month ended 30 November 1995 and clearly showing the total sales for the period.

5   Prepare the cash account for November showing clearly the total drawings made by Natasha during the month.

A SUGGESTED ANSWER TO THIS PRACTICE CENTRAL ASSESSMENT IS GIVEN ON PAGE 371.

Practice Central Assessment 3: Explosives

PRACTICE CENTRAL ASSESSMENT 3: EXPLOSIVES (JUNE 1996)

SECTION 1

The suggested time allocation for this extended trial balance exercise is 85 minutes.

Melanie Lancton trades under the name of Explosives and operates out of a store and warehouse. She is a sole trader and has been in the clothes business for approximately ten years. Explosives deals mainly in jeans and speciality T shirts. All of the sales out of the store are for cash but the warehouse is used to supply other clothing retailers throughout the UK on a credit basis. Occasionally, orders are received on a limited scale from shops in northern France.

You are employed by Melanie to assist with the book-keeping. This is currently a manual system and consists of a general ledger, where double entry takes place, a sales ledger and a purchases ledger. The individual accounts of debtors and creditors are therefore regarded as memoranda accounts. Day books are used and totals from their various columns are transferred periodically into the general ledger.

The following balances were extracted from the general ledger at the end of the financial year on 31 May 1996.

	£	£
Stock at 1 June 1995	180,420	
Purchases	610,080	
Sales		840,560
Purchases returns		2,390
Sales returns	2,650	
Motor expenses	5,430	
Bank	20,415	
Cash	3,420	
Rent	11,000	
Lighting and heating	4,180	
Stationery and advertising	6,120	
Provision for bad debts		5,620
Debtors control account	120,860	
Creditors control account		102,860
Salaries	96,200	
Bad debts	7,200	
Drawings	31,600	
Discounts allowed	20,520	
Discounts received		18,400
Motor vehicles: at cost	60,480	
provision for depreciation		12,590
Office furniture and equipment: at cost	26,750	
provision for depreciation		3,170
VAT		10,260
Capital account at 1 June 1995		211,475
	1,207,325	1,207,325

Having extracted the above figures, the following errors were found in the books.

(a)   The purchases day book totals for the month of March were as follows.

		£
Total		50,160
VAT		7,471
Net		42,689
Goods for resale		40,463
Other items		2,226

    (i)   An invoice for £200 plus £35 VAT received from Just Jeans Ltd had been entered as £2,000 plus £35 VAT thus causing errors in both the net and total columns.

    (ii)   The total of the net column was debited to the purchases account. An analysis of 'other items' showed £1,201 for lighting and heating and £1,025 for stationery and advertising. No entries had been passed in these accounts.

(b)   A credit note received from Astra Clothing for £40 plus £7 VAT had, in error, been left out altogether from the returns outwards day book.

(c)   Cash sales of £1,645 (inclusive of £245 VAT) had been entered as follows.

Dr Cash book   £1,645
Cr Sales   £1,645

(d)   An invoice had been received and correctly entered in the books from Kay Imports Ltd for £1,080 plus £180 VAT, total £1,260. A payment by cheque was made for £1,206 but the discount had been omitted from the discount column of the cash book.

The following adjustments also need to be taken into account.

(1)   Depreciation is to be provided as follows.

Motor vehicles - 20% per annum on cost
Office furniture and equipment - 10% per annum reducing balance method

It should be noted that no depreciation is charged on assets in their year of purchase or in their year of sale. On 10 January 1996 a new vehicle had been purchased for £9,800.

(2)   Rent payable on the store and warehouse is £1,000 per month.

(3)   The stationery and advertising figure includes the sum of £1,560 paid to the Wise Advertising Agency for a series of newspaper advertisements covering all of Explosives' products and due to appear during the period October to December 1996.

(4)   Stock has been valued on 31 May 1996 at £208,540. This figure excludes £2,300 of jeans (cost price) which had been damaged by a leak in the roof of the warehouse. The jeans were considered worthless and were thrown out. The Regal Insurance Company has agreed to pay a claim for the full cost of the jeans although as yet no payment has been received.

(5)   The provision for bad debts is to be adjusted to a figure representing 5% of debtors.

Task 1

Prepare journal entries to correct the errors (a) to (d) shown on Page 258. Dates and narratives are not required.

Use the blank journal on Page 260 for your answer.

Task 2

Enter the corrected balances into the first two columns of the extended trial balance provided on Page 261.

Note. It is the *corrected* balances that should be used, thus taking into account the journal entries prepared for Task 1. Total the two columns ensuring that the two totals agree.

Task 3

Make appropriate entries in the adjustment columns of the extended trial balance to take account of the adjustments (1) to (5) above.

Task 4

Extend the figures into the extended trial balance columns for profit and loss and balance sheet. Total all of these columns, transferring the balance of the profit or loss as appropriate.

BPP
PUBLISHING

JOURNAL

Details	DR £	CR £

EXPLOSIVES	Trial balance		Adjustments		Profit and Loss a/c		Balance Sheet	
Account	Debit £	Credit £	Debit £	Credit £	Debit £	Credit £	Debit £	Credit £
Opening Stock								
Purchases								
Sales								
Purchases returns								
Sales returns								
Motor expenses								
Bank								
Cash								
Rent								
Lighting and heating								
Stationery and advertising								
Provision for bad debts								
Debtors control account								
Creditors control account								
Salaries								
Bad debts								
Drawings								
Discount allowed								
Discount received								
Motor vehicles (cost)								
Office furniture & equipment (cost)								
Motor vehicles (prov for depreciation)								
Office furniture & equipment (prov for depreciation)								
VAT								
Capital								
Depreciation								
Regal Insurance Company								
Closing stock (P&L)								
Closing stock (B/S)								
Provision for bad debts (adjustment)								
Prepayments / accruals								
Subtotal								
Profit for the year								
TOTAL								

SECTION 2

The following short answer questions are mainly based on the scenario outlined in Section 1. You may have to refer back to the information in that exercise in order to answer the questions.

The suggested time allocation for this set of short answer questions is 40 minutes.

1   Indicate with a circle the effect on the calculation of profit and on the assets in the balance sheet if capital expenditure is treated as revenue expenditure.

    (a)   Profit would be: Overstated/Understated

    (b)   The value of the assets would be: Overstated/Understated

2   Explosives makes a credit sale to Dillon Clothes for £600 plus VAT £105. (*Note.* State clearly for each entry the name of the account, the amount and whether debit or credit.)

    (a)   What double entry is made in the general ledger to record the sale?

    (b)   What double entry is made in the general ledger to record the debtor clearing the debt by cheque?

3   Expenditure on applied research may be capitalised should a company so wish.

    (a)   State whether or not you agree with the above statement. (Assume the expenditure is not on fixed assets.)

    (b)   Explain *briefly* the reason for your answer to (a), referring to the relevant statement of standard accounting practice.

4   Julie Owens is a credit customer of Explosives and currently owes approximately £5,000. She has recently become very slow in paying for purchases and has been sent numerous reminders for most of the larger invoices issued to her. A cheque for £2,500 sent to Explosives has now been returned by Julie Owens' bankers marked 'refer to drawer'. Which accounting concept would suggest that a provision for doubtful debts should be created to cover the debt of Julie Owens?

5   It is found that cash sales have, in error, been credited to purchases instead of sales. In correcting this error and adjusting the profit, would profit be increased, reduced or stay the same?

6   At the end of a previous accounting period, a suspense account with a £200 credit balance had been opened to agree the trial balance. It was subsequently found that only one error had been made, which related to cash drawings. Two debit entries had been made for the same amount instead of a debit and a credit. What entries should be passed to correct the error? (*Note.* State clearly for each entry the name of the account, the amount and whether debit or credit.)

7   You have received the following note from Melanie Lancton.

'I have been looking at the draft final accounts you have produced. In the valuation of the closing stock you have included some of the jeans at less than cost price. The figure you used is net realisable value and this has effectively reduced the profit for the period. The closing stock will be sold in the next financial period and my understanding of the accruals concept is that the revenue from selling the stock should be matched against the cost of that stock. This is not now possible since part of the cost of the stock has been written off in reducing the closing stock valuation from cost price to net realisable value.'

Write a suitable response to Melanie Lancton in the form of a memorandum. Your answer should include references to relevant accounting concepts and to SSAP 9.

SECTION 3

The suggested time allocation for this exercise is 55 minutes.

Melanie Lancton is considering taking over a small clothing wholesalers which belongs to Rahul Gupta. You have been asked to prepare some figures for Melanie from the records kept for the business.

You are presented with the following.

Rahul Gupta assets and liabilities at 31 May 1995

	£
Freehold buildings at cost	80,000
Less depreciation to date	16,000
	64,000
Fixtures and fittings at cost	17,500
Less depreciation to date	12,000
	5,500
Stock	33,200
Debtors	39,470
Prepaid general expenses	550
Cash	900
	74,120
Creditors	35,960
Bank overdraft	17,390
	53,350

Summary of the business bank account for the year ended 31 May 1996

	£		£
Cash sales	147,890	Balance b/d	17,390
From debtors	863,740	To creditors	607,650
Sale proceeds fixtures and fittings	1,360	General expenses	6,240
		Salaries	94,170
		Security devices	5,100
		Drawings	28,310
		Balance c/d	254,130
	1,012,990		1,012,990

Other information

(a)   The profit margin achieved on all sales is 40%. At the end of the year on 31 May 1996 the stock was valued at £38,700. However, Rahul Gupta is convinced that various items have been stolen during the year. To prevent further theft the premises were fitted out with various security devices on 31 May 1996.

(b)   Depreciation is calculated on a *monthly* basis as follows.

Premises   2% on cost
Fixtures and fittings   10% on cost

Fixtures and fittings purchased on 1 June 1990 for £4,000 were sold on 30 November 1995, the purchaser paying by cheque.

(c)   The proceeds of cash sales are held in tills and paid into the bank at the end of the day, apart from a float which is retained on the premises to be used at the start of the following day. During May 1996 a decision was made to increase the size of the float from the £900 held at the beginning of the year to £1,000.

(d)   On 31 May 1996 creditors amounted to £49,310, debtors £45,400 and £170 was owing for general expenses. During the year bad debts of £2,340 have been written off.

Tasks

1   Draw up a total debtors account (debtors control account) showing clearly the total value of the credit sales for the year ended 31 May 1996.

2   Calculate the total sales for the year ended 31 May 1996.

3   Draw up a total creditors account (creditors control account) showing clearly the total purchases for the year ended 31 May 1996.

4   Calculate the value of the stock stolen during the year.

5   Calculate the profit or loss made from the sale of fixtures and fittings on 30 November 1995.

6   Calculate the figure for general expenses which would be included in the calculation of profit for the year ended 31 May 1996.

A SUGGESTED ANSWER TO THIS PRACTICE CENTRAL ASSESSMENT IS GIVEN ON PAGE 379.

Practice Central Assessment 4: Castle Alarms

PRACTICE CENTRAL ASSESSMENT 4: CASTLE ALARMS (DECEMBER 1996)

SECTION 1

The suggested time allocation for this extended trial balance exercise is 80 minutes.

Andrew Hallgrove is the proprietor of Castle Alarms, which specialises in supplying domestic and commercial burglar alarm systems. Although the business operates throughout the UK, the offices and warehouse are located in the north of England.

You are employed within the business to assist with the bookkeeping. This is currently a manual system and consists of a general ledger, where double entry takes place, a sales ledger and a purchases ledger. The individual accounts of debtors and creditors are therefore regarded as memoranda accounts. Day books are used and totals from the various columns of these are transferred periodically into the general ledger.

At the end of the financial year of 31 October 1996, the balances were extracted from the general ledger and entered into an extended trial balance as shown on Page 269.

Task 1

Make appropriate entries in the adjustment columns of the extended trial balance to take account of the following.

(a) Depreciation is to be provided as follows.

Motor vehicles: 20% per annum straight line method
Equipment: 10% per annum reducing balance method

(b) The bank loan of £50,000 was taken out on 31 January 1996. The interest rate charged on the loan is fixed at 10% per annum.

(c) In August a system invoiced at £3,400 was installed at a local restaurant. Unfortunately no money was received in payment, the restaurant closed and the owner disappeared. A decision has now been made to write off the debt.

(d) Having written off all bad debts, the provision for bad debts is to be adjusted to 6% of remaining debtors.

(e) At the stocktake on 31 October 1996 the stock was valued at £289,400 cost price. However, this figures includes the following.

(i) Five system costing £1,200 each which have now been replaced by improved models. It is thought that in order to sell them the price of each system will have to be reduced to £1,000.

(ii) A system costing £2,000 was damaged in the warehouse. Repairs will cost £200 before it can be used in an installation.

(f) The business took advantage of an offer to advertise on local radio during October 1996 at a cost of £2,250. Although the invoice has now been received no entries have been made.

(g) Rent for the business property is £2,100 payable monthly in advance. This has been the figure payable over the last 12 months and a rent review is not due at the present time.

(h) On 30 October 1996 £5,000 cash was withdrawn from the bank for use within the business. To date no entries have been made to reflect this transaction.

(i)   A credit note received from Ashito Electronics and relating to goods returned has just been found in a pile of correspondence. The credit note, dated 20 October 1996, is for £2,900 and has not been entered in any of the books of the business.

Task 2

Extend the figures into the extended trial balance columns for profit and loss and balance sheet. Total all of these columns, transferring the balance of the profit or loss as appropriate.

CASTLE ALARMS

Account	Trial balance Debit £	Trial balance Credit £	Adjustments Debit £	Adjustments Credit £	Profit and Loss a/c Debit £	Profit and Loss a/c Credit £	Balance Sheet Debit £	Balance Sheet Credit £
Sales		1,200,000						
Purchases	667,820							
Sales returns	96,570							
Purchases returns		52,790						
Opening Stock	301,840							
Debtors control account	189,600							
Cash	1,200							
Bank	25,300							
Creditors control account		95,000						
Provision for bad debts		12,000						
Bad debts	10,100							
Discount allowed	6,320							
Salaries	103,030							
Drawings	26,170							
Rent	27,300							
General expenses	14,310							
Capital		121,860						
VAT		22,600						
Bank loan		50,000						
Interest on bank loan	2,500							
Advertising	11,450							
Motor vehicles (cost)	32,600							
Equipment (cost)	48,860							
Motor vehicles (prov for depreciation)		4,100						
Equipment (prov for depreciation)		6,620						
Depreciation								
Loan interest owing								
Closing stock (P&L)								
Closing stock (B/S)								
Provision for bad debts (adjustment)								
Prepayments / accruals								
Subtotal	1,564,970	1,564,970						
Profit for the year								
TOTAL	1,564,970	1,564,970						

SECTION 2

The following short answer questions are mainly based on the scenario outlined in Section 1. You may have to refer back to the information in that exercise in order to answer the questions.

The suggested time allocation for this set of short answer questions is 30 minutes.

1   Andrew Hallgrove bought a calculator costing £10 for use in the office. Referring to the relevant accounting concept, briefly explain why the purchase would normally be treated as revenue rather than as capital expenditure, despite the fact that the calculator will probably be used for several years.

2   At the end of a particular quarter, Castle Alarms' VAT account showed a balance of £2,100 debit. Explain briefly what the balance represents.

3   Andrew Hallgrove is considering leasing a car for use by one of his sales staff. He understands that leases are classified as operating leases or finance leases and the two types affect the books of a business in different ways. Which type of lease would have to be capitalised in the books of Castle Alarms?

4   Castle Alarms makes a credit sale to Turnbull Haircare for £200 plus £35 VAT. Unfortunately, in error, the sale invoice is not entered in the sales day book.

    (a)   Would the error be detected by drawing up a trial balance?

    (b)   Briefly explain the reason for your answer to (a)

5   A motor vehicle which has been purchased by Castle Alarms for £10,450 was eventually sold for £3,000, when it had a net book value of £4,100. What is the total charge to the profits of Castle Alarms with respect to the capital cost of the vehicle, during the life of the asset?

6   Castle Alarms purchases an alarm from Ace Electronics. Ace Electronics normally sells the alarm at a price of £2,400, but Castle Alarms is given a 20% trade discount. Ace Electronics charges £10 for delivery to Castle Alarms' premises. Castle Alarms puts a price on the alarm of £2,425. What value would be placed on this particular item by Castle Alarms in valuing the stock of the business?

7   Castle Alarms purchases 20 alarm sirens from Northern Imports Ltd. The price charged for each siren is £40 plus VAT calculated at 17.5%. A 10% cash discount is offered by Northern Imports Ltd provided that payment is made within 14 days. (*Note*. State clearly for each entry the name of the account, the amount and whether it is debit or credit.)

    (a)   What double entry is made in the general ledger to record the purchase (the date of payment has not yet been determined)?

    (b)   What double entry is made in the general ledger to record Castle Alarms' clearing the debt by cheque whilst at the same time taking advantage of the discount offered?

8   Although Andrew Hallgrove has proved to be a good businessman, his knowledge of accounting is rather limited. In particular he does not understand how it is possible for a business to make a profit whilst at the same time the bank balance can remain static or even decrease. He has asked you to provide some guidance.

    Draft a memorandum to him clearly stating how profit is measured and giving examples of why the movement of the bank balance does not necessarily reflect the profits made.

SECTION 3

The suggested time allocation for this exercise is 80 minutes.

Data

(a) Andrew Hallgrove decided to open a shop selling cheap alarm systems and security equipment direct to the public. Trading was to start at the beginning of October 1996. He decided to call the shop and business 'Total Security'.

(b) On 1 September he opened a new bank account and paid in £50,000 of his own money as his investment in the business.

(c) During September he purchased shop fixtures and fittings at £22,500 and stock at £47,300. He paid £9,000 for 6 months' rent covering the period 1 September 1996 to 28 February 1997. Insurance of £480 covering the 12 months from 1 September 1996 was also paid, as were various items of general expenditure totalling £220.

(d) Since it was convenient to make some of the payments in cash he withdrew a lump sum from the bank.

(e) Unfortunately, his £50,000 investment was insufficient to cover all of the expenditure. However, he managed to negotiate a bank loan and all the monies from this were paid into the business's bank account.

(f) The interest rate for the bank loan was fixed at 12% per annum.

(g) At the end of September he had a £10,000 balance remaining in the bank account and £500 in cash.

(h) A summary of the business bank account for October 1996 is shown below.

	£		£
Balance b/d	10,000	To creditors	20,250
Cash banked	22,000	Drawings	3,500
		General expenses	500
		Stationery	320
		Customer refund	2,000
		Balance c/d	5,430
	32,000		32,000

(i) The cash banked all came from sales to customers. However, before banking the takings, £2,400 had been paid out as wages. The cash float at the end of October remained at £500.

(j) In paying his creditors he had been able to take advantage of discounts totalling £1,250. At the end of the month not all creditors had been paid, however, and he calculated that the total of the unpaid invoices amounted to £3,400.

(k) Depreciation is calculated on the fixtures and fittings at 20% per annum on cost.

(l) On 31 October 1996 a customer returned an alarm system which he had decided was not appropriate for his premises. He was given a refund by cheque.

(m) Unsold stock on 31 October was valued at £55,000, but this did not include the returned system. The profit margin on this type of system is 30%.

Tasks

1   Calculate the amount of the bank loan taken out in September, clearly showing your workings.

2   List the business assets as at 30 September 1996 together with their value. (Depreciation for September should be ignored.)

3   Calculate the value of the purchases made during October 1996

4   Prepare a draft statement calculating the net profit for the month ended 31 October 1996.

A SUGGESTED ANSWER TO THIS PRACTICE CENTRAL ASSESSMENT IS GIVEN ON PAGE 384.

Practice Central Assessment 5: Electronics World Ltd

PRACTICE CENTRAL ASSESSMENT 5: ELECTRONICS WORLD LTD (JUNE 1997)

SECTION 1

The suggested time allocation for this extended trial balance exercise is 75 minutes.

The company Electronics World Ltd operates out of offices and a warehouse located in Wales. The company purchases hi-fi systems, televisions and other electronic goods from manufacturers world-wide. Customers are mainly UK based shops specialising in electronic items.

- You are employed by Electronics World Ltd to assist with the bookkeeping.

- The company is relatively new and is still considering an appropriate computerised accounting system.

- The manual system currently in use consists of a general ledger, a sales ledger and a purchases ledger.

- Double entry takes place in the general ledger and the individual accounts of debtors and creditors are therefore regarded as memoranda accounts.

- Day books consisting of a purchases day book, a sales day book, a purchases returns day book and a sales returns day book are used. Totals from the various columns of the day books are transferred periodically into the general ledger.

The following balances were extracted by a colleague from the general ledger on 24 May 1997, one week before the end of the financial year, which is on 31 May 1997.

	£
Share capital	600,000
Premises	360,000
Fixtures and fittings (F and F) at cost	140,000
Provision for depreciation (F and F)	65,000
Purchases	972,140
Sales	1,530,630
Salaries	206,420
Sales returns	23,200
Purchases returns	17,350
General expenses	74,322
Insurance	16,390
Bad debts	7,506
Provision for bad debts	6,000
Debtors control account	237,855
Creditors control account	121,433
Stock at 1 June 1996	188,960
Bank	65,200
Bank deposit account	150,000
Bank interest received	3,750
Motor vehicles (MV) at cost	22,400
Provision for depreciation (MV)	3,800
VAT (credit balance)	24,720
Profit and loss	91,710

During the last week of the financial year a number of transactions took place and these are summarised below.

Purchases day book	*Total*	*VAT*	*Net*
	£	£	£
	23,970	3,570	20,400

Sales day book	*Total*	*VAT*	*Net*
	£	£	£
	35,955	5,355	30,600

Sales returns day book	*Total*	*VAT*	*Net*
	£	£	£
	1,410	210	1,200

Cheques issued	£
Payable to various creditors in settlement of debts	5,000

Task 1

Complete the table below to show the double entry which would have to be carried out in order to update the balances extracted on 24 May 1997, to take account of the summarised transactions shown above.

DOUBLE ENTRY TO UPDATE BALANCES EXTRACTED ON 24 MAY 1997		
Names of accounts	*Dr* £	*Cr* £
Entries from purchases day book		
Entries from sales day book		
Entries from sales returns day book		
Entries from cheques issued		

Task 2

Enter the updated balances into the first two columns of the extended trial balance provided on Page 278. Total the two columns ensuring that the two totals agree.

Note. It is the *updated* balances that should be used taking into account the effects of the entries prepared for Task 1.

Task 3

Make appropriate entries in the adjustment columns of the extended trial balance to take account of the following.

(a) Depreciation is to be provided as follows.

Motor vehicles: 20% per annum on cost
Fixtures and fittings: 10% per annum reducing balance method

No depreciation is charged on assets in their year of purchase or in their year of sale. On 12 November 1996 new fixture and fittings costing £6,000 had been purchased.

(b) The £150,000 was invested in the bank deposit account on 30 November 1996 at a fixed rate of interest of 6% per annum.

(c) The general expenses figure includes the sum of £2,400 paid to a company to clean the offices of Electronics World Ltd during the period 1 April 1997 to 30 September 1997.

(d) Stock has been valued on 31 May 1997 at £198,650. This figure excludes a television which was damaged beyond repair and had to be scrapped (no sale proceeds). Regis Insurance has agreed to cover the loss incurred in writing off the television.

Cost price of television: £420
Sales price of television: £630

(e) A cheque for £60 was issued at the beginning of May 1997 to pay for insurance cover which expired on 31 May 1997. A bank statement showed that the cheque was paid on 20 May. As yet no entries have been made in the books of Electronics World Ltd.

(f) The provision for bad debts is to be adjusted to a figure representing 5% of debtors.

| ELECTRONICS WORLD | Trial balance | | Adjustments | |
Account	Debit	Credit	Debit	Credit
	£	£	£	£
Share capital				
Premises				
Fixtures & fittings at cost				
Fixtures & fittings (prov for depreciation)				
Purchases				
Sales				
Salaries				
Sales returns				
Purchases returns				
General expenses				
Insurance				
Bad debts				
Provision for bad debts				
Debtors control account				
Creditors control account				
Stock at 1 June 1996				
Bank				
Bank deposit account				
Bank interest received				
Motor vehicles (cost)				
Motor vehicles (prov for depreciation)				
VAT: Credit balance				
Profit and loss				
Depreciation				
Regis Insurance				
Closing stock (P&L)				
Closing stock (B/S)				
Provision for bad debts (adjustment)				
Bank interest owing				
Prepayments				
Subtotal				
Profit for the year				
TOTAL				

SECTION 2

The following short answer questions are mainly based on the scenario outlined in Section 1. You may have to refer back to the information in that exercise in order to answer the questions.

The suggested time allocation for this set of short answer questions is 50 minutes.

1   On 31 May 1997, the balances of the accounts in the sales ledger were listed, totalled then compared with the balance of the debtors control account. The total of the list of balances amounted to £274,189. Investigations were carried out and the following errors discovered.

(a)   A customer balance of £484 had been listed as £448.

(b)   A customer balance of £1,490 had been listed twice.

(c)   A discount of £100 allowed to a customer had been debited to the account in the sales ledger.

(d)   Although goods of £135 (inclusive of VAT) had been returned by a customer, no entry had been made in the sales ledger.

Enter the appropriate adjustments in the table shown below. For each adjustment show clearly the amount involved and whether that amount is to be added or subtracted.

		£
Total from listing of balances		274,189
Adjustment for (a)	add/subtract	....
Adjustment for (b)	add/subtract	....
Adjustment for (c)	add/subtract	....
Adjustment for (d)	add/subtract	....
Revised total to agree with debtors control account		....

2   Stock has always been valued by Electronics World Ltd on a FIFO basis and this includes the closing stock figure of £198,650 as at 31 May 1997. It has been suggested that the closing stock figure should now be recalculated on a LIFO basis.

(a)   Assuming that the prices of electronic goods have been gradually rising throughout the year would the change suggested increase profit for the year ended 31 May 1997, decrease profit or would profit remain the same?

(b)   Which accounting concept states that the company should not normally change its basis for valuing stock unless it has very good reasons for doing so?

3   Electronics World Ltd recently arranged for a local builder to design and build an extension to the company offices. An invoice is received from the builder on completion of the work showing two main categories of expenditure: materials (bricks, doors, windows, frames etc) and labour. It has been suggested that:

'Since salaries and wages are normally shown in the profit and loss account the labour cost in the invoice should be written off as an expense whilst the cost of the materials should be debited to the premises account.'

(a)   Do you agree with the above statement?

(b)   Briefly explain the reason for your answer.

4   You are reviewing some accounting records on 10 June 1997 and discover an error in the sales day book. Although the VAT and net columns have been correctly totalled, the total column itself has been miscast. The appropriate figures have then been transferred from the day book into the ledgers.

Preparation of which of the following, if any, would be likely to detect the error?

Bank reconciliation statement/Trial balance/VAT return/None of these

5   For some months Electronic World Ltd has been purchasing a range of CD racks from Arun Divan, a small local supplier, who deals exclusively with the company. Initially invoices received from this business did not include VAT but the last invoice did have VAT, calculated at 17.5%, added to the cost of the racks. Jackie Brown, a colleague, is confused about the regulations regarding VAT and the implications of the change. A note is left for you by Jackie raising the following specific points.

(a)   If Electronics World Ltd is now having to pay more money for the CD racks then this must affect the profits of the company.

(b)   Arun Divan has now registered for VAT. Since the increased money he receives from Electronics World Ltd is payable to HM Customs and Excise then his profitability must remain unchanged.

Prepare a memo to Jackie Brown covering both of the points raised.

SECTION 3

The suggested time allocation for this exercise is 55 minutes.

Lucy Barber previously worked full-time for a furniture manufacturing company. Approximately two years ago, however, she decided to set up a part-time business making and selling speaker stands for hi-fi systems. She now has an arrangement to sell exclusively to Electronics World Ltd and you have been asked to assist her in preparing her accounts for the year ended 30 April 1997.

The following information is available.

(a)   Tools and equipment costing £3,000 were purchased for the business on 31 July 1995.

(b)   A van costing £4,800 was purchased on 31 October 1995, again for use in the business.

(c)   Lucy Barber rents a small workshop on a light industrial estate. The rent payable was £100 a month until 31 October 1996 but then it was increased to £120 a month and this remains as the current rate. On 30 April 1996 one month's rent was owing to the landlord.

(d)   During Lucy Barber's first period of trading, which ended on 30 April 1996, all of the transactions were for cash. On 30 April 1996 the cash balance of the business was £4,250. On 1 May 1996 she opened a business bank account and a private bank account. The £4,250 was paid into the business account but no funds were paid at that time into the private account. From 1 May 1996 all business transactions passed through the business bank account with the exception of some cheques from Electronics World Ltd (see below).

(e)   From 1 May 1996 sales to Electronics World Ltd were on credit as were purchases from her supplier, Johnson Materials Ltd. Cheques received from Electronics World were all paid into the business bank account apart from three which Lucy Barber paid directly into her private account.

(f)   Throughout the year ended 30 April 1997 Lucy Barber withdrew £200 a month cash from her private account for personal spending. No other transactions passed through the account other than the three cheques paid in from Electronics World Ltd. On the 30 April 1997 the balance of the account was £600.

(g) During the year ended 30 April 1997 she made and sold 500 pairs of speaker stands. In determining the price charged for each pair she calculated the cost of materials used for the pair then doubled this figure.

(h) On 30 April 1997.

    (i)   £4,400 was owed to the business by Electronics World Ltd.

    (ii)   £1,500 was owed by the business to Johnson Materials Ltd.

    (iii) Materials were in stock to make 120 pairs of speaker stands.

(i) Lucy Barber does not have a record of the materials that were in stock on 30 April 1996.

(j) The van is to be depreciated at 10% per annum on cost. The tools and equipment are to be depreciated at 20% per annum on cost.

(k) The following is a summary made by Lucy Barber of the entries which passed through the business bank account during the year ended 30 April 1997.

	£
Money received	
Electronics World Ltd	17,600
Money paid out	
Rent	1,300
Johnson Materials Ltd	12,000
Tools and equipment	250
Electricity	640
Telephone	560

Tasks

1   Calculate the total sales made by Lucy Barber during the year ended 30 April 1997.

2   Calculate the selling price for one pair of speaker stands.

3   Calculate the cost of materials used in making one pair of speaker stands.

4   Calculate the total cost of goods sold during the year ended 30 April 1997 (ie the cost of materials used in making the sales calculated in Task 1).

5   Calculate the cost of materials purchased by Lucy Barber during the year ended 30 April 1997.

6   Calculate the stock of materials held by Lucy Barber on 30 April 1996

7   Calculate the capital invested in the business by Lucy Barber on 30 April 1996.

8   Calculate the figure for rent which would be included in the calculation of profit for the year ended 30 April 1997.

A SUGGESTED ANSWER TO THIS PRACTICE CENTRAL ASSESSMENT IS GIVEN ON PAGE 388.

Practice Central Assessment 6: Drew Installations

PRACTICE CENTRAL ASSESSMENT 6: DREW INSTALLATIONS (DECEMBER 1997)

SECTION 1

The suggested time allocation for this extended trial balance exercise is 75 minutes.

Colin Drew is the proprietor of Drew Installations, a firm specialising in the supply and installation of kitchens and bathrooms. The showroom, warehouse and offices are located in London and most of the work carried out by the business is in the London area.

- You are employed by Colin Drew to assist with the bookkeeping.

- The business currently operates a manual system consisting of a general ledger, a sales ledger and a purchases ledger.

- Double entry takes place in the general ledger and the individual accounts of debtors and creditors are therefore regarded as memoranda accounts.

- Day books consisting of a purchases day book, a sales day book, a purchases returns day book and a sales returns day book are used. Totals from the various columns of the day books are transferred periodically into the general ledger.

At the end of the financial year on 31 October 1997, the balances were extracted from the general ledger and entered into an extended trial balance as shown on page 286.

Unfortunately in preparing the extended trial balance it was found that the total of the debit column did not agree with the total of the credit column. A suspense account was opened as a temporary measure.

Task 1

Make appropriate entries in the adjustment columns of the extended trial balance on page 286 to take account of the following.

(a) Depreciation calculated on a monthly basis is to be provided as follows:

Motor vehicles - 20% per annum straight line method
Equipment - 10% per annum reducing balance method

On 30 April 1997 a new motor vehicle costing £12,000 had been purchased.

(b) The bank loan had originally been taken out on 30 April 1996 when the sum of £60,000 had been borrowed, repayable by six annual repayments of £10,000. The first repayment had been made as agreed on 30 April 1997. Interest is charged on the loan at 8% per annum.

(c) Rent payable by the business is as follows:

Showroom and offices - £3,000 per month
Warehouse - £2,000 per month

(d) The motor vehicle expenses include a payment of £260 paid out of the business bank account to service Colin Drew's family car which is not used in the business.

(e) Insurance includes an annual buildings policy which runs from 1 August 1997. The premium paid was £2,400.

(f) The provision for bad debts is to be adjusted to a figure representing 8% of debtors.

(g) Stock has been valued at cost on 31 October 1997 at £107,300. However, this includes some discontinued kitchen cabinets the details of which are as follows:

Cost	£2,300
Normal selling price	£3,500
Net realisable value	£1,800

Task 2

Subsequent to the preparation of the extended trial balance the following errors were found, some of which had caused the opening of the suspense account. Prepare journal entries to record the correction of the errors using the blank journal on page 287. Dates and narratives are not required.

(a) The VAT column of the sales returns day book had been overcast by £200.

(b) Motor vehicle expenses of £40 had been debited to Motor Vehicles (any adjustment to depreciation can be ignored).

(c) Sales returns of £160 had been credited to purchases returns. The VAT element of the returns had been entered correctly.

(d) Purchases of £2,340 had been transferred from the rent column of the day book and into the purchases account as £2,430.

(e) A cheque for £2,450 paid to Ashwood Kitchens, a credit supplier, had been entered in the cash book but not in the relevant control account.

DREW INSTALLATIONS	Trial balance		Adjustments	
Account	Debit	Credit	Debit	Credit
	£	£	£	£
Purchases	339,500			
Sales		693,000		
Purchases returns		6,320		
Sales returns	1,780			
Carriage inwards	8,250			
Salaries and wages	106,200			
Bad debts	4,890			
Provision for bad debts		4,500		
Debtors control account	46,800			
Creditors control account		28,760		
Stock at 1 November 1996	113,450			
Motor vehicles expenses	5,780			
Motor vehicles (cost)	86,000			
Motor vehicles (prov for depreciation)		12,800		
Equipment (cost)	24,500			
Equipment (prov for depreciation)		6,700		
Rent	58,000			
Drawings	32,900			
Insurance	5,720			
Bank	8,580			
Bank loan account		50,000		
Bank interest paid	2,400			
VAT (credit balance)		12,400		
Capital		32,750		
Suspense account	2,480			
Depreciation				
Closing stock (P&L)				
Closing stock (B/S)				
Provision for bad debts (adjustment)				
Loan interest owing				
Subtotal	847,230	847,230		
Profit for the year				
TOTAL	847,230	847,230		

Note. Only the above columns of the extended trial balance are required for this exercise.

JOURNAL		
Details	DR £	CR £

SECTION 2

The following short answer questions are mainly based on the scenario outlined in Section 1. You may have to refer back to the information in that exercise in order to answer the questions.

The suggested time allocation for this set of short answer questions is 40 minutes.

1   Colin Drew is considering part-exchanging one of the business motor vehicles for a new model. The garage has offered him £2,500 in part-exchange and he will need to pay a further £10,000 by cheque. it has been calculated that the loss on disposal on the old vehicle will be £500. The vehicle was originally purchased at a price of £9,000.

   What would have been the total depreciation charge to profits during the life of the asset excluding the loss on disposal?

2   Assume that before Colin Drew was registered for VAT, Drew Installations had purchased goods costing £400 plus VAT £70 for cash.

   Note. State clearly for both (a) and (b) the names of the accounts, the amounts and whether each entry is a debit or credit.

   (a)   What would have been the double entry made in Drew Installation's books to record the purchase?

   (b)   What would have been the double entry made in the seller's books to record the sale to Drew Installations?

3   Colin Drew is thinking of manufacturing some of the kitchen cabinets supplied to customers. He estimates that in the first year of production 15,000 units could be made, with sales of 10,000 units. Costs associated with the kitchen cabinets would be as follows:

Direct materials used	£20,000
Direct labour used	£5,000
Direct production overheads	£5,000
Selling and distribution expenses	£3,000

   If Colin Drew were to proceed on this basis, what would be the estimated value of the closing stock of 5,000 units?

4   The three figures shown on a sales invoice of £4,080 plus VAT £714, total £4,794, were mistakenly entered in the sales day book of Drew Installations as £4,800 plus VAT £714, total £5,514. Would the error be detected by drawing up a trial balance? Briefly explain the reason for your answer.

5   You have received the following note from Colin Drew.

   'I have been looking at the valuation of the closing stock prepared for the trial balance and the final accounts. It occurs to me that the current range of deluxe bathroom suites is selling so well that we are almost certain to sell the existing stock. In view of this, if we were to include the stock at selling price the costs of goods sold would effectively be reduced and the gross profit would therefore be increased. I am anxious to show as high a profit as possible and would like to have your thoughts on this proposal.'

   Write a suitable response to Colin Drew in the form of a memo. Your answer should include references to SSAP 2 and SSAP 9.

SECTION 3

The suggested time allocation for this exercise is 65 minutes.

During Colin Drew's early years in business trading as Drew Installations, he had very little administrative help and kept minimal records. A number of queries have now arisen and it has become necessary to calculate some figures relating to the year ended 31 October 1992. You have been asked to provide assistance. The information available from Drew Installations is as follows:

- Assets at 1 November 1991:

	£	£
Stock		30,400
Debtors		22,800
Motor vehicles at cost	8,750	
Less provision for depreciation	2,690	
		6,060
Equipment at cost	5,200	
Less provision for depreciation	840	
		4,360

- Liabilities at 1 November 1991:

	£
Creditors	15,600
Bank overdraft	4,300
Accrued expenses	1,000

- Payment made during the year ended 31 October 1992:

	£
To creditors	120,750
Expenses	52,800
Equipment purchased 30 April 1992	4,500
Drawings	unknown

- Receipts during the year ended 31 October 1992:

	£
From debtors	unknown

- Profit margin 50% on all sales

- Depreciation calculated on a monthly basis was provided as follows:

  Motor vehicles - 20% per annum straight line method
  Equipment - 10% per annum reducing balance method

- Assets at 31 October 1992

	£
Stock	32,700
Debtors	21,700
Motor vehicles at cost	8,750
Equipment at cost	9,700
Bank	15,850
Prepaid expenses	1,500

- Liabilities at 31 October 1992

	£
Creditors	16,850

Tasks

1 Calculate the cost of goods sold during the year ended 31 October 1992.

2 Calculate the gross profit for the year ended 31 October 1992.

3 Calculate the sales for the year ended 31 October 1992.

4 Calculate the receipts from debtors for the year ended 31 October 1992.

5 Calculate the drawings made by Colin Drew during the year ended 31 October 1992.

6 Calculate the net profit for the year ended 31 October 1992.

A SUGGESTED ANSWER TO THIS PRACTICE CENTRAL ASSESSMENT IS GIVEN ON PAGE 393.

Practice Central Assessment 7: Fair Sounds

PRACTICE CENTRAL ASSESSMENT 7: FAIR SOUNDS (JUNE 1998)

SECTION 1

The suggested time allocation for this extended trial balance exercise is 70 minutes.

Caroline Fairley is the proprietor of Fair Sounds, a business which repairs, buys and sells musical instruments. It is situated in the middle of England and takes work from all over the country.

- You are employed by Caroline Fairley to assist with the bookkeeping.

- The business currently operates a manual system consisting of a general ledger, a sales ledger and a purchases ledger.

- Double entry takes place in the general ledger and the individual accounts of debtors and creditors are therefore regarded as memoranda accounts.

- Day books consisting of a purchases day book, a sales day book, a purchases returns day book and a sales returns day book are used. Totals from the various columns of the day books are transferred periodically into the general ledger.

At the end of the financial year on 30 April 1998, the balances were extracted from the general ledger and entered into an extended trial balance as shown on page 294.

Task 1

Make appropriate entries in the adjustment columns of the extended trial balance to take account of the following.

(a) Depreciation is to be provided as follows:

   Motor vehicles - 20% per annum reducing balance method
   Equipment - 10% per annum straight line method

(b) The £22,500 in the bank deposit account was invested on 1 July 1997 at a fixed rate interest of 8% per annum.

(c) On reviewing the debtors at 30 April 1998, it was decided that one of them would probably not pay and the debt should be written off. The amount owing was £1,800. No entries have been made to reflect this. Any VAT implications are to be ignored.

(d) The provision for doubtful debts should be adjusted to a figure of 5% of the outstanding debtors.

(e) Closing stock was valued at cost at £43,795. However, this figure includes two items, cost price £175 each, which have been damaged in storage. It has been estimated that if a total of £35 was spent on repairing them, they could be sold for £140 each.

(f) Insurance is paid quarterly in arrears on 31 January, 30 April, 31 July and 31 October each year. The instalment due on 30 April 1998 was overlooked and a cheque, for £90, was not raised until 15 May 1998.

Task 2

Extend the figures into the extended trial balance columns for the profit and loss and balance sheet. Total all of these columns, transferring the balance of the profit or loss as appropriate.

Extended trial balance at 30 April 1998

DESCRIPTION	Ledger balance		Adjustments		Profit and Loss a/c		Balance Sheet	
	Debit	Credit	Debit	Credit	Debit	Credit	Debit	Credit
	£	£	£	£	£	£	£	£
Purchases	127,680							
Sales		184,784						
Purchases returns		360						
Sales returns	502							
Stock at 1 May 1997	40,650							
Salaries	22,590							
General expenses	14,580							
Insurance	270							
Motor vehicle (MV) at cost	9,600							
Provision for depreciation (MV)		4,685						
Equipment (EQ) at cost	17,100							
Provision for depreciation (EQ)		5,130						
Bad debt	2,025							
Provision for doubtful debts		1,485						
Debtors control account	31,200							
Creditors control account		25,232						
Drawings	17,892							
Capital		82,493						
Bank overdraft		261						
Cash	426							
VAT		1,685						
Bank interest received		900						
Bank deposit account	22,500							
Depreciation								
Closing stock - P&L								
Closing stock - balance sheet								
Bank interest owing								
Provision for doubtful debts - adjustment								
Other accruals								
Profit								
	307,015	307,015						

Task 3

Subsequent to the completion of the extended trial balance, certain errors were discovered. Prepare journal entries to record the correction of the following errors, using the blank journal below. Dates and narratives are not required.

(a) Sales returns of £96 (net of VAT) had been debited to the purchases returns account. The VAT element of the returns had been entered correctly.

(b) An invoice had been received from a supplier for cleaning materials, totalling £188. It had been wrongly assumed that this amount included VAT. However, on inspection of the original invoice, it was found that the supplier was not registered for VAT and therefore no VAT had in fact been charged.

JOURNAL		
Details	DR £	CR £

SECTION 2

The following short answer questions are mainly based on the scenario outlined in Section 1. You may have to refer back to the information in that exercise in order to answer the questions.

The suggested time allocation for this set of short answer questions is 40 minutes.

1   Assume the motor vehicle costing £9,600 as shown in the trial balance was sold on 1 May 1998 for £4,400.

(a)   What would the profit or loss on disposal be? (*Note.* State clearly the value and whether a profit or a loss.)

(b)   What would have been the double entry made in the books of Fair Sounds to record the disposal of the motor vehicle, including the transfer to the profit and loss account? (*Note.* State clearly for each entry the name of the account, the amount and whether it is a debit or a credit.)

2   The drawings figure in the trial balance is £17,892.

(a)   Where is this figure shown? Profit and loss account or the Balance sheet?

(b)   Briefly explain the reason for your answer.

3   Discounts allowed had been wrongly credited to discounts received.

On correction of this error would the reported profits be increased, decreased or stay the same?

4   The list of balances on page 294 includes an amount of £1,685 as VAT.

(a)   To whom is this amount payable?

(b)   Explain fully how this balance has come about.

5   You have received the following note from Caroline Fairley.

'I have been looking at the figures in the profit and loss account, in particular the expenses. I notice that the insurance figure is higher by £90 than originally shown in the trial balance. I assume that this £90 is something to do with the cheque which was raised on 15 May 1998. If this cheque was raised after the year end, I can see no reason why it should be included with the expenses for the year ended 30 April 1998. I am concerned that this could have reduced my profits and I would be grateful for an explanation.'

Write an appropriate memo to Caroline Fairley, explaining your treatment. Your answer should include relevant references to SSAP 2. Use the headed paper on page 297 for your answer.

(NB Two pages are included for this memo to allow for notes and candidates with large writing. It is anticipated that the majority of candidates will find one page sufficient.)

MEMORANDUM

To:
From:
Ref:
Date:

SECTION 3

The suggested time allocation for this exercise is 70 minutes.

Caroline Fairley's brother, Richard Fairley, has been watching Caroline's growing success and is tempted also to set up business on his own. He has found a small newsagent which would be ideal. The current owner of the business, Babek Assidian, is equally keen to sell the business and has therefore very kindly given Richard Fairley some information which he could use to asses the viability of the business.

Unfortunately, the information provided is incomplete, so Richard Fairley has passed the information to you so that you can calculate some of the necessary figures.

The following is the information provided.

Assets as at 31 December 1996

	£	£
Fixtures and fittings at cost	17,500	
Less provision for depreciation	12,250	
		5,250
Motor vehicle at cost	12,500	
Less provision for depreciation	6,250	
		6,250
Stock		15,750
Debtors		630
Insurance prepayment		495
Cash		355
		28,730
Creditors	4,750	
Bank overdraft	3,490	
		8,240
		20,490

Other information

(a) The normal gross profit margin on all sales is 30%. Babek Assidian has no idea what the value of the stock is at 31 December 1997. However, he does know that he has taken stock which has a cost price of £270 for his own private use.

(b) Depreciation is calculated as follows.

Fixture and fittings	10% on cost
Motor vehicle	25% on cost

(c) The proceeds of cash sales and receipts from debtors for credit sales are all paid into the bank account at the end of the day, apart from the float which is retained on the premises to be used at the start of the following day.

(d) On 31 December 1997, the creditors amounted to £7,400 and the debtors amounted to £290.

(e) Also, on 31 December 1997, it was discovered that there was £260 owing for electricity costs and the buildings insurance had not yet been paid. The insurance should have been paid in November 1997 to provide cover from 1 December 1997 for the following twelve months, but Babek Assidian forgot to pay until mid-January 1998. The annual insurance premium was £600.

(f) A summary of the business bank account for the year ended 31 December 1997 showed:

	£		£
Receipts from sales	126,790	Balance b/d	3,490
		To creditors	83,410
		General expenses	16,060
		Salaries	5,110
		Drawings	17,500
		Balance c/d	1,220
	126,790		126,790

Note. General expenses includes electricity and insurance.

Tasks

1 Calculate the total sales for the year ended 31 December 1997.

2 Calculate the total purchases for the year ended 31 December 1997.

3 Calculate the total cost of sales for the year ended 31 December 1997.

4 Calculate the value of the closing stock as at 31 December 1997.

5 Calculate the figure for general expenses which would be included in the calculation of profit for the year ended 31 December 1997.

6 Calculate the figure for net profit for the year ended 31 December 1997.

A SUGGESTED ANSWER TO THIS PRACTICE CENTRAL ASSESSMENT IS GIVEN ON PAGE 396.

Practice Central Assessment 8: Tulips

PRACTICE CENTRAL ASSESSMENT 8: TULIPS (DECEMBER 1998)

SECTION 1

The suggested time allocation for this extended trial balance exercise is 85 minutes.

Donald Johnson is the proprietor of Tulips, a business which specialises in the growing, buying and selling of flowers. The growing of the flowers take places in greenhouses, which are large glass buildings specially designed for this purpose.

- You are employed by Donald Johnson as the bookkeeper.

- The business currently operates a manual system consisting of a general ledger, a sales ledger and a purchases ledger.

- Double entry takes place in the general ledger and the individual accounts of debtors and creditors are therefore regarded as memoranda accounts.

- Day books consisting of a purchases day book, a sales day book, a purchases returns day book and a sales returns day book are used. Totals from the various columns of the day books are transferred periodically into the general ledger.

The following list of balances had been extracted from the general ledger on 30 November 1998, which is the financial year end for Tulips.

	£
Sales	313,746
Sales returns	971
Purchases	186,574
Purchases returns	714
Stock	25,732
Wages	40,000
Rent and rates	18,608
Light and heat	11,940
Office expenses	9,530
Greenhouse running expenses	11,290
Motor expenses	4,782
Sundry expenses	5,248
Motor vehicles (cost)	25,810
Motor vehicles (provision for depreciation) at 1 December 1997	5,162
Greenhouses (cost)	25,500
Greenhouses (provision for depreciation) at 1 December 1997	7,650
Cash	100
Bank current account (debit balance)	3,020
Bank loan	30,000
Debtors' control account	6,860
Creditors' control account	4,720
Capital account	21,112
Drawings	11,000
VAT account (credit balance)	3,587
Suspense account (credit balance)	274

After all the above balances had been extracted from the books of Tulips, the following additional information became available.

(i) For one month only, the drawings for Donald Johnson had been posted, in error, to the wages account. The drawings had amounted to £1,000.

(ii) A cheque received from a debtor, J Willis, had been credited, in error, to the creditors' control account. The amount of the cheque was £280.

(iii) In one month, the total of the columns in the sales returns day book for £560, net of VAT, had been correctly treated in the sales returns account, and the debtors' control account had been correctly posted with the gross amount. However, the VAT element had not been posted to the VAT account.

(iv) In August 1998, the total of the columns in the purchase returns day book showed net £480, VAT £84 and total £564. Although the net amount and the VAT amount had been correctly treated in the general ledger, the total amount had been credited to the creditors' control account.

(v) A receipt of £1,500 had been shown in the bank statement in November 1998. Originally, you had not known what this was for, so an entry was made in the bank account and in the suspense account. On investigation, you discovered that one of the greenhouses had been sold in November 1998, and the £1,500 represented the proceeds from that disposal. The greenhouse had cost £2,500 and its accumulated depreciation on 1 December 1997 amounted to £750. The business has a policy of not depreciating an asset in the year of disposal.

Task 1

Prepare the journal entries to record the correction of the errors and omissions listed on page 303. Use the blank journal on page 305. Dates and narratives are not required.

(NB Your journal should include the completion of the disposal account with the transfer to the profit or loss on disposal.)

Task 2

Enter the updated account balances into the first two columns of the extended trial balance provided on page 306 Total the two columns.

Note. It is the updated balances that should be used, ie after taking into account the effect of the journal entries prepared in Task 1.

Task 3

Make appropriate entries in the adjustment columns of the extended trial balance to take account of the following.

(a) Depreciation is to be provided as follows:

Motor vehicles - 20% per annum straight line method
Greenhouses - 10% per annum straight line method

(b) On reviewing the debtors on 30 November 1998, it was decided that a provision for doubtful debts should be made. This provision is to be 5% of the outstanding debtors.

(c) Closing stock was valued at cost at £24,895.

(d) Rent is paid quarterly in advance on 1 January, 1 April, 1 July and 1 October each year. The instalment due on 1 October 1998 was overlooked and a cheque, for £4,500, was not raised until 10 December 1998.

Task 1

JOURNAL		
Details	DR £	CR £

Tasks 2 and 3

DESCRIPTION	LEDGER BALANCES		ADJUSTMENTS	
	Dr	Cr	Dr	Cr
	£	£	£	£
Sales				
Sales returns				
Purchases				
Purchases returns				
Stock at 1 December 1997				
Wages				
Rent and rates				
Light and heat				
Office expenses				
Greenhouse running expenses				
Motor expenses				
Sundry expenses				
Motor vehicle (MV) at cost				
Provision for depreciation MV				
Greenhouses (GH) at cost				
Provision for depreciation GH				
Cash				
Bank current account				
Bank loan				
Debtors' control account				
Creditors' control account				
Capital account				
Drawings account				
VAT account				
Suspense account				
Profit or loss on disposal of fixed asset				
Depreciation				
Provision for doubtful debts - P&L				
Provision for doubtful debts - balance sheet				
Closing stock - P&L				
Closing stock - balance sheet				
Accrual				

Note. Only the above columns of the extended trial balance are required for this central assessment.

SECTION 2

The suggested time allocation for this set of short answer questions is 35 minutes.

Task 1

Donald Johnson has a small number of watering cans that are used in the greenhouses. Each watering can costs £5 and is expected to last for approximately four years. The policy of the business is to charge the full cost of these items to the profit and loss account when purchased.

(a) Is this treatment acceptable accounting practice?

(b) Briefly explain the reason for your answer.

Task 2

Assume that during the annual physical stock count, the closing stock figure shown in the business had been wrongly undercast by £1,000 and that error had been undetected.

Indicate what the effect would be:

(a) On this year's profit?
(b) On next year's profit?

Task 3

Included in Tulips' stock are some rose bushes. At the beginning of November 1998 there were 40 rose bushes in stock, each costing £6. Stock movements during the month of November 1998 were as follows:

Purchases 5/11/98	40 at £6.5
Sales 12/11/98	50
Sales 15/11/98	10
Purchases 23/11/98	30 at £6

Each rose bush is sold for £11. Stock is valued on a FIFO basis.

Calculate the value of the following.

(a) Sales of rose bushes for November 1998.
(b) Closing stock of rose bushes on 30 November 1998.
(c) Cost of goods sold of rose bushes for November 1998.

Task 4

Donald Johnson is considering entering into a contract with a large retail shop. Tulips will supply all the shop's gardening needs. This contract will probably be under a sale or return basis. As Donald Johnson is not fully aware of what this type of contract involves, he has asked your advice.

Write an appropriate memo to Donald Johnson explaining what 'sale or return basis' means. Your answer should include how the accounts would reflect these transactions. Use the headed paper on page 308 for your answer.

MEMORANDUM

To:
From:
Ref:
Date:

SECTION 3

The suggested time allocation for this exercise is 60 minutes.

A friend of Donald Johnson, Sheena Gordon, has been trading for just over twelve months as a dressmaker. She has kept no accounting records at all, and she is worried that she may need professional help to sort out her financial position. Knowing that Donald Johnson runs a successful business, Sheena Gordon approached him for advice. He recommended that you, his bookkeeper, should help Sheena Gordon.

You meet with Sheena Gordon and discuss the information that you require her to give you. Sometime later, you receive a letter from Sheena Gordon providing you with the information that you requested, as follows.

(a) She started her business on 1 October 1997. She opened a business bank account and paid in £5,000 of her savings.

(b) During October she bought the equipment and the stock of materials that she needed. The equipment cost £4,000 and the stock of materials cost £1,800. All of this was paid for out of the business bank account.

(c) A summary of the business bank account for the twelve months ended 30 September 1998 showed the following.

	£		£
Capital	5,000	Equipment	4,000
Cash banked	27,000	Opening stock of materials	1,800
		Purchases of materials	18,450
		General expenses	870
		Drawings	6,200
		Balance c/d	680
	32,000		32,000

(d) All of the sales are on a cash basis. Some of the cash is paid into the bank account while the rest is used for cash expenses. She has no idea what the total value of her sales is for the year, but she knows that she has spent £3,800 on materials and £490 on general expenses. She took the rest of the cash not banked for her private drawings. She also keeps a cash float of £100.

(e) The gross profit margin on all sales is 50%.

(f) She estimates that all the equipment should last for five years. You therefore agree to depreciate it using the straight line method.

(g) On 30 September 1998, the creditors for materials amounted to £1,400.

(h) She estimates that the cost of stock of materials that she had left at the end of the year was £2,200.

Tasks

1 Calculate the total purchases for the year ended 30 September 1998.

2 Calculate the total cost of sales for the year ended 30 September 1998.

3 Calculate the sales for the year ended 30 September 1998.

4 Show the entries that would appear in Sheena Gordon's cash account.

5 Calculate the total drawings made by Sheena Gordon throughout the year.

6 Calculate the figure for net profit for the year ended 30 September 1998.

A SUGGESTED ANSWER TO THIS PRACTICE CENTRAL ASSESSMENT IS GIVEN ON PAGE 401.

Practice Central Assessment 9: Pine Warehouse

PRACTICE CENTRAL ASSESSMENT 9: PINE WAREHOUSE (December 1998)

SECTION 1

The suggested time allocation for this extended trial balance exercise is 70 minutes.

Pat Hall is the proprietor of The Pine Warehouse, a business which buys, repairs and supplies pine furniture.

- You are employed by Pat Hall to assist with the bookkeeping.

- The business currently operates a manual system consisting of a general ledger, a sales ledger and a purchases ledger.

- Double entry takes place in the general ledger and the individual accounts of debtors and creditors are therefore regarded as memoranda accounts.

- Day books consisting of a purchases day book, a sales day book, a purchases returns day book and a sales returns day book are used. Totals from the various columns of the day books are transferred periodically into the general ledger.

At the end of the financial year, on 30 November 1998, the balances were extracted from the general ledger and entered into an extended trial balance as shown on page 315.

Task 1

Make appropriate entries in the adjustment columns of the extended trial balance on page 315 to take account of the following.

(a) Stock was initially valued on 30 November 1998 at £136,000. However, it was later found that this figure included some pine chairs which had been valued at selling price rather than at cost. The selling price valuation of the chairs was £9,600 and the profit mark-up for the chairs was 50%.

(b) Depreciation calculated on a monthly basis is to be provided as follows.

Motor vehicles - 20% per annum straight line method
Machinery - 10% per annum reducing balance method
Equipment - 10% per annum reducing balance method

Note. The machinery figure shown in the extended trial balance includes some new machinery purchased on 31 May 1998 at a cost of £6,000.

(c) The advertising figure includes £7,200 paid for 3 newspaper adverts each costing the same amount and due to appear on:

10 August 1998
10 October 1998
10 December 1998

(d) Rent payable by the business is £2,460 per month.

(e) An invoice relating to goods received by The Pine Warehouse on 1 November 1998 has been lost and no entries have therefore been made. The goods supplied cost £1,800 plus £315 VAT and have been included in the valuation of the closing stock on 30 November 1998.

(f) A standing order has been set up to transfer £3,000 on the 28th day of each month from the business bank account into Pat Hall's private bank account. The transfer for 28 November 1998 has not been entered into the accounts of the business.

(g) The provision for bad debts is to be adjusted to a figure representing 5% of debtors.

Task 2

After the preparation of the extended trial balance the following errors, which had caused the opening of the suspense account, were found. Prepare journal entries to record the correction of all the errors using the blank journal on page 316. Dates and narratives are not required.

(a) Sales of £10,810 had been transferred from the total column of the sales day book into the debtors' control account as £10,180.

(b) The VAT column of the purchases day book had been overcast by £500.

(c) The net column of the sales day book had been overcast by £4,450.

(d) A cheque for £1,200 received from a debtor had been entered into the cash book but not into the relevant control account.

(e) Discounts allowed of £40 had been credited to the discounts received account.

Task 1

Extended Trial Balance at November 1998

DESCRIPTION	LEDGER BALANCES		ADJUSTMENTS	
	Dr	Cr	Dr	Cr
	£	£	£	£
Sales		1,240,600		
Purchases	826,400			
Debtors control account	93,340			
Creditors control account		70,870		
Bad debts	8,750			
Provision for bad debts		4,010		
Motor vehicles (MV) at cost	80,500			
Provision for depreciation (MV)		15,760		
Machinery (Mach) at cost	24,000			
Provision for depreciation (Mach)		2,000		
Equipment (Equip) at cost	27,400			
Provision for depreciation (Equip)		5,850		
Drawings	33,000			
Cash	3,000			
Bank		12,500		
Lighting and heating	3,250			
Insurance	1,020			
Advertising	10,620			
VAT (credit balance)		13,600		
Stock at 1 December 1997	125,560			
Motor expenses	8,670			
Discounts allowed	4,200			
Discounts received		1,200		
Salaries and wages	120,650			
Rent	24,600			
Capital		32,030		
Suspense	3,460			
Prepayments				
Depreciation				
Closing stock - P&L				
Closing stock - balance sheet				
Provision for bad debts - adjustment				
Accrued expenses				
	1,398,420	1,398,420		

Note. Only the above columns of the extended trial balance are required for this central assessment.

Task 2

JOURNAL		
Details	DR £	CR £

SECTION 2

The suggested time allocation for this set of short answer questions is 50 minutes.

Tasks

1   On 30 November 1998 the balances of the accounts in the purchases ledger were listed, totalled, and then compared with the updated balance of the creditors' control account. The total of the list of balances amounted to £76,670. After investigations the following errors were found.

   (a)   A credit purchase of £235 (inclusive of VAT) had been omitted from a supplier's account in the purchases ledger

   (b)   A payment of £1,600 to a supplier had been credited to the supplier's account in the purchases ledger

   (c)   A supplier's balance of £1,194 had been listed as £1,914.

   Enter the appropriate adjustments in the table shown below. For each adjustment show clearly the amount involved and whether the amount is to be added or subtracted.

2   A credit sale, made by the Pine Warehouse, was correctly entered into the general ledger but was then credited to the customer's account in the sales ledger.

   (a)   Would the error be detected by drawing up a trial balance?

   (b)   Briefly explain the reason for your answer to (a).

3   On 1 December 1998 a motor vehicle, which had been purchased on 1 December 1997 for £10,000, was part-exchanged for a new vehicle. The disposal account showed a £500 profit on disposal. A further £3,000 was paid for the new vehicle by cheque. (Depreciation on motor vehicles is calculated on a monthly basis at 20% per annum straight line method.)

   Calculate the purchase price of the new vehicle.

4   Pat Hall is the treasurer of a local tennis club which has 420 members. The subscription details for the club are as follows.

   Subscription for year to 31 December 1997 - £220 per member

   Subscription for year to 31 December 1998 - £240 per member

   Subscription for year to 31 December 1999 - £250 per member

   On 31 December 1997 6 members had prepaid their subscriptions for 1998.

   By 31 December 1998 8 members will have prepaid their subscriptions for 1999.

   All other members have paid, and will continue to pay, their subscriptions during the relevant year.

   (a)   What is the subscriptions figure to be entered in the income and expenditure account for the year ended 31 December 1998?

   (b)   What will be the total amount of money received for subscriptions during the year ended 31 December 1998?

5   On 30 November 1998 The Pine Warehouse made a cash sale of some pine tables and chairs. These had originally cost £1,000 and were sold for £1,500. Although the sale was immediately recorded in the accounts of the business and the cash had been paid at the time of the sale, the customer asked for delivery to take place on 22 December 1998. The tables and chairs were therefore still in stock at the financial year end. Pat Hall has suggested that the tables

and chairs should be included in the valuation of the closing stock at the selling price of £1,500. Pat Hall comments to you: 'this seems to be in accordance with the prudence concept since profits can be recognised once they are realised.'

Using the headed paper on page 319, write a memo to Pat Hall stating whether or not you agree with the proposed accounting treatment for the tables and chairs. Clearly explain the reasons for your answer.

Task 5

MEMORANDUM

To:
From:
Ref:
Date:

SECTION 3

The suggested time allocation for this exercise is 60 minutes.

Pat Hall also owns a small manufacturing business, Hall Products, which makes and supplies some of the furniture for The Pine Warehouse. The financial year for Hall Products ends on 30 November and Pat Hall asks you to produce some information from the following figures for the year ended 30 November 1998.

	£
• Stocks	
Stock of raw material at 1 December 1997	4,300
Raw materials purchased	95,600
Stock of raw materials at 30 November 1998	9,400
Stock of finished goods at 1 December 1997	10,360
Stock of finished goods at 30 November 1998	12,510

Note. Work in progress can be ignored

	£
• Staff costs	
Furniture production wages	38,000
Factory supervisory wages	28,000
Office wages	16,000

	£
• Business fixed assets	
Factory premises at cost 1 December 1990	80,000
Office premises at cost 1 December 1990	30,000
Factory machinery at cost 1 December 1995	20,000
Office equipment at cost 1 December 1996	10,000

•   Depreciation

Premises: 2% per annum straight line method
Machinery and equipment: 10% per annum straight line method

	£
• Other expenses	
Factory overheads	12,500
Office expenses	8,300

	£
• Debtors and creditors for stock	
Debtors at 1 December 1997	22,200
Debtors at 30 November 1998	24,500
Creditors at 1 December 1997	12,100
Creditors at 30 November 1998	13,300
Received from debtors during the year	294,700

•   *Note.* All payments and receipts pass through the business bank account.

Task 1

Calculate the prime cost of the goods produced by Hall Products during the year ended 30 November 1998.

Task 2

Calculate the total production cost of the goods made by Hall Products during the year ended 30 November 1998.

Task 3

Calculate the total sales made by Hall Products during the year ended 30 November 1998.

Task 4

Calculate the gross profit made by Hall Products during the year ended 30 November 1998.

Task 5

The opening balance of Hall Products' bank account on 1 December 1997 was an overdraft of £3,600. Calculate the closing balance of the bank account on 30 November 1998.

A SUGGESTED ANSWER TO THIS PRACTICE CENTRAL ASSESSMENT IS GIVEN ON PAGE 405.

Practice Central Assessment 10: Automania

PRACTICE CENTRAL ASSESSMENT 10: AUTOMANIA (JUNE 1999)

SECTION 1

The suggested time allocation for this extended trial balance exercise is 80 minutes.

Ananda Carver is the proprietor of Automania, a business which supplies car parts to garages to use in servicing and repair work.

- You are employed by Ananda Carver to assist with the bookkeeping.

- The business currently operates a manual system consisting of a general ledger, a sales ledger and a purchases ledger.

- Double entry takes place in the general ledger and the individual accounts of debtors and creditors are therefore regarded as memoranda accounts.

- Day books consisting of a purchases day book, a sales day book, a purchases returns day book and a sales returns day book are used. Totals from the various columns of the day books are transferred into the general ledger.

At the end of the financial year, on 30 April 1999, the balances were extracted from the general ledger and entered into an extended trial balance as shown on page 326.

Task 1

Make appropriate entries in the adjustments columns of the extended trial balance to take account of the following:

(a) Rent payable by the business is as follows:
     For period to 31 July 1998   -£1,500 per month
     From 1 August 1998   -£1,600 per month

(b) The insurance balance includes £100 paid for the period 1 May 1999 to 31 May 1999.

(c) Depreciation is to be calculated as follows:
     Motor vehicles   -20% per annum straight line method
     Fixtures and Fittings   -10% per annum reducing balance method

(d) The provision for bad debts is to be adjusted to a figure representing 2% of debtors.

(e) Stock has been valued at cost on 30 April 1999 at £119,360. However, this figure includes old stock, the details of which are as follows:

     Cost price of old stock   -£3,660

     Net realisable value of old stock   -£2,060

     Also included is a badly damaged car door which was to have been sold for £80 but will now have to be scrapped. The cost price of the door was £60.

(f) A credit note received from a supplier on 5 April 1999 for goods returned was filed away with no entries having been made. The credit note has now been discovered and is for £200 net plus £35 VAT.

Extended Trial Balance at 30th April 1999

DESCRIPTION	LEDGER BALANCES		ADJUSTMENTS	
	Dr £	Cr £	Dr £	Cr £
Capital		135,000		
Drawings	42,150			
Rent	17,300			
Purchases	606,600			
Sales		857,300		
Sales returns	2,400			
Purchases returns		1,260		
Salaries and wages	136,970			
Motor vehicles (M.V.)at cost	60,800			
Provision for depreciation (M.V)		16,740		
Fixtures and fittings (F&F) at cost	40,380			
Provision for depreciation (F&F)		21,600		
Bank		3,170		
Cash	2,100			
Lighting and heating	4,700			
VAT		9,200		
Stock at 1 May 1998	116,100			
Bad debts	1,410			
Provision for bad debts		1,050		
Debtors control account	56,850			
Creditors control account		50,550		
Sundry expenses	6,810			
Insurance	1,300			
Accruals				
Prepayments				
Depreciation				
Provision for bad debts - Adjustment				
Closing stock - P&L				
Closing stock - Balance sheet				
Totals	1,095,870	1,095,870	-	-

COMMERCIAL BANK PLC
Bank Statement

Automania   **Account Number: 80261995**

Date	Detail	Debit	Credit	Balance
1999		£	£	£
17 May	Balance			8,700
17 May	Cheque 704182	290		8,410
18 May	Credit		360	8,770
19 May	Cheque 704184	310		8,460
20 May	Cheque 704183	200		8,260
20 May	Credit		1,080	9,340
21 May	Cheque 704185	1,360		7,980
21 May	Cheque 704186	2,750		5,230
24 May	Credit		1,400	6,630
24 May	Bank charges	140		6,490
25 May	Standing order: Anzac property	1,600		4,890
26 May	BACS credit		125	5,015
26 May	Cheque 704188	475		4,540
27 May	Cash withdrawal	200		4,340
28 May	Cheque 704187	2,970		1,370

The following is an extract from the cash book for the same period.

Bank Account

1999			£	1999			Cheque No.	£
May	17	Balance b/d	7,900	May	17	Auto Parts	185	1,360
	17	L White	360		18	Slick Oils	186	2,750
	18	Field garages	750		21	Stealth Wheels	187	2,970
	19	H Smith	330		21	K Mason	188	475
	20	L Sprig	190		24	P Curtis	189	395
	21	Kay Cars	1,210		27	K Fabrications	190	1,880
	27	Halliwells	685		28	Auto Parts	191	4,200
	28	Reece Motors	470					
	28	Balance c/d	2,135					
			14,030					14,030

Task 2

Prepare a statement reconciling the £7,900 opening balance of the cash book with the £8,700 opening balance of the bank statement. Show clearly the individual items which have caused the opening balance of the cash book to differ from the opening balance of the bank statement.

Task 3

Showing clearly the individual debits and credits, update the closing balance of the cash book.

Task 4

Prepare a book reconciliation statement as at 28 May 1999.

SECTION 2

The suggested time allocation for this set of short answer questions is 50 minutes.

Task 1

Some cash sales of £470, inclusive of VAT, were entered into the books of Automania as follows:

Dr Cash   £470
Cr Sales   £470

If the error is not detected and corrected:

(a) **Would profits calculated at the end of the next financial period be overstated, understated or unaffected?**

(b) **Would the balance of the cash account prior to any reconciliation be overstated, understated or unaffected?**

(c) **What entries should be made to correct the error?**

> **NOTE: State clearly the names of the accounts, the amounts and whether each entry is a debit or a credit.**

Task 2

You overhear a conversation between Sam Bell, who is another bookkeeper employed by Automania, and a supplier. The supplier has telephoned to see when he can expect to receive a cheque in settlement of a debt which is a few days overdue. Sam Bell tells him the following:

'A cheque for £2,150 was sent off to you yesterday. However, Automania's overdraft is over the limit set by the bank at the moment and it would therefore be a good idea if you waited a few days before paying in the cheque.'

Briefly comment on the statement made by Sam Bell to the supplier.

Task 3

A motor vehicle which had originally been purchased on 31 October 1997 for £12,000 was part exchanged for a new vehicle on 31 May 1999. The new vehicle cost £15,000 and was paid for using the old vehicle and a cheque for £5,000.

Prepare a disposals account for the old vehicle showing clearly the transfer to the profit and loss account. (Depreciation for motor vehicles is calculated on a monthly basis at 20% per annum straight line method assuming no residual value.)

Task 4

At the end of May a trial balance is produced. The two sides do not agree and a suspense account is opened on a temporary basis. The error which had caused the problem is then found. Cash drawings of £250 had been credited both to the cash account and to the drawings account.

What would have been the balance of the suspense account?

Task 5

Ananda Carver is considering expanding Automania into the manufacture of car seat covers. The following estimated figures for the next financial period have been produced:

	£
Direct labour	26,000
Materials used	14,000
Production overheads	20,000
Closing stock – work in progress	2,000

Calculate the production cost of goods completed.

Task 6

You receive the following note from Ananda Carver:

'As you know, I am considering expanding Automania by manufacturing car seat covers. If this goes ahead there will be a need to purchase some new machinery. I am, however, concerned about the effects of the purchase on the profits of the business. To avoid depreciation charges altogether I suggest that the total cost of the machinery is taken out of the bank account at the time of the purchase by paying by cheque. There will therefore be no need to take the cost out of profits in future years. Please let me know if you have any comments to make regarding this suggestion.'

Using the headed paper on pages 330 and 331 write a memo to Ananda Carver responding to the above note. Your answer should refer to appropriate Statements of Standard Accounting Practice and should clearly state whether or not you agree with the suggestion made by Ananda Carver to avoid depreciation charges.

NOTE: Two pages have been included for this memo. However, it is anticipated that the majority of candidates will find one page sufficient.

Task 6

MEMORANDUM

To:
From:
Ref:
Date:

Task 6 (continued)

SECTION 3

The suggested time allocation for this exercise is 50 minutes.

Ananda Carver is the treasurer of the City Fields Tennis Club. As treasurer he needs to prepare some financial statements and asks you to provide assistance.

The following information is available at the year end on 31 December 1998:

Bank Account Summary

	£		£
Balance b/d (1 January 1998)	1,200	Purchase of refreshments	10,600
Subscriptions	30,000	Club staff wages	28,000
Sale of refreshments	15,260	Electricity	1,780
Donations	500	Sundry expenses	1,820
Loan	6,000	Repairs to tennis courts	800
		Clubhouse improvements	6,400
		Rent of land	3,400
		Balance c/d (31 December 1998)	160
	52,960		52,960

- Balances at 1 January 1998:

	£
Stock of refreshments	120
Creditors for refreshments	860
Clubhouse at cost	24,000
Provision for depreciation – clubhouse	7,200
Subscriptions in advance	400

- Balances at 31 Decmeber 1998

Stock of refreshments	230
Creditors for refreshments	780
Subscriptions in advance	550

- Depreciation on the clubhouse is calculated at the rate of 5% of cost at the end of the financial year.

- 15% of wages relate to refreshments, 85% to other activities.

- 20% of electricity relates to refreshments, 80% to other activities.

- The loan was taken out on 30 June 1998 at a rate of interest of 10% per annum.

- Club rules state that donations over £1,000 should be capitalised.

Task 1

List separately the opening assets and liabilities of the club at 1 January 1998 and calculate the accumulated fund at that date.

Task 2

Calculate the subscriptions figure to be used in the calculation of the surplus or deficit for the year ended 31 December 1998.

Task 3

Calculate the purchases of refreshments for the year ended 31 December 1998.

Task 4

Prepare a statement calculating the profit or loss on refreshments for the year ended 31 December 1998.

Task 5

By listing the various items of income and expenditure, prepare a statement calculating the surplus or deficit of income over expenditure for the year ended 31 December 1998.

A SUGGESTED ANSWER TO THIS PRACTICE CENTRAL ASSESSMENT IS GIVEN ON PAGE 411.

Trial Run Central Assessment

TRIAL RUN CENTRAL ASSESSMENT (December 1999)

This central assessment is in TWO sections. Section 1 contains two parts, part A and part B. Part A is made up of longer questions whilst part B consists of short answer questions. You are reminded that competence must be achieved in each section. You should therefore attempt and aim to complete EVERY task in EACH section.

All essential workings should be included within your answer where appropriate.

SECTION 1

PART A

The suggested time allocation for this extended trial balance exercise is 60 minutes.

Phil Townsend is the proprietor of Infortec Computers, a wholesale business which buys and sells computer hardware and software.

- You are employed by Phil Townsend to assist with the bookkeeping.

- The business currently operates a manual system consisting of a general ledger, a sales ledger and a purchases ledger.

- Double entry takes place in the general ledger and the individual accounts of debtors and creditors are therefore regarded as memoranda accounts.

- Day books consisting of a purchases day book, a sales day book, a purchases returns day book and a sales returns day book are used. Totals from the various columns of the day books are transferred into the general ledger.

At the end of the financial year, on 30 November 1999, the following balances were extracted from the general ledger.

	£
Capital	134,230
Purchases	695,640
Sales	836,320
Stock at 1 December 1998	84,300
Rent paid	36,000
Salaries	37,860
Motor Vehicles (M.V.) at cost	32,400
Provision for depreciation (M.V.)	8,730
Fixtures and fittings (F&F) at cost	50,610
Provision for depreciation (F&F)	12,340
Purchases returns	10,780
Sales returns	5,270
Drawings	55,910
Insurance	4,760
Debtors control account	73,450
Creditors control account	56,590
Bad debts	3,670
Provision for doubtful debts	3,060
Bank overdraft	10,800
Cash	1,980
VAT (credit balance)	5,410
Discounts allowed	6,770
Discounts received	4,380

Task 1

Enter the balances into the columns of the trial balance provided below. Total the two columns and enter an appropriate suspense account balance to ensure that the two totals agree.

Extended Trial Balance at 30th November 1999

DESCRIPTION	Dr £	Cr £
Capital		
Purchases		
Sales		
Stock at 1 December 1998		
Rent paid		
Salaries		
Motor vehicles (M.V.)at cost		
Provision for depreciation (M.V.)		
Fixtures and fittings (F&F) at cost		
Provision for depreciation (F&F)		
Purchase returns		
Sales returns		
Drawings		
Insurance		
Debtors control account		
Creditors control account		
Bad debts		
Provision for doubtful debts		
Bank overdraft		
Cash		
VAT (credit balance)		
Discounts allowed		
Discounts received		
Suspense account		
Totals	-	-

Subsequent to the preparation of the trial balance a number of errors were discovered which are detailed below.

(a) Drawings of £400 had been debited to the salaries account.

(b) The net column of the sales day book had been undercast by £100.

(c) The VAT column of the sales returns day book had been overcast by £60.

(d) A cheque for £120 paid to a credit supplier had been entered in the cash book but not in the relevant control account.

(e) A £3,000 cheque paid for rent had been debited to both the bank account and the rent paid account.

(f)   The total column of the purchases day book had been overcast by £10.

(g)   The discounts received column of the cash book had been overcast by £40.

(h)   A £65 cheque paid for insurance, although correctly entered in the cash book, had been entered in the insurance account as £55.

Task 2

Prepare journal entries to record the correction of these errors. Dates and narratives are not required. Use the blank journal on page 340.

Task 2

JOURNAL	Dr £	Cr £

The individual balances of the accounts in the sales ledger were listed, totalled and compared with the £73,450 balance of the debtors control account. The total of the list came to £76,780 and after investigation the following errors were found.

(a) A customer account with a balance of £400 was omitted from the list.

(b) A £50 discount allowed had been debited to a customer's account.

(c) A customer's account with a balance of £2,410 was included twice in the list.

(d) A customer's balance of £320 was entered in the list as £230.

(e) A customer with a balance of £540 had been written off as a bad debt in October but the balance was still included in the list.

(f) Sales returns totalling £770 (including VAT) had been omitted from the relevant customer accounts.

Task 3

Make appropriate adjustments to the total of the list using the table below. For each adjustment show clearly the amount involved and whether the amount is to be added or subtracted.

	£
Total from listing of balances	76,780
Adjustment for a) add / subtract*	....
Adjustment for b) add / subtract*	....
Adjustment for c) add / subtract*	....
Adjustment for d) add / subtract*	....
Adjustment for e) add / subtract*	....
Adjustment for f) add / subtract*	....
Revised total to agree with debtors control account	....

*Circle your answer to show add or subtract.

PART B

The suggested time allocation for this set of short answer questions is 50 minutes.

Task 4

On 1 December 1998 Infortec Computers owned motor vehciles costing £28,400. During the year ended 30 November 1999 the following changes to the motor vehicles took place:

		£
1 March 1999	Sold vehicle – original cost	18,000
1 June 1999	Purchased new vehicle – cost	10,000
1 September 1999	Purchased new vehicle – cost	12,000

Depreciation on motor vehicles is calculated on a monthly basis at 20% per annum on cost.

Complete the table below to calculate the total depreciation charge to profits for the year ended 30 November 1999.

	£
Depreciation for vehicle sold 1 March 1999	....
Depreciation for vehicle purchased 1 June 1999	....
Depreciation for vehicle purchased 1 September 1999	....
Depreciation for other vehicles owned during the year	....
	....
Total depreciation for the year ended 30 November 1999	....

Task 5

At the end of the previous financial year, on 30 November 1998, Phil Townsend had produced an extended trial balance. Prior to the calculation of the profit the balance sheet columns showed a total of £247,000 for the debit balances and £231,000 for the credit balances. The balances included capital of £164,230 and drawings of £46,000.

(a) **Calculate the profit or loss for the year ended 30 November 1998.**

£ .... profit / loss

(b) **Calculate the final capital balance representing the investment by Phil Townsend in the business on 30 November 1998.**

£ ....

Task 6

Infortec Computers needs to have use of a powerful computer for 3 months to carry out some development work. Phil Townsend has two choices. He can lease the computer for £500 a month or he can purchase it for £8,000, in which case he calculates that it could be sold 3 months later for £7,000. The payment of £8,000 would increase the business overdraft by that sum for the 3 months. Interest is payable on the overdraft at 12% per annum.

Calculate the total charge to the profits of the business over the 3-month period.

(a) **If the computer was leased over the 3 months (Ignore the effect of the lease payments on the overdraft).**

....

(b) **If the computer was purchased and then sold at the end of the 3 months.**

....

....

....

Task 7

Phil Townsend is the treasurer of a computer club. During the year ended 31 December 1999 the club will have received £230,000 in cash and cheques from members which includes £10,000 prepaid for the following year. £240,000 is to be entered into the income and expenditure account for 1999. No members are in arrears with their subscriptions at either the beginning or end of 1999.

If the subscription payable per member is £200 per annum.

(a) **Calculate the number of members in the club for 1999.**

....

....

....

(b) **Calculate the number of members who prepaid their 1999 subscription during the year ended 31 December 1998.**

....

....

....

....

Task 8

You receive the following note from Phil Townsend:

"I have been looking at the stock valuation for the year end and I have some concerns about the Mica 40z PCs.

We have ten of these in stock each of which cost £500 and are priced to sell to customers at £580. Unfortunately they all have faulty hard drives which will need to be replaced before they can be sold. The cost is £100 for each machine.

However, as you know, the Mica40z is now out of date and having spoken to some computer retailers I am fairly certain that we are going to have to scrap them or give them away for spares. Perhaps for now we should include them in the closing stock figure at cost. Can you please let me have your views."

Using the headed paper on page 344 and 345, write a memo in reply to Phil Townsend's note. Your memo should refer to alternative stock valuations and to appropriate statements of standard accounting practice.

(N.B. Two pages have been included for this memo. However, it is anticipated that the majority of candidates will find one page sufficient.)

Task 8

MEMORANDUM

To: Phil Townsend
From:
Ref: Valuation of stock
Date: 29 November 1999

Task 8 (continued)

N.B. This page will not be needed by all candidates

SECTION 2

The suggested time allocation for this exercise is 60 minutes.

Phil Townsend is planning to manufacture computers with effect from 1 January 2000. If he decides to go ahead then he would open a new business called Infortec Manufacturing. He has produced the following estimated figures for the year ended 31 December 2000 and has asked you to help in preparing some information.

	£
• Raw materials to be purchased	180,000
• Production wages	41,750
• Production supervisory wages	22,000
• Other production overheads	15,170
• Selling and distribution expenses	38,800

In order to set up the business Phil Townsend would need to do the following with effect from 1 January 2000.

- Open a new business bank account.

- Take out a business bank loan of £40,000. (Interest at 8% per annum to be paid out of the new business bank account).

- Place £50,000, which includes the £40,000 from the bank loan, into the new business bank account to cover future expenditure.

- Purchase, out of his own personal money, new production machinery and equipment costing £72,500. (Depreciation on this is to be calculated at 10% per annum at cost.)

On 31 December 2000:

	£
• Closing stock of raw materials	15,600
• Closing stock of work in progress	10,170
• Closing stock of finished goods	20,400
• Closing debtors estimated to be $^{1}/_{12}$ of sales for the year	
• Closing creditors estimated to be $^{1}/_{12}$ of raw materials purchased for the year	

NOTE:

- The profit mark up is to be 20% on factory cost of sales.

- All payments and receipts to pass through the new business bank account.

Task 1

Calculate the capital which would be invested by Phil Townsend in the business on 1 January 2000.

....

....

....

....

....

....

....

....

....

Task 2

Calculate the prime cost of production of Infortec Manufacturing for the year ending 31 December 2000.

....

....

....

....

....

....

....

....

....

Task 3

Calculate the total production cost of the finished goods to be made by Infortec Manufacturing during the year ending 31 December 2000.

....

....

....

....

....

....

....

....

....

BPP PUBLISHING

Task 4

Produce a statement showing the planned sales, factory cost of sales, gross profit and net profit of Infortec Manufacturing for the year ending 31 December 2000.

....

....

....

....

....

....

....

....

....

Task 5

Produce a summary of the business bank account for the year ending 31 December 2000 showing clearly the payments, the receipts and the closing balance.

....

....

....

....

....

....

....

....

....

A SUGGESTED ANSWER TO THIS TRIAL RUN CENTRAL ASSESSMENT IS GIVEN ON PAGE 419.

SAMPLE CENTRAL ASSESSMENT

INTERMEDIATE STAGE - NVQ/SVQ3

Unit 5

Maintaining Financial Records

and Preparing Accounts

(AAT Specimen)

This Sample Central Assessment is the AAT's Specimen Central Assessment for Unit 5. Its purpose is to give you an idea of what an AAT central assessment looks like. It is not intended as a definitive guide to the tasks you may be required to perform.

The suggested time allowance for this Assessment is three hours. You are advised to spend approximately 80 minutes on Section 1, 40 minutes on Section 2 and 60 minutes on Section 3.

Calculators may be used but no reference material is permitted.

**DO NOT OPEN THIS PAPER UNTIL YOU ARE READY TO START
UNDER TIMED CONDITIONS**

INSTRUCTIONS

This Central Assessment is designed to test your ability to maintain financial records and prepare accounts.

The Central Assessment is in **three** sections, all of which relate to the firm Creative Catering.

You are provided with data which you must use to complete the tasks, and space to set out your answers.

You are allowed **three hours** to complete your work. You are reminded that competence must be achieved in each section. You should therefore attempt and aim to complete **every** task in **each** section. All essential workings should be included within your answer where appropriate.

A high level of accuracy is required. Check your work carefully.

Correcting fluid may be used in moderation. Errors should be crossed out neatly and clearly. You should write in black ink, not pencil.

A suggested answer to this Assessment is given on Page 427.

CREATIVE CATERING

SECTION 1 (Suggested time allocation: 80 minutes)

Data

Jane Sutton is the proprietor of Creative Catering, a firm that provides catering services for a variety of events and functions. Creative Catering's premises are located in Bristol and most of the firm's customers can be found in the west of England.

- You are employed by Jane Sutton to assist with the bookkeeping.

- The business currently operates a manual system consisting of a general ledger, a sales ledger and a purchases ledger.

- Double entry takes place in the general ledger and the individual accounts of debtors and creditors are therefore regarded as memoranda accounts.

- Day books consisting of a purchases day book, a sales day book, a purchases returns day book and a sales returns day book are used. Totals from the various columns of the day books are transferred periodically into the general ledger.

At the end of the financial year on 30 April 1998, the balances were extracted from the general ledger and entered into an extended trial balance as shown on page 353.

Task 1

Make appropriate entries in the adjustment columns of the extended trial balance to take account of the following.

(a) The stock consists of food and drink and has been valued on 30 April 1998 at £6,240. This figure includes some frozen food that had cost £860 but will have to be thrown out due to a problem with a freezer. Although the Polar Insurance Company has agreed to pay for the full cost of the food, no money has yet been received. Also included in the stock valuation figure are 20 bottles of wine. These had originally cost £8.50 each but since they are not popular they are to be sold off at £6.50 per bottle.

(b) Depreciation calculated on a monthly basis is to be provided as follows.

Motor vehicles - 20% per annum straight line method
Equipment - 10% per annum reducing balance method

(c) The sum of £20,000 was invested in the bank deposit account on 1 May 1997. The interest rate is fixed at 7% per annum.

(d) Rent payable by the business is as follows.

Up to 31 October 1997   £1,200 per month
From 1 November 1997   £1,300 per month

(e) The provision for bad debts is to be adjusted to a figure representing 5% of debtors.

(f) On 29 April 1998 Jane Sutton withdraw £5,000 from the bank account for her own use. The entries made were:

Dr   Cash   £5,000
Cr   Bank   £5,000

(g) A series of adverts were broadcast during April 1998 by Western Radio at a cost to Creative Catering of £2,750. The invoice has yet to be received from Western Radio and no entries have been made.

352

CREATIVE CATERING	Trial balance		Adjustments	
Account	Debit	Credit	Debit	Credit
	£	£	£	£
Sales		620,700		
Purchases	410,650			
Purchases returns		390		
Salaries and wages	90,820			
Rent	16,300			
Debtors control account	51,640			
Creditors control account		33,180		
Bad debts	6,550			
Provision for bad debts		3,100		
Motor vehicles (cost)	60,700			
Motor vehicles (prov for depreciation)		12,600		
Equipment (cost)	24,200			
Equipment (prov for depreciation)		6,300		
Drawings	28,500			
Cash	7,000			
Bank	6,250			
Lighting and heating	2,100			
Insurance	760			
Advertising	3,470			
VAT (credit balances)		8,400		
Stock at 1 May 1997	5,660			
Motor expenses	4,680			
Bank deposit amount	20,000			
Bank interest received		700		
Capital		54,010		
Polar Insurance Company				
Depreciation				
Closing stock (P&L)				
Closing stock (B/S)				
Provision for bad debts (adjustment)				
Deposit account interest owing				
Prepayments / accruals				
Subtotal	739,380	739,380		
Profit for the year				
TOTAL	739,380	739,380		

Note. Only the above columns of the extended trial balance are required for this central assessment.

The bank statement shown below was received by Creative Catering on 1 June 1998 and was compared with the bank account section of the cash book also shown below.

MIDWEST BANK LTD

Bank statement

Creative Catering   **Account Number: 60419776**

Date	Detail	Debit	Credit	Balance
1998		£	£	£
14 May	Balance			6,300
14 May	Cheque 606842	120		6,180
14 May	Bank Giro Credit		230	6,410
15 May	Credit		320	6,730
18 May	Cheque 606844	260		6,470
19 May	Cheque 606843	440		6,030
20 May	Credit		375	6,405
21 May	Credit		2,650	9,055
22 May	Cheque 606846	1,100		7,955
22 May	Credit		860	8,815
26 May	Cheque 606848	1,650		7,165
27 May	Cheque	470		6,695
28 May	Credit		1,950	8,645

Bank account

May	15	Balance b/d	5,800	May	16	J Champion	845	620
	18	P Donald	175		16	Catering Services	846	1,100
	18	Mayes Ltd	200		20	Witworth Drinks	847	490
	19	A Palmer	230		20	K J Foods	848	1,650
	19	Rugby Club	1,260		22	D Andrews	849	470
	20	Town Institute	1,390		26	Catering Services	850	260
	22	P Whelan	860		27	Days Bakery	851	320
	25	P Whitehead	1,950		29	K J Foods	852	1,400
	28	Tennis Club	1,810		29	Balance c/d		7,365
			13,675					13,675

Task 2

Prepare a statement reconciling the £5,800 opening balance of the cash book with the £6,300 opening balance of the bank statement.

....

....

....

....

....

....

....

....

....

....

Task 3

Prepare a bank reconciliation statement as at 29 May 1998.

....

....

....

....

....

....

....

....

....

....

....

SECTION 2 (Suggested time allocation: 40 minutes)

Answer each of the following questions in the space provided.

1   One of the vans used by Creative Catering was originally purchased on 1 November 1995 for £12,360. If the van was sold on 1 June 1998 for £6,500:

    (a)   **What would be the book value of the van at the date of sale?**

        £.................................

    (b)   **What would be the profit or loss on disposal of the van?**

        £................................. profit/loss

2   Jane Sutton is a member of the local golf club and occasionally assists with the club accounts. For the year to 31 December 1997 the club had 380 members. On 1 January 1997 six members owed the subscription for the previous year, but all of them subsequently paid the amount owing (£250 per member). At this time, no subscriptions were prepaid. On 31 December 1997 ten members had prepaid their subscription for the following year (£250 per member). During the year ended 31 December 1997, £98,000 was received in subscriptions. The amount payable for the year was again £250 per member.

    Calculate the number of members who had not paid their subscription on 31 December 1997.

....

....

....

....

3   Creative Catering provides catering for Barrett & Co, a small local business that is not registered for VAT. The sales invoice issued to Barrett & Co shows a total sum of £329, which includes £49 VAT. Barrett & Co treats the invoice as a hospitality expense in its books.

Note. State clearly for both (a) and (b) the names of the accounts, the amounts and whether each entry is a debit or credit.

(a)   **What would be the double entry made in Creative Catering's books to record the sale to Barrett & Co?**

....

....

....

(b)   **What would be the double entry made in Barrett & Co's books to record the purchase from Creative Catering?**

....

....

....

4   Jane Sutton decides to purchase some new equipment for Creative Catering on hire purchase.

When does Creative Catering record the equipment as a fixed asset in the books of the business?

| When the equipment is acquired | When the final instalment is paid | The equipment is never shown as a fixed asset |

5   A credit sale made to the Bristol Rowing Club is entered in error into the account of the Bristol Rugby Club in the sales ledger.

(a)   **Would the error be detected through use of the debtors control account?**

Yes / No

(b)   **Briefly explain the reason for your answer.**

....

....

....

....

....

....

....

6   After the end of the financial year on 30 April 1998 and after the profit for the year has been calculated, an invoice dated 20 April 1998 is found in a pile of letters. The invoice relates to a £500 purchase of soft drinks and has not been entered into the books of Creative Catering. Jane Sutton discusses the matter with you and says she is concerned that in leaving out the invoice the calculation of profit might have been affected. However, she finally decides that since all the drinks have been included in the valuation of the closing stock, none could have been sold during the year. She is therefore satisfied that all is well from an accounting point of view and tells you 'since none of the drinks were included in either the sales or purchases figure, the profits were not affected'.

She asks you to think about what she has said and to confirm her conclusions.

Write an appropriate memo to Jane Sutton covering the points she has raised relating to the calculation of profit for the financial year ended 30 April 1998. Use the headed paper on page 358 for your answer.

BPP PUBLISHING

MEMORANDUM

To: Ref:

From: Date:

Subject:

_____

SECTION 3 (Suggested time allocation: 60 minutes)

Note. Clearly show your workings for all tasks.

Jane Sutton obtains her supplies of bread and cakes mainly from a small bakery owned by Pat Day. The goods are sold to various caterers, retailers and direct to the public through a shop attached to the bakery and also owned by Pat Day. The bakery and the shop have both recently been put up for sale and Jane Sutton is interested in buying them. She has been able to obtain some figures from the agent acting for Pat Day and these relate to the year ended 31 December 1997. Jane Sutton asks you to produce some information from these figures.

Figures for Pat Day's bakery and shop - available from the agent.

- Stocks:

	£
Stock of baking materials at 1 January 1997	1,000
Baking materials purchased	84,000
Stock of baking materials at 31 December 1997	3,000

  All finished goods are sold and no finished goods are therefore held in stock.

- Staff costs

Bakery production wages	44,000
Bakery supervisory wages	25,000
Shop wages	30,000

- Business fixed assets

Bakery premises at cost 1 January 1970	100,000
Shop premises at cost 1 January 1970	80,000
Bakery equipment at cost 1 June 1990	50,000
Shop equipment at cost 1 June 1990	40,000

- Depreciation - calculated on a monthly basis:

  Premises 2% per annum straight line method
  Equipment 10% per annum straight line method

- Other business expenses

Bakery overheads	22,000
Shop expenses	30,000

- Sales

  Two thirds of production is sold with a 50% mark-up to caterers and retail outlets.
  All these sales are on credit.
  One third of production is passed to the shop to then be sold with a 100% mark up.
  All these sales are for cash.

- Debtors and creditors

Debtors at 1 January 1997	12,000
Creditors at 1 January 1997	6,000
Debtors at 31 December 1997	Unknown
Creditors at 31 December 1997	7,000
Received from debtors during the year	179,500
Paid to creditors during the year	Unknown

Task 1

Calculate the prime cost of the goods produced by the bakery during the year ended 31 December 1997.

....

....

....

....

....

....

....

....

....

....

Task 2

Calculate the total production cost of the goods made by the bakery during the year ended 31 December 1997.

....

....

....

....

....

....

....

....

....

....

Task 3

Calculate the total combined gross profit made by the shop and the bakery during the year ended 31 December 1997.

....

....

....

....

....

....

....

....

....

....

Task 4

Calculate the amount paid to creditors during the year ended 31 December 1997.

....

....

....

....

....

....

....

....

....

....

Task 5

Calculate the sum of money owed by debtors on 31 December 1997.

....

....

....

....

....

....

....

....

....

....

Answers to Practice
Central Assessments

ANSWERS TO PRACTICE CENTRAL ASSESSMENT 1:HIGHBURY DISCS

SECTION 1

Task 1

See extended trial balance on Page 367.

Task 2

	Depreciation charge for the year ended 31 May 1995
	£
Motor vehicles	3,576
Equipment	9,550
Total	13,126

Task 3

Stock sheets	*Value*
	£
Total b/f from previous pages	18,000
Bambino choir of Prague	3,500
The Joyful Singers sing Wesley	1,200
Bach at St Thomas's	5,000
Value of stock as at 31 May 1995	27,700

Task 4

JOURNAL		Page 1
Details	**£**	**£**
(a) DEBIT Artists' fees and royalties	4,500	
CREDIT Sundry creditors		4,500
Being royalties due to artists for the quarter ended 31 May 1995.		
DEBIT Artists' fees and royalties	252	
CREDIT Sundry creditors		252
Being correction of under-calculation of royalties due to Mr Willis-Brown for quarter ended 31 December 1994		
(b) DEBIT Debtors	220	
CREDIT Bank		220
Being dishonoured cheque		
(c) DEBIT Drawings	2,110	
CREDIT Motor expenses		2,110
Being correct posting of private motoring expenses		

Tasks 5 and 6

HIGHBURY DISCS Account	Trial balance Debit £	Trial balance Credit £	Adjustments Debit £	Adjustments Credit £	Profit and Loss a/c Debit £	Profit and Loss a/c Credit £	Balance Sheet Debit £	Balance Sheet Credit £
Artists' fees and royalties	41,120		4,752		45,872			
Bank and cash	1,420			220			1,200	
Capital		26,449						26,449
Drawings	14,500		2,110				16,610	
Employer's NI	3,619				3,619			
Equipment (cost)	38,200						38,200	
Motor vehicles (cost)	29,800						29,800	
Equipment (prov for depreciation)		19,100		9,550				28,650
Motor vehicles (prov for depreciation)		17,880		3,576				21,456
Loan		10,000						10,000
Loan interest	1,350		150		1,500			
Mastering and production costs	143,400				143,400			
Motor expenses	6,330			2,110	4,220			
Recording costs	12,550				12,550			
Rent	13,000			1,000	12,000			
Sales		307,800				307,800		
Stocks of compact discs	22,500				22,500			
Sundry creditors		4,080						4,080
Sundry debtors	12,500		220				12,720	
Sundry expenses	1,270				1,270			
VAT (amount owing)		3,250						3,250
Wages and salaries	47,000				47,000			
Depreciation			13,126		13,126			
Closing stock (B/S)			27,700				27,700	
Closing stock (P&L)				27,700		27,700		
Prepayments / accruals			1,000	4,902			1,000	4,902
Subtotal	388,559	388,559	49,058	49,058	307,057	335,500	127,230	98,787
Profit for the year					28,443			28,443
TOTAL	388,559	388,559	49,058	49,058	335,500	335,500	127,230	127,230

367

SECTION 2

1   (a)   The credit balance on the VAT account represents the excess of VAT collected on sales (output tax) over VAT paid on purchases or expenses (input tax).

     (b)   This amount is owed to HM Customs & Excise.

2   The microphones could become obsolete as a newer, better model comes onto the market.

3   A case could be made for capitalising the cost of the tapes, on the grounds that they are for use over a number of accounting periods. Highbury Discs has not, however, adopted this treatment because, at only £8 each, the cost of the tapes is not material. They have therefore been expensed in the year of purchase.

     It should be emphasised that this type of decision is not always clear cut. In particular, what is material to a small business may not be to a large one.

4   (a)   This year's profit would be overstated since closing stock is a deduction from cost of sales.

     (b)   Next year's profit would be understated since opening stock is an addition to cost of sales.

5   The accruals or matching concept.

6

MEMORANDUM

To: Anthony Sedgewick   Ref:
From: Accounting Technician   Date: 6 June 1995
Subject: *Rules for stock valuation*

The fundamental accounting concept of prudence dictates that profits are not anticipated but losses are taken into account as soon as they are foreseen.

This cautious approach is adopted in SSAP 9 *Stocks and long-term contracts* which states that stock should be valued at the lower of cost and net realisable value (NRV). Cost, here, is the cost of producing the discs, together with a share of manufacturing overheads. Net realisable value is the estimated selling price less any further costs required to sell the product or get the product into saleable form.

It should be noted further that the comparison of cost and NRV should be carried out for each item separately. It is not sufficient to compare the total cost of all stock items with their total NRV.

When net realisable value is lower than cost, net realisable value should be used. Applying this principle to the Bambino Choir discs, NRV is higher than costs, because we expect to earn a profit on them, even if this profit is delayed.

However, in the case of the 'Joyful Singers' discs, net realisable value is £3.00 each, which is lower than cost of £5.00 each. Thus we will make a loss of $400 \times (£5 - £3)$ ie £800, which, following the prudence concept we must take to the P&L as soon as it is foreseen.

Turning now to the Bach at St Thomas's discs, we see an application of *net* realisable value. The discs cost £3.50 each. While they can be sold for £4.00, this would only be after incurring further costs of £1.50 per disc. The net realisable value of each disc is therefore £4.00 less £1.50, that is £2.50 per disc. Since this is below cost, this is the figure that must be used.

SECTION 3

Tutorial notes

(1) Be careful when calculating the discounts received figure. The £30,060 paid to creditors is 90% of the normal price, so the discount is £30,060 $\times \dfrac{10\%}{90\%}$, ie £3,340.

(2) The van owned at the beginning of the year is shown at net book value. It has been depreciated for one year, so the original cost was £7,500 × 4/3 = £10,000.

BANK			
	£		£
Balance b/f	323	Trade creditors	30,060
Cash	2,770	Drawings	12,000
Trade debtors	43,210	Motor van	4,800
Capital	10,000	Rent	5,330
		Motor expenses	3,400
		Balance c/d	713
	56,303		56,303
Balance b/d	713		

CASH			
	£		£
Balance b/f	25	Bank	2,770
Trade debtors	8,340	Motor expenses	600
		Drawings (bal fig)	4,961
		Balance c/d	34
	8,365		8,365
Balance b/d	34		

MOTOR EXPENSES			
	£		£
Bank	3,400	Balance b/f	174
Cash	600	Profit and loss	4,035
Balance c/d	209		
	4,209		4,209
		Balance b/d	209

MOTOR VAN(S)			
	£		£
Balance b/f	7,500	Depreciation charge (P&L)	
Bank	4,800	£(10,000 ÷ 4) + (4,800 ÷ 4 × $^4/_{12}$)	2,900
		Balance c/d	9,400
	12,300		12,300
Balance b/d	9,400		

RENT AND INSURANCE			
	£		£
Balance (insurance) b/f	180	Balance (rent) b/f	250
Bank	5,330	Profit and loss	5,060
		Balance (insurance) c/d	200
	5,510		5,510
Balance (insurance) b/d	200		

MATERIALS USED

	£		£
Balance b/f	1,530	Profit and loss	33,910
Purchases	33,980	Balance c/d	1,600
	35,510		35,510
Balance b/d	1,600		

TRADE CREDITORS

	£		£
Bank	30,060	Balance b/f	3,650
Discounts received		Purchases (bal fig)	33,980
(£30,060 × $^{10\%}/_{90\%}$)	3,340		
Balance c/d	4,230		
	37,630		37,630
		Balance b/d	4,230

TRADE DEBTORS

	£		£
Balance b/f	1,550	Bank	43,210
Work done	52,000	Bad debts	480
		Cash (bal fig)	8,340
		Balance c/d £(2,000 – 480)	1,520
	53,550		53,550
Balance b/d	1,520		

DRAWINGS

	£		£
Bank	12,000	Capital	16,961
Cash	4,961		
	16,961		16,961

BPP PUBLISHING

ANSWERS TO PRACTICE CENTRAL ASSESSMENT 2: JASON BROWN

SECTION 1

Task 1

See extended trial balance on Page 372.

Task 2

(a) *Depreciation*

Delivery vans: $£(12,800 - 3,520) \times 20\% = £1,856$

Equipment $£22,800 \times 10\% = £2,280$

Total depreciation $= £4,136$

(b) *Interest*

$£30,000 \times 6\% = £1,800$

∴ $£600$ accrued interest is receivable.

(c) *Bad debts*

	£
Debtors control account balance	41,600
Debt written off: M C Millar	2,460
	39,140

Provision for doubtful debts required
$= 5\% \times £39,140 = £1,957$ ∴ reduce current provision of £1,980 by £23.

(d) *Stock*

The damaged chairs must be valued at the lower of cost and net realisable value.

		£
Cost ($£230 \times 4$)		920
NRV:	selling price ($£190 \times 4$)	760
	less repairs	40
		720

∴ Reduce stock by $£(920 - 720) = £200$
Closing stock is $£(58,394 - 200) = £58,194$

(e) *JB Office Supplies*

This payment has not in fact been made, so the original entry must be reversed.

DEBIT	Bank overdraft	£1,260	
CREDIT	Creditors control a/c		£1,260

(f) *Insurance*

Premium prepaid $= £260 \times 6/12 = £130$

(g) *Rent*

Total rent payable $= £200 \times 12 = £2,400$

∴ $£200$ must be accrued

JASON BROWN

Account	Trial balance Debit £	Trial balance Credit £	Adjustments Debit £	Adjustments Credit £	Profit and Loss a/c Debit £	Profit and Loss a/c Credit £	Balance Sheet Debit £	Balance Sheet Credit £
Purchases	170,240				170,240			
Sales		246,412				246,412		
Purchases returns		480				480		
Sales returns	670				670			
Opening Stock	54,200				54,200			
Salaries	30,120				30,120			
Rent	2,200		200		2,400			
Insurance	360			130	230			
Delivery vans (cost)	12,800						12,800	
Equipment (cost)	22,800						22,800	
Delivery vans (prov for depn)		3,520		1,856				5,376
Equipment (prov for depn)		5,760		2,280				8,040
Bad debts	2,700		2,460		5,160			
Provision for bad debts		1,980	23					1,957
Debtors control account	41,600			2,460			39,140	
Creditors control account		33,643		1,260				34,903
Drawings	10,522						10,552	
Capital		83,171						83,171
Bank overdraft		348	1,260				912	
Cash	568						568	
VAT		2,246						2,246
Bank interest received		1,200		600		1,800		
Bank deposit account	30,000						30,000	
Suspense account		20						20
Depreciation			4,136		4,136			
Bank interest owing			600				600	
Closing stock (P&L)				58,194		58,194		
Closing stock (B/S)			58,194				58,194	
Provision for bad debts (adjustment)				23		23		
Prepayments / accruals			130	200			130	200
Subtotal	378,780	378,780	67,003	67,003	267,156	306,909	175,666	135,913
Profit for the year					39,753			39,753
TOTAL	378,780	378,780	67,003	67,003	306,909	303,909	175,666	175,666

Task 3

See extended trial balance on Page 372.

Task 4

See journal below.

Note. These journals clear the suspense account, as shown in the ledger account.

SUSPENSE ACCOUNT

	£		£
Debtors control a/c	60	Balance on TB	20
Sales	570	Discounts	250
		Purchases	360
	630		630

JOURNAL		Page 1
Details	**£**	**£**
(a) DEBIT Suspense a/c	60	
CREDIT Debtors control a/c		60
Being receipt from debtor not recorded in control a/c		
(b) DEBIT Discounts received	125	
DEBIT Discounts allowed	125	
CREDIT Suspense account		250
Being correction of double entry and correct account for discount allowed		
(c) DEBIT Purchase a/c	360	
CREDIT Suspense a/c		360
Being correction of purchases day book transposition		
(d) DEBIT Suspense a/c	570	
CREDIT Sales		570
Being correction of undercast in sales day book		

SECTION 2

1 (a) *Book value of van at sale*

	£
Cost	6,000
Accumulated depreciation 1.11.93 - 31.10.94 = £6,000 × 20%	1,200
	4,800
1.11.94 - 31.10.95 = £4,800 × 20%	960
	3,840
1.11.95 - 30.4.95 = £3,840 × 20% × $^6/_{12}$	384
Book value at date of sale	3,456

BPP PUBLISHING

(b) *Disposals account*

MOTOR VANS DISPOSAL ACCOUNT			
	£		£
Vans: cost	6,000	Motor vans: provision for depreciation £(6,000 – 3,456)	2,544
		Cash	3,200
		Profit and loss a/c	256
	6,000		6,000

2   The argument in favour of including the advertising costs in the calculation of profit for the year ended 31 October 1997 is based on the *accruals concept*. The costs of advertising will be 'matched' with the associated revenues of the service. (However, the prudence concept might dictate that the costs should be written off against current profits if there is no guarantee that the consultancy will be profitable.)

3   (a)   Decreased by £250

   (b)   Decreased by £360

4   (a)   *Sales for October*

   (2 + 4 + 6) × £50 = £600

   (b)   *Cost of goods sold for October*

	£
Sale 13.10.95: Cost = 2 × £30	60
Sale 18.10.95: Cost = 4 × £30	120
Sale 30.10.95: Cost = 4 × £30	120
2 × £32	64
12	364

   (c)   *Closing stock*

	£
10 at £32	320
10 at £31	310
	630

5   This statement is not true because fixed assets must be depreciated over their useful economic lives. The periodic depreciation charge passes through the profit and loss account as an expense, thus reducing profit. The benefit obtained from use of the asset is thus matched against its cost.

6   (a)   It excludes VAT.

   (b)   SSAP 5 *Accounting for VAT* requires all figures in the accounts, in particular sales and purchases, to be shown net of VAT, where VAT is recoverable.

MEMORANDUM

To: Jason Brown   Ref:

From: Accounting Technician   Date: 8 December 1995

Subject: *Profit and accounting rules*

There are various problems with the changes you propose to make next year to improve profitability.

(a) At the year end the cost of sales is matched with sales to calculate profit. Where stocks are held at the year end, these must be matched against future sales (under the accruals, or matching concept), and so they are deducted from the current cost of sales. You can see then that running down stocks at the year end would therefore have no impact, for example:

	Higher year end stocks	*Lower year end stocks*
	£	£
Purchases (and opening stock)	120,000	100,000
Closing stock	30,000	10,000
	90,000	90,000

There is no effect on profit, just a lower closing stock figure in the balance sheet, and a higher cash balance (fewer purchases made).

(b) The prudence concept states that all losses must be recognised as soon as they are foreseen. It is therefore not acceptable to 'put off' writing off a debt until the following year (when in any case it would have just as bad an effect on profit).

(c) It is not acceptable to change the method of depreciation of assets from year to year because of the consistency concept. This requires items to be treated in the same way over time in order to allow comparison between accounts from year to year.

I am afraid that the only real ways to increase profitability are to increase sales and cut costs!

MEMORANDUM

To: Jason Brown   Ref:

From: Accounting Technician   Date: 8 December 1995

Subject: *Sales ledger errors*

The error discovered, that £96.20 had not been posted to the account of John Pearce Furniture Ltd, will not be discovered by a trial balance because the account in question is not part of the system of accounts. It is, rather, a 'personal' account kept as a memorandum of how much an individual owes your business, along with all other such accounts in the sales ledger.

The account within the system which relates to debtors, the debtors control account, is an impersonal, summary account which shows only the *total* owed to your business by debtors.

These accounts are both posted from the same sources (such as the sales day book and the cash book), but the debtors control account postings are in total, whereas the personal accounts in the sales ledger are posted with individual transactions.

The control account balance should therefore, in theory, be equal to the total of all the balances in the personal accounts in the sales ledger. In practice, discrepancies arise, and by comparing the two totals and investigating these discrepancies, errors can be found in both types of account and thereby corrected.

This is a good way of making sure that the figure from the control account, which appears under debtors in the balance sheet, is correct, as well as ensuring that you receive the correct amounts from the individual debtors of the business.

SECTION 3

Task 1

	£
Premises	74,400
Fixtures and fittings	28,800
Stocks £(15,613 – 10,000)	5,613
	108,813
Less bank loan	48,000
	60,813
Surplus funds	1,220
Original capital invested	62,033

Task 2

CARLTON OFFICE SUPPLIES				
	£			£
Oct 95		*Oct 95*		
		Credit purchases		10,000
Nov 95		*Nov 95*		
Bank	9,800	Credit purchases		12,500
Discount received	200	Credit purchases		8,600
Bank	12,250			
Discount received	250			
Creditor c/f	8,600			
	31,100			31,100

Task 3

	£
Carlton Office Supplies	
October	10,000
November £(12,500 + 8,600)	21,100
Cash purchases £(187 + 5,613)	5,800
	36,900

Task 4

Profit for November 1995

	£	£
Sales (balancing figure)		32,125
Cost of sales		
Purchases	36,900	
Closing stock	11,200	
		25,700
Gross profit (£25,700 × 25/100)		6,425
Discounts received		450
		6,875
Expenses		
Insurance (384 × 1/12)	32	
Depreciation		
Premises (2% × £74,400 × 1/12)	124	
Fixtures (10% × £28,800 × 1/12)	240	
Computer (1/3 × £(1,402 – 250) × 1/12)	32	
Interest (£48,000 × 10% × 1/12)	400	
Postages	43	
Sundry £(52 + 61)	113	
		984
Net profit		5,891

Task 5

CASH ACCOUNT				
	£			£
Sales	32,125	Postages		43
		Cash purchases		187
		Sundry expenses		52
		Cash banked		30,408
		Drawings (bal)		1,435
	32,125			32,125

ANSWERS TO PRACTICE CENTRAL ASSESSMENT 3: EXPLOSIVES

SECTION 1

Task 1

JOURNAL		Page 1
Details	**£**	**£**
(a) (i) DEBIT Creditors control a/c	1,800	
CREDIT Purchases		1,800
Being correction of overstatement of purchases and creditors		
(ii) DEBIT Light and heat	1,201	
DEBIT Stationery and advertising	1,025	
CREDIT Purchases		2,226
Being posting of other expenses from purchases		
(b) DEBIT Creditors control a/c	47	
CREDIT Purchase returns		40
CREDIT VAT		7
Being purchase return omitted		
(c) DEBIT Sales	245	
CREDIT VAT		245
Being correction of misposting of VAT		
(d) DEBIT Creditors control a/c	54	
CREDIT Discounts received		54
Being posting of omitted discount received		

Task 2

See extended trial balance on Page 381.

Task 3

See extended trial balance on Page 381. Workings are shown below.

(1) *Depreciation*

Motor vehicles = 20% × £(60,480 – 9,800) = £10,136

Office furniture and equipment = 10% × £(26,750 – 3,170) = £2,358

Total depreciation = £(10,136 + 2,358) = £12,494

(2) *Rent*

An accrual is required as the rent expense for the year should be £1,000 × 12 = £12,000.

(3) *Stationery and advertising*

Advertising of £1,560 has been prepaid.

(4) *Stock and insurance*

The damaged stock is correctly excluded from the stock balance. **The amount due from the insurance company is a debtor.**

(5) *Provision for bad debts*

	£
Debtors control account balance	120,860

	£
Provision required £120,860 × 5% =	6,043
Current provision	5,620
Adjustment required	423

Task 4

See extended trial balance on Page 381.

EXPLOSIVES

Account	Trial balance Debit £	Trial balance Credit £	Adjustments Debit £	Adjustments Credit £	Profit and Loss a/c Debit £	Profit and Loss a/c Credit £	Balance Sheet Debit £	Balance Sheet Credit £
Opening Stock	180,420				180,420			
Purchases	606,054			2,300	603,754			
Sales		840,315				840,315		
Purchases returns		2,430				2,430		
Sales returns	2,650				2,650			
Motor expenses	5,430				5,430			
Bank	20,415						20,415	
Cash	3,420						3,420	
Rent	11,000		1,000		12,000			
Lighting and heating	5,381				5,381			
Stationery and advertising	7,145			1,560	5,585			
Provision for bad debts		5,620		423				6,043
Debtors control account	120,860						120,860	
Creditors control account		100,959						100,959
Salaries	96,200				96,200			
Bad debts	7,200				7,200			
Drawings	31,600						31,600	
Discount allowed	20,520				20,520			
Discount received		18,454				18,454		
Motor vehicles (cost)	60,480						60,480	
Office furniture & equipment (cost)	26,750						26,750	
Motor vehicles (prov for depreciation)		12,590		10,136				22,726
Office furniture & equipment (prov for depreciation)		3,170		2,358				5,528
VAT		10,512						10,512
Capital		211,475						211,475
Depreciation			12,494		12,494			
Regal Insurance Company			2,300				2,300	
Closing stock (P&L)				208,540		208,540		
Closing stock (B/S)			208,540				208,540	
Provision for bad debts (adjustment)			423		423			
Prepayments / accruals			1,560	1,000			1,560	1,000
Subtotal	1,205,525	1,205,525	226,317	226,317	952,057	1,069,739	475,925	358,243
Profit for the year					117,682			117,682
TOTAL	1,205,525	1,205,525	226,317	226,317	1,069,739	1,069,739	475,925	475,925

SECTION 2

1 (a) Understated

   (b) Understated

			£	£
2	(a) DEBIT	Debtors control account	705	
	CREDIT	Sales		600
	CREDIT	VAT		105
	(b) DEBIT	Bank	705	
	CREDIT	Debtors control account		705

3 (a) Disagree

   (b) SSAP 13 *Accounting for research and development expenditure* states that both pure and applied research should be written off as incurred. Only development costs relating to new products which are technically and financially feasible may be capitalised.

4 The prudence concept suggests that Julie Owens' debt of £5,000 should be provided for as it is likely that Explosives will lose the entire amount.

5 Stay the same.

6	DEBIT	Suspense account	£200	
	CREDIT	Cash		£200

(The original credit entry should have been to cash.)

7

MEMORANDUM

To: Melanie Lancton   Ref:

From: Accounting technician   Date: 8 July 1996

Subject: *Stock valuation*

Statement of Standard Accounting Practice 9 (SSAP 9) *Stocks and long-term contracts* requires stock to be valued at the lower of cost and net realisable value (where NRV is the selling price less any further costs to be incurred to bring the stocks to a saleable condition).

Normally, the accruals concept requires the matching of income and expenditure, as you note. However, where the prudence concept and accruals concept conflict, prudence prevails (according to SSAP 2 *Disclosure of accounting policies*).

The prudence concept requires losses to be provided for as soon as they are foreseen. Here, the 'loss' is the difference between the cost and the NRV of the stock and it must therefore be written off immediately.

I hope this answers your query satisfactorily.

SECTION 3

Task 1

DEBTORS CONTROL A/C				
	£			£
1 June 1995 Balance b/f	39,470	Cash from debtors		863,740
Credit sales (balance)	872,010	Bad debts written off		2,340
		31 May 1996 Balance c/f		45,400
	911,480			911,480

Task 2

	£
Credit sales (see above)	872,010
Cash sales	147,890
Adjustment to float	100
	1,020,000

Task 3

CREDITORS CONTROL A/C			
	£		£
Cash to creditors	607,650	1 June 1995 Balance b/f	35,960
31 May 1996 Balance c/f	49,310	Purchases (balance)	621,000
	656,960		656,960

Task 4

	£	£
Sales		1,020,000
Cost of sales		
Opening stock	33,200	
Purchases	621,000	
	654,200	
Closing stock (balance)	42,200	
		612,000
Gross profit (£1,020,000 × 40%)		408,000

Stolen stock = £42,200 – £38,700 = £3,500.

Task 5

	£	£
Sales proceeds		1,360
Net book value		
Cost	4,000	
Depreciation		
10% for 66 months	2,200	
		1,800
Loss on disposal		440

Task 6

	£
Prepaid general expenses at 31 May 1995	550
General expenses paid	6,240
Owed at year end	170
Profit and loss account	6,960

ANSWERS TO PRACTICE CENTRAL ASSESSMENT 4: CASTLE ALARMS

SECTION 1

Task 1

See extended trial balance on Page 385. Workings are as follows.

(a) *Depreciation*

Motor vehicles: £32,600 × 20% = £6,520

Equipment: £(48,860 – 6,620) × 10% = £4,224

Total depreciation = £10,744

(b) *Bank loan interest*

Interest for 9 months $= £50,000 \times 10\% \times 9/12$
$= £3,750$

Accrued interest = £3,750 – £2,500 = £1,250

(c) and (d)

Bad debts

	£
Debtors control account balance	189,600
Debt written off: restaurant	3,400
	186,200

Provision required = 6% × £186,200 = £11,172

Adjustment required = £12,000 – £11,172 = £828

(e) *Stock*

	£
Stock at cost	289,400
Reduction to NRV of 5 system £(1,200 – 1,000) × 5	(1,000)
Damaged system	(200)
	288,200

(f) *Advertising*

DEBIT	Advertising	£2,250	
CREDIT	Accruals		£2,250

(g) *Rent*

Rent for year = £2,100 × 12 = £25,200

∴£27,300 – £25,200 = £2,100 is prepaid

DEBIT	Prepayments	£2,100	
CREDIT	Rent		£2,100

(h) *Cash withdrawn*

DEBIT	Cash	£5,000	
CREDIT	Bank		£5,000

(i) *Credit note*

DEBIT	Creditor's control account	£2,900	
CREDIT	Purchases returns		£2,900

Task 2

See extended trial balance on Page 385.

CASTLE ALARMS

Account	Trial balance Debit £	Trial balance Credit £	Adjustments Debit £	Adjustments Credit £	Profit and Loss a/c Debit £	Profit and Loss a/c Credit £	Balance Sheet Debit £	Balance Sheet Credit £
Sales		1,200,000				1,200,000		
Purchases	667,820				667,820			
Sales returns	96,570				96,570			
Purchases returns		52,790		2,900		55,690		
Opening Stock	301,840				301,840			
Debtors control account	189,600			3,400			186,200	
Cash	1,200		5,000				6,200	
Bank	25,300			5,000			20,300	
Creditors control account		95,000	2,900					92,100
Provision for bad debts		12,000	828					11,172
Bad debts	10,100		3,400		13,500			
Discount allowed	6,320				6,320			
Salaries	103,030				103,030			
Drawings	26,170						26,170	
Rent	27,300			2,100	25,200			
General expenses	14,310				14,310			
Capital		121,860						121,860
VAT		22,600						22,600
Bank loan		50,000						50,000
Interest on bank loan	2,500		1,250		3,750			
Advertising	11,450		2,250		13,700			
Motor vehicles (cost)	32,600						32,600	
Equipment (cost)	48,600						48,860	
Motor vehicles (prov for depreciation)		4,100		6,520				10,620
Equipment (prov for depreciation)		6,620		4,224				10,844
Depreciation			10,744		10,744			
Loan interest owing				1,250				1,250
Closing stock (P&L)				288,200		288,200		
Closing stock (B/S)			288,200				288,200	
Provision for bad debts (adjustment)				828		828		
Prepayments / accruals			2,100	2,250			2,100	2,250
Subtotal	1,564,970	1,564,970	316,672	316,672	1,256,784	1,544,718	610,630	322,696
Profit for the year					287,934			287,934
TOTAL	1,564,970	1,564,970	316,672	316,672	1,544,718	1,544,718	610,630	610,630

385

SECTION 2

1   Under the materiality concept it is acceptable to write off such items to revenue rather than capitalise them. Such a small amount depreciated over the life of the calculator would have no real impact on the balance sheet or the profit and loss account.

2   This balance represents the amount owed to Castle Alarms by HM Customs & Excise. Over the quarter Castle Alarms' VAT inputs (purchases) have been higher than its VAT output (sales) and so it can reclaim the excess VAT.

3   Finance lease only.

4   (a)   No.

    (b)   Errors of omission are not detected by a trial balance. Both the debits and credits in the trial balance are understated by £235.

5   The total charge represents deprecation charged plus/minus the loss/profit on disposal.

	£
Depreciation (£10,450 – £4,100)	6,350
Loss on disposal (£4,100 – £3,000)	1,100
Total charge to capital	7,450

6   Stock should be valued at the lower of cost and net realisable value (NRV).

	£
List price	2,400
Less 20% discount	(480)
Plus delivery charge	10
Value in accounts	1,930

7   (a)

DEBIT	Purchases (£40 × 20)	£800	
DEBIT	VAT (£800 × 90% × 17.5%)	£126	
CREDIT	Creditors		£926

    (b)

DEBIT	Creditors	£926	
CREDIT	Discount received (£40 × 10% × 20)		£80
CREDIT	Cash		£846

8

MEMORANDUM

To: Andrew Hallgrove   Ref: Bank balance and profits
From: Accounting Technician   Date: XX/XX/XX

The profits of a business do not represent its cash flows because of the use of *accrual accounting*. Under this method transactions are recorded, not when cash is received or paid, but when revenues have been earned or costs incurred. This means that a company can make a large sale, recording a substantial profit, but the customer may not pay immediately. The amount owing is recorded as a debtor to the business, but the cash has yet to be received.

The business may have a large amount of stock at the year end. The cost of this stock will not be matched against revenue (ie affecting profit) until the following period but, if the stock has been paid for, the business's bank balance will be adversely affected.

The bank balance will also reflect purchases of fixed assets for cash, whereas profit will only be affected by the smaller impact of depreciation.

I hope these explanations are satisfactory.

SECTION 3

Task 1

	£	£
1 September balance paid in		50,000
Payments		
Fixtures and fittings	22,500	
Stock	47,300	
Rent	9,000	
Insurance	480	
General	220	
		(79,500)
		(29,500)
Balance c/f		
Bank	10,000	
Cash	500	
		(10,500)
Loan from bank		40,000

Task 2

Business assets at 30 September 1996

	£
Fixtures and fittings	22,500
Stock	47,300
Prepayments	
Rent (£9,000 × 5/6)	7,500
Insurance (£480 × 11/12)	440
Bank	10,000
Cash	500

Task 3

TRADE CREDITORS

	£		£
Discount received	1,250	Balance b/f	-
Cash paid	20,250	Purchases on credit (bal fig)	24,900
Balance c/f	3,400		
	24,900		24,900

Task 4

Statement of net profit for October 1996

	£	£
Sales (£20,000 + £2,400)		22,400
Cost of sales		
Opening stock	47,300	
Purchases	24,900	
	72,200	
Closing stock (£55,000 + (£2,000 × 70%))	(56,400)	
		15,800
Gross profit		6,600
Discount received		1,250
		7,850
Expenses		
Wages	2,400	
Depreciation: fixtures and fittings (20% × £22,500 × 1/12)	375	
Bank interest (£40,000 × 12% × 1/12)	400	
Stationery	320	
General expenses	500	
Rent (£9,000 × 1/6)	1,500	
Insurance (£480 × 1/12)	40	
		(5,535)
Net profit		2,315

ANSWERS TO PRACTICE CENTRAL ASSESSMENT 5: ELECTRONICS WORLD

SECTION 1

Task 1

	Debit	*Credit*
	£	£
Entries from purchases day book		
Purchases	20,400	
VAT	3,570	
Creditors control account		23,970
Entries from sales day book		
Debtors control account	35,955	
VAT		5,355
Sales		30,600
Entries from sales returns day book		
Sales returns	1,200	
VAT	210	
Debtors control account		1,410
Cheques issued		
Creditors control account	5,000	
Bank		5,000

Task 2

See extended trial balance on Page 389 .

Task 3

For entries on the extended trial balance: see Page 389.

(a) *Depreciation*

Motor vehicles: £22,400 × 20% = £4,480

Fixtures and fittings: £(140,000 – £6,000 – £65,000) × 10% = £6,900

Total deprecation = £11,380

(b) *Interest*

Interest due = £150,000 × 6% × 6/12 = £4,500

Bank interest owing = £4,500 – £3,750 = £750

(c) *General expenses*

Prepaid £2,400 × 4/6 = £1,600

(d) *Stock*

Valued at cost = £198,650

Insurance proceeds:

DEBIT	Regis Insurance	£420	
CREDIT	Purchases		£420

(e) *Insurance*

DEBIT	Insurance	£60
CREDIT	Bank	£60

(f) *Provision for bad debts*

	£
Existing provision	6,000
Provision required (£272,400 × 5%)	13,620
Additional provision	7,620

ELECTRONICS WORLD	Trial balance		Adjustments	
Account	Debit	Credit	Debit	Credit
	£	£	£	£
Share capital		600,000		
Premises	360,000			
Fixtures & fittings at cost	140,000			
Fixtures & fittings (prov for depreciation)		65,000		6,900
Purchases (972,140 + 20,400)	992,540			420
Sales (1,530,630 + 30,600)		1,561,230		
Salaries	206,420			
Sales returns (23,200 + 1,200)	24,400			
Purchases returns		17,350		
General expenses	74,322			1,600
Insurance	16,390		60	
Bad debts	7,506			
Provision for bad debts		6,000		7,620
Debtors control account (£237,855 + £35,955 - £1,410)	272,400			
Creditors control account (£121,433 + £23,970 - £5,000)		140,403		
Stock at 1 June 1996	188,960			
Bank (65,200 + 5,000)	60,200			60
Bank deposit account	150,000			
Bank interest received		3,750		750
Motor vehicles (cost)	22,400			
Motor vehicles (prov for depreciation)		3,800		4,480
VAT: Credit balance (24,720 - 3,570 + 5,355 - 210)		26,295		
Profit and loss		91,710		
Depreciation			11,380	
Regis Insurance			420	
Closing stock (P&L)				198,650
Closing stock (B/S)			198,650	
Provision for bad debts (adjustment)			7,620	
Bank interest owing			750	
Prepayments			1,600	
Subtotal	2,515,538	2,515,538	220,480	220,480
Profit for the year				
TOTAL	2,515,538	2,515,538	220,480	220,480

SECTION 2

1

		£
	Total from listing of balances	274,189
(a)	Add error in customer balance (£484 – £448)	36
(b)	Subtract customer balance listed twice	(1,490)
(c)	Subtract discount misposting × 2	(200)
(d)	Subtract goods returned	(135)
		272,400

2 (a) Profit would decrease under LIFO.

   (b) The consistency concept would prevent the basis for valuation of stock being changed.

3 (a) No.

   (b) The cost of the asset shown in the balance sheet should be the full cost of bringing the asset to its present location and condition. SSAP 12 *Accounting for depreciation* requires this treatment, so that self-built assets of this nature are treated in the same way as finished assets purchased. If the company had brought a competed office building, the labour cost would be taken into account in the purchase price asked.

4 Trial balance.

5

MEMORANDUM

To: Jackie Brown   Ref: VAT
From: Accounting Technician   Date: XX/XX/XX

You have raised two queries regarding the VAT which began to appear on invoices from Arun Divan Ltd just recently.

(a) Although Electronics World Ltd pays more money to Arun Divan for the CD racks, profit is not affected because Electronics World Ltd can claim the VAT back from HM Customs & Excise on its next VAT return. The money will therefore be recouped either by a refund of VAT or a reduction in the VAT owed. The purchase is recorded net of VAT, so that VAT is not charged against profit.

(b) This statement is true, for the same reasons given above. It is, in effect, the other side of the same coin as in (a).

You can see from this that, as far as VAT is concerned, the only person or body who pays VAT is the final consumer (not registered for VAT) and the only person or body who gains from VAT is HM Customs & Excise (ie the government). The profitability of a company may be affected, but only to the extent that, for a final consumer, goods which have no VAT charged on them (or which are zero-rated) will be cheaper (and so more attractive) than goods with VAT charged on them.

I hope that this has cleared up your misunderstanding.

SECTION 3

Task 1

Total sales: year ended 30 April 1997

	£
Private bank account	
Balance b/f	-
Drawings (£200 × 12)	2,400
Balance c/f	600
Cheques from Electronics World	3,000

ELECTRONICS WORLD LTD

	£		£
Balance b/f	-	Cash received (business a/c)	17,600
Sales (bal fig)	25,000	Cash received (private a/c)	3,000
		Balance c/f	4,400
	25,000		25,000

Task 2

Selling price for 1 pair speaker stands

500 pairs sold for £25,000

$$\therefore \text{ Price per pair paid} = \frac{£25,000}{500} = £50$$

Task 3

Cost of materials for 1 pair speaker stands

$$\text{Cost per pair} = \frac{£50}{2} = £25$$

Task 4

Cost of goods sold

Total = £25.00 × 500 = £12,500

Task 5

Purchases

JOHNSON MATERIALS LTD

	£		£
Cash paid	12,000	Balance b/f	-
Balance c/f	1,500	Purchases (bal fig)	13,500
	13,500		13,500

Task 6

Closing stock at 30 April 1997 = 120 × £25 = £3,000

To find opening stock at 30 April 1996:

	£
Opening stock (balancing figure)	2,000
Purchases (Task 5)	13,500
Less: closing stock at 30 April 1997	(3,000)
Cost of goods sold (Task 4)	12,500

Task 7

Capital invested on 30 April 1996

	£	£
Assets		
Tools and equipment	3,000	
Less depreciation (£3,000 × 20% × $^9/_{12}$)	(450)	
		2,550
Van	4,800	
Less depreciation (£4,800 × 10% × $^6/_{12}$)	(240)	
		4,560
Stock		2,000
Bank		4,250
		13,360
Rent owed		(100)
Capital		13,260

Task 8

Rent to 30 April 1997

	£
1 May 1996 - 31 October 1996 (£100 × 6)	600
1 November 1996 - 30 April 1997 (£120 × 6)	720
Rent for year	1,320

ANSWERS TO PRACTICE CENTRAL ASSESSMENT 6: DREW INSTALLATIONS

SECTION 1

Task 1

DREW INSTALLATIONS	Trial balance		Adjustments	
Account	Debit	Credit	Debit	Credit
	£	£	£	£
Purchases	339,500			
Sales		693,000		
Purchases returns		6,320		
Sales returns	1,780			
Carriage inwards	8,250			
Salaries and wages	106,200			
Bad debts	4,890			
Provision for bad debts		4,500	756	
Debtors control account	46,800			
Creditors control account		28,760		
Stock at 1 November 1996	113,450			
Motor vehicles expenses	5,780			260
Motor vehicles (cost)	86,000			
Motor vehicles (prov for depreciation)		12,800		16,000
Equipment (cost)	24,500			
Equipment (prov for depreciation)		6,700		1,780
Rent	58,000		2,000	
Drawings	32,900		260	
Insurance	5,720			1,800
Bank	8,580			
Bank loan account		50,000		
Bank interest paid	2,400		2,000	
VAT (credit balance)		12,400		
Capital		32,750		
Suspense account	2,480			
Depreciation			17,780	
Closing stock (P&L)				106,800
Closing stock (B/S)			106,800	
Provision for bad debts (adjustment)				756
Loan interest owing				2,000
Prepayments / Accruals			1,800	2,000
Subtotal	847,230	847,230	131,396	131,396
Profit for the year				
TOTAL	847,230	847,230	131,396	131,396

Task 2

	Dr £	Cr £
Suspense	200	
VAT		200
Motor Vehicle expenses	40	
Motor Vehicles		40
Sales returns	160	
Purchases returns	160	
Suspense		320
Suspense	90	
Purchases		90
Creditors control account	2,450	
Suspense		2,450

SECTION 2

1   £6,000

2   (a)   Dr   Purchases   £470
              Cr   Cash   £470

    (b)   Dr   Cash   £470
              Cr   Sales   £400
              Cr   VAT   £70

3   £10,000

4   (a)   No

    (b)   The trial balance only detects errors where the debit entry(ies) for a transaction are not the same as the credit entry(ies). In this case £5,514 would have been debited to the debtors control account, £4,800 credited to sales and £714 credited to VAT. Since the value of the debit is the same as the total value of the credits, the error would not have been detected.

5

> **MEMORANDUM**
>
> To: Colin Drew   Ref: Closing stock valuation
> From: Date:
>
> I refer to your recent note concerning the valuation of the closing stock. The suggestion you have made to include stock at selling price would increase the gross profit since the effect would be to include the profit from the stock of deluxe bathroom suites in this year's accounts rather than in the accounts for the period when the suites are sold. However, I do need to draw to your attention the requirements of SSAP 2 and SSAP 9. The prudence concept, which is covered in SSAP 2, states that profits should not be anticipated and should only be recognised once they are realised. This would take place when the suites are sold. SSAP 9 reinforces the point by stating that the value of stock should be taken at the lower of cost and net realisable value. Both standards therefore reject the idea of valuing stock at selling price and we are not therefore able to proceed on that basis.
>
> I hope this fully covers the issue raised in your note.

SECTION 3

Task 1

	£
Opening stock	30,400
Purchases (120,750 + 16,850 – 15,600)	122,000
	152,400
Closing stock	32,700
Cost of goods sold	119,700

Task 2

Gross profit	£119,700

Task 3

	£
Cost of goods sold	119,700
Gross profit	119,700
Sales	239,400

Task 4

	£
Sales	239,400
Add opening debtors	22,800
	262,200
Less closing debtors	21,700
Receipts from debtors	240,500

Task 5

Bank

	£		£
Debtors	240,500	Balance b/d	4,300
		Creditors	120,750
		Expenses	52,800
		Equipment	4,500
		Drawings	42,300
		Balance c/d	15,850
	240,500		240,500

Task 6

		£
Gross profit		119,700
Less		
Expenses (52,800 – 1,000 – 1,500)	50,300	
Depreciation Motor Vehicles	1,750	
Depreciation Equipment	661	
		52,711
Net profit		66,989

ANSWERS TO PRACTICE CENTRAL ASSESSMENT 7: FAIR SOUNDS (JUNE 1998)

Tasks 1 and 2

Extended trial balance at 30 April 1998

DESCRIPTION	Ledger balance Debit £	Ledger balance Credit £	Adjustments Debit £	Adjustments Credit £	Profit and Loss a/c Debit £	Profit and Loss a/c Credit £	Balance Sheet Debit £	Balance Sheet Credit £
Purchases	127,680				127,680			
Sales		184,784				184,784		
Purchases returns		360				360		
Sales returns	502				502			
Stock at 1 May 1997	40,650				40,650			
Salaries	22,590				22,590			
General expenses	14,580				14,580			
Insurance	270		90		360			
Motor vehicle (MV) at cost	9,600						9,600	
Provision for depreciation (MV)		4,685		983				5,668
Equipment (EQ) at cost	17,100						17,100	
Provision for depreciation (EQ)		5,130		1,710				6,840
Bad debt	2,025		1,800		3,825			
Provision for doubtful debts		1,485		15				1,470
Debtors control account	31,200			1,800			29,400	
Creditors control account		25,232						25,232
Drawings	17,892						17,892	
Capital		82,493						82,493
Bank overdraft		261						261
Cash	426						426	
VAT		1,685						1,685
Bank interest received		900		600		1,500		
Bank deposit account	22,500						22,500	
Depreciation			2,693		2,693			
Closing stock - P&L				43,690		43,690		
Closing stock - balance sheet			43,690				43,690	
Bank interest owing			600				600	
Provision for doubtful debts - adjustment				15		15		
Other accruals				90				90
Profit					17,469			17,469
	307,015	307,015	48,888	48,888	230,349	230,349	141,208	141,208

Task 3

JOURNAL		
Details	DR £	CR £
Sales returns	96	
Purchases returns		96
Cleaning materials or general expenses	28	
VAT account		28

SECTION 2

Task 1

(a) A profit of £468

			£	£
(b)	Dr	Disposal Account	9,600	
	Cr	Motor Vehicle Cost Account		9,600
	Dr	Provision for Depreciation (MV) Account	5,668	
	Cr	Disposal Account		5,668
	Dr	Bank Account	4,400	
	Cr	Disposal Account		4,400
	Dr	Disposal Account	468	
	Cr	Profit and Loss Account		468

Task 2

(a) In the balance sheet

(b) Drawings are a balance sheet figure as Caroline Fairley is not an employee of the business. The figure represents the amount she has withdrawn from the business. It cannot be treated as salary.

Task 3

Decreased, as the amount should have been debited to discounts allowed.

Task 4

(a) To HM Customs and Excise

(b) This balance is the excess of VAT payable on Fair Sound's sales over the VAT reclaimable on purchases and other inputs.

Task 5

MEMORANDUM

To: Caroline Fairley
From: Accounting Technician
Ref: XXXX
Date: 15 June 1998

Thank you for your note regarding the amounts charged to expenses for this years accounts, in particular the amount of £90 for insurance. This amount relates to the years accounts as the insurance covered this period.

Under SSAP 2 the expenses relating to the accounting period should be matching to the relevant sales. This is known as the matching concept.

As you correctly state, the profit for the year will be reduced by £90, but this is the correct accounting treatment.

SECTION 3

Task 1

	£
Bank receipts	126,790
Debtors at 31/12/97	290
Debtors at 31/12/96	(630)
	126,450

Task 2

	£
Bank payments	83,410
Creditors at 31/12/97	7,400
Creditors at 31/12/96	(4,750)
Purchases	86,060

Task 3

	£
Sales (from Task 1)	126,450
Gross profit (30%)	(37,935)
Cost of sales	88,515

Task 4

	£
Opening stock	15,750
Purchases (from Task 2)	86,060
Goods for own use	(270)
	101,540
Cost of sales (from Task 3)	(88,515)
Closing stock	13,025

Task 5

	£
General expenses - from bank	16,060
Accrual – electricity	260
Accrual – insurance (1/12 × £600)	50
Prepayment for insurance	495
	16,865

Task 6

	£	£
Gross profit (from Task 3)		37,935
General expenses (from Task 5)	16,865	
Salaries	5,110	
Dep'n - F&F	1,750	
MV	3,125	
		(26,850)
Net profit		11,085

ANSWERS TO PRACTICE CENTRAL ASSESSMENT 8: TULIPS

SECTION 1

Task 1

JOURNAL		
Details	DR £	CR £
Drawings account	1,000	
Wages		1,000
Creditors' control account	280	
Debtors' control account		280
VAT account	98	
Suspense account		98
Creditors' control account	1,128	
Suspense account		1,128
Suspense account	1,500	
Disposal account		1,500
Disposal account	2,500	
Greenhouse cost account		2,500
Greenhouse depreciation account	750	
Disposal account		750
Loss on disposal	250	
Disposal account		250

Tasks 2 and 3

DESCRIPTION	LEDGER BALANCES		ADJUSTMENTS	
	Dr	Cr	Dr	Cr
	£	£	£	£
Sales		313,746		
Sales returns	971			
Purchases	186,574			
Purchases returns		714		
Stock at 1 December 1997	25,732			
Wages	39,000			
Rent and rates	18,608		3,000	
Light and heat	11,940			
Office expenses	9,530			
Greenhouse running expenses	11,290			
Motor expenses	4,782			
Sundry expenses	5,248			
Motor vehicle (MV) at cost	25,810			
Provision for depreciation MV		5,162		5,162
Greenhouses (GH) at cost	23,000			
Provision for depreciation GH		6,900		2,300
Cash	100			
Bank current account	3,020			
Bank loan		30,000		
Debtors' control account	6,580			
Creditors' control account		3,312		
Capital account		21,112		
Drawings account	12,000			
VAT account		3,489		
Suspense account	-	-		
Profit or loss on disposal of fixed asset	250			
Depreciation			7,462	
Provision for doubtful debts - P&L			329	
Provision for doubtful debts - balance sheet				329
Closing stock - P&L				24,895
Closing stock - balance sheet			24,895	
Accrual				3,000
	384,435	384,435	35,686	35,686

SECTION 2

Task 1

(a) It is an acceptable accounting practice

(b) The materiality concept prevails in this case. The watering cans are few in number and low in value. It would not be appropriate to show assets of such low value on the balance sheet.

Task 2

(a) It would be understated
(b) It would be overstated

Task 3

(a) 60 bushes @ £11 each = £660

(b) 20 bushes @ £6.5 = £130

   30 bushes @ £6 = £180

   Total closing stock = £310

(c) 40 bushes @ £6 = £240

   20 bushes @ £6.5 = £130

   Cost of sales = £240 + £130 = £370

   Or alternatively:

   Opening stock = 40 bushes @ £6.5 = £260

   Purchases =   40 bushes @ £6.5 = £260

                     30 bushes @ £6 = £180

   Closing stock = see (b) above = £310

   Cost of sales = 240 + 260 + 180 – 310 = £370

Task 4

MEMORANDUM

To: Donald Johnson
From: Accounting Technician
Ref: Sale or Return Basis
Date: 30 November 1998

Thank you for your recent query regarding the sale or return based contract you are considering.

This contract would mean that the goods you supplied to the shop would continue to be Tulip's stocks until they were sold to a third party. When the sale was made stocks would be reduced accordingly If stocks are returned by the shops then no transaction is made. If you enter into the contract then accurate records of the transactions will need to be made. You need to ensure that the shops records are adequate and that you can rely on them to keep you up to date on sales and stock amounts.

SECTION 3

Task 1

	£
Opening stock	1,800
Payments : bank	18,450
: cash	3,800
Creditors	1,400
Total purchases	25,450

Task 2

	£
Purchases (from Task 1)	25,450
Closing stock	(2,200)
Total cost of sales	23,250

Task 3

	£
Cost of sales (from Task 2)	23,250
Total sales (x2)	46,500

Task 4

	£	£
Sales (from Task 3)		46,500
Payments Materials	3,800	
General expenses	490	
Bank account	27,000	
Drawings (bal fig)	15,110	
		(46,400)
Float		100

Task 5

	£
Bank account	6,200
Cash account (From Task 4)	15,110
Total drawings	21,310

Task 6

	£	£
Sales (From Task 3)		46,500
Cost of sales (From Task 2)		(23,250)
Gross profit		23,250
General expenses (870 + 490)	1,360	
Depreciation (4,000 × 20%)	800	
		(2,160)
Net profit		21,090

ANSWERS TO PRACTICE CENTRAL ASSESSMENT 9: PINE WAREHOUSE

SECTION 1

Task 1

DESCRIPTION	LEDGER BALANCES		ADJUSTMENTS	
	Dr	Cr	Dr	Cr
	£	£	£	£
Sales		1,240,600		
Purchases	826,400		1,800	
Debtors' control account	93,340			
Creditors' control account		70,870		2,115
Bad debts	8,750			
Provision for bad debts		4,010		657
Motor vehicles (MV) at cost	80,500			
Provision for depreciation (MV)		15,760		16,100
Machinery (Mach) at cost	24,000			
Provision for depreciation (Mach)		2,000		1,900
Equipment (Equip) at cost	27,400			
Provision for depreciation (Equip)		5,850		2,155
Drawings	33,000		3,000	
Cash	3,000			
Bank		12,500		3,000
Lighting and heating	3,250			
Insurance	1,020			
Advertising	10,620			2,400
VAT (credit balance)		13,600	315	
Stock at 1 December 1997	125,560			
Motor expenses	8,670			
Discounts allowed	4,200			
Discounts received		1,200		
Salaries and wages	120,650			
Rent	24,600		4,920	
Capital		32,030		
Suspense	3,460			
Prepayments			2,400	
Depreciation			20,155	
Closing stock - P&L				132,800
Closing stock - balance sheet			132,800	
Provision for bad debts - adjustment			657	
Accrued expenses				4,920
	1,398,420	1,398,420	166,047	166,047

Task 2

JOURNAL

Details	DR £	CR £
Debtors' control account	630	
Suspense		630
Suspense	500	
VAT		500
Sales	4,450	
Suspense		4,450
Suspense	1,200	
Debtors' control account		1,200
Discounts allowed	40	
Discounts received	40	
Suspense		80

Proof

Suspense account balance	3460
Add (500+1200)	1700
Less (630+4450+ 80)	5160
Balance	NIL

SECTION 2

Task 1

	£
Total from listing of balances	76,670
Adjustment for (a) add	235
Adjustment for (b) subtract	(3,200)
Adjustment for (c) subtract	(720)
Revised total to agree with creditors' control account	72,985

Task 2

(a) No

(b) The sales ledger is a memorandum account and so the balance is not used in preparing the trial balance. The trial balance is prepared from the general ledger which, as stated, has the correct entry for the credit sale.

Task 3

	£
Purchase price of vehicle	10,000
Depreciation on vehicle	(2,000)
Net book value	8,000
Profit on disposal of vehicle	500
Value against new vehicle	8,500
Cheque payment	3,000
Purchase price of new vehicle	11,500

Task 4

(a) The subscriptions figure for income and expenditure - 420 members @ £240 each = £100,800.

(b)

	£
Subscriptions received (420-6) members @ £240	99,360
Plus 8 pre-paid members @£250	2,000
Total receipts	101,360

Task 5

MEMORANDUM

To: Pat Hall
From: Accounting Technician
Ref: Closing stock valuation
Date: 30 November 1998

I am writing regarding the pine furniture which was sold in the year but is not to be delivered until 22 December 1998. Although the furniture is still present in your stocks it should not be included in the year end figures. It has been sold and is therefore the property of the customer, this is reflected in both the sales figure and the cost of sales figure.

If you were to include the furniture in the closing stocks this would reduce the cost of sales figure and therefore not match the cost of the furniture against the sales figure.

Please contact me if you would like to discuss this matter further.

SECTION 3

Task 1

	£
Opening stock : raw materials	4,300
Purchases : raw materials	95,600
	99,900
Closing stock: raw materials	(9,400)
Raw materials used	90,500
Wages: furniture production	38,000
Prime cost	128,500

Task 2

	£
Prime cost (from Task 1)	128,500
Wages: factory supervisory	28,000
Factory overheads	12,500
Depreciation: factory premises	1,600
Depreciation: factory machinery	2,000
Production cost	172,600

Task 3

	£
Receipts from debtors	294,700
Less debtors at 1 December 1997	(22,200)
	272,500
Add debtors at 30 November 1998	24,500
Total sales	297,000

Task 4

	£	£
Sales (from Task 3)		297,000
Less cost of goods sold:		
Opening stock finished goods	10,360	
Add production cost of finished goods (from Task 3)	172,600	
	182,960	
Closing stock of finished goods	(12,510)	
		(170,450)
Gross profit		126,550

Task 5

	£
Purchases	95,600
Add creditors at 1 December 1997	12,100
	107,700
Less creditors at 30 November 1998	(13,300)
Payments to creditors	94,400

Bank

	£		£
Debtors	294,700	Balance b/d	3,600
		Creditors	94,400
		Production wages	38,000
		Supervisory wages	28,000
		Office wages	16,000
		Factory overheads	12,500
		Office expenses	8,300
		Balance c/d	93,900
	294,700		294,700

ANSWERS TO PRACTICE CENTRAL ASSESSMENT 10: AUTOMANIA

SECTION 1

Task 1

See trial balance on page 412.

Workings

(a)	Rent:	$(3 \times £1,500) + (9 \times £1,600)$	= £18,900
		£18,900 less £17,300	= £1,600 accrual

(b)	Insurance:	£100 prepayment	

(c)	Depreciation MV:	£60,800 @20%	= £12,160
	FF:	$(£40,380 - £21,600)$ @10%	= £1,878

(d)	Provision for bad debts:	£56,850 @2%	=£1,137
		Existing provision	£1,050
		New provision	£1,137
		Adjustment	£87

		£	£
(e)	Stock:		
	Valued @	119,360	
	Old stock cost	(3,660)	
	NRV of old stock	2,060	
	Car door cost	(60)	
		117,700	

		£	£
(f)	Credit Note:		
	Dr Creditors control	235	
	Cr Purchase returns		200
	Cr VAT		35

Extended Trial Balance at 30th April 1999

DESCRIPTION	Ledger balances		Adjustments	
	Dr	Cr	Dr	Cr
	£	£	£	£
Capital		135,000		
Drawings	42,150			
Rent	17,300		1,600	
Purchases	606,600			
Sales		857,300		
Sales returns	2,400			
Purchases returns		1,260		200
Salaries and wages	136,970			
Motor vehicles (M.V.)at cost	60,800			
Provision for depreciation (M.V)		16,740		12,160
Fixtures and fittings (F&F) at cost	40,380			
Provision for depreciation (F&F)		21,600		1,878
Bank		3,170		
Cash	2,100			
Lighting and heating	4,700			
VAT		9,200		35
Stock at 1 May 1998	116,100			
Bad debts	1,410			
Provision for bad debts		1,050		87
Debtors control account	56,850			
Creditors control account		50,550	235	
Sundry expenses	6,810			
Insurance	1,300			100
Accruals				1,600
Prepayments			100	
Depreciation			14,038	
Provision for bad debts - Adjustment			87	
Closing stock - P&L				117,700
Closing stock - Balance sheet			117,700	
Totals	1,095,870	1,095,870	133,760	133,760

Task 2

	£
Cash book: opening balance as at 17 May 1999	7,900
Unpresented cheques	
No 704182	290
704183	200
704184	310 800
Bank balance as at 17 May 1999	8,700

Task 3

BANK ACCOUNT

	£		£
BACS credit	125	Balance b/d	2,135
		Bank charges	140
		Standing order	1,600
Balance c/d	3,950	Cash withdrawal	200
	4,075		4,075

Task 4

		£
Cash book balance as at 28 May 1999		(3,950)
Unpresented cheques		
No 704189	395	
704190	1,880	
704191	4,200	
		6,475
Uncleared lodgements		
Halliwells	685	
Reece Motors	470	(1,155)
Bank balance as at 28 May 1999		1,370

SECTION 2

Task 1

(a)   Overstated (by the £70 VAT)

(b)   Unaffected (£470 of cash **was** received)

(c)   Dr Sales   £70

      Cr VAT   £70

Task 2

Cheques should not be issued if they are not going to be honoured by the bank. The supplier will rightly be concerned by this. The supplier will also think twice about delivering any more goods to Automania until it is satisfied that there are no further cashflow problems.

Sam Bell should not have given this confidential and potentially damaging information out to the supplier without the permission of a senior member of staff.

Task 3

DISPOSALS ACCOUNT

	£		£
Vehicle at cost	12,000	Accumulated depreciation (W1)	3,800
		Part exchange value	10,000
Profit on disposal	1,800	(15,000 – 5,000)	
	13,800		13,800

W1

Vehicle held for 19 months.

Depreciation is $12,000 @ 20\% \times 1\,^7/_{12} = 3,800$

Task 4

£500 Debit. The drawings account should have been **debited** by £500.

Task 5

	£
Direct labour	26,000
Direct materials	14,000
	40,000
Production overheads	20,000
	60,000
Less closing stocks	(2,000)
Production cost of goods completed	58,000

MEMORANDUM

To: Ananda Carver   Ref: Machinery
From: Accounting Technician   Date: 14 June 1999

I read your note regarding the machinery required for car seat cover manufacturing and my comments are as follows.

All accounting transactions are subject to the rules of double entry. This means that the cash paid for the machinery is only one side of the entry. The other is to debit fixed assets with the machinery's value.

Under FRS 15 (previously SSAP 12) all fixed assets (except land) must be depreciated.

Depreciation reflects the wearing out or consumption of the asset over its useful life. This reflects the concept of matching, as laid out in SSAP 2.

Your alternative suggestion is not allowed under FRS 15. If we were to implement it, it is likely we would have to write the cost of the asset off in the year of purchase. This would affect this year's profit by the cost of the asset.

Hopefully the car seat cover project will be profitable enough to more than offset the effects of the yearly depreciation charge.

SECTION 3

Task 1

Assets

	£
NBV of Clubhouse (24,000 – 7,200)	16,800
Stocks	120
Cash at bank	1,200
	18,120

Liabilities

Creditors	860	
Subscriptions in advance	400	
		(1,260)
Accumulated fund @1 January 1998		16,860

Task 2

	£
Subscriptions in advance @1 January 1998	400
Subscriptions	30,000
Subscriptions in advance @31 December 1998	(550)
Subscriptions for the year	29,850

Task 3

	£
Amount paid for refurbishments	10,600
Opening creditors	(860)
Closing creditors	780
Purchases	10,520

Task 4

	£	£
Sales of refreshments		15,260
Opening stocks	120	
Purchases (from Task 3)	10,520	
	10,640	
Closing stocks	(230)	
		(10,410)
Gross profit		4,850
Expenses		
Wages (15% of 28,000)	4,200	
Electricity (2% of 1,780)	356	
		(4,556)
Net Profit		294

Task 5

		£
Income		
Subscriptions (from **Task 2**)		29,850
Donations		500
Profit on refreshments		294
		30,644
Expenditure		
Wages (85% of 28,000)	23,800	
Electricity (80% of 1,780)	1,424	
Sundry expenses	1,820	
Repairs to tennis court	800	
Rent of land	3,400	
Depreciation of clubhouse ([24,000+6,400]@5%)	1,520	
Loan interest ([6,000@10%]×$^6/_{12}$)	300	
		33,064
Deficit for the year		2,420

Answers to Trial Run Central Assessment

ANSWERS TO TRIAL RUN CENTRAL ASSESSMENT

SECTION 1: PART A

Task 1

Extended Trial Balance at 30th November 1999

DESCRIPTION	Dr £	Cr £
Capital		134,230
Purchases	695,640	
Sales		836,320
Stock at 1 December 1998	84,300	
Rent paid	36,000	
Salaries	37,860	
Motor vehicles (M.V.)at cost	32,400	
Provision for depreciation (M.V)		8,730
Fixtures and fittings (F&F) at cost	50,610	
Provision for depreciation (F&F)		12,340
Purchase returns		10,780
Sales returns	5,270	
Drawings	55,910	
Insurance	4,760	
Debtors control account	73,450	
Creditors control account		56,590
Bad debts	3,670	
Provision for doubtful debts		3,060
Bank overdraft		10,800
Cash	1,980	
VAT (credit balance)		5,410
Discounts allowed	6,770	
Discounts received		4,380
Suspense account		5,980
Totals	1,088,620	1,088,620

Task 2

JOURNAL		
Details	DR £	CR £
a) Drawings account	400	
Salaries		400
b) Suspense	100	
Sales		100
c) Suspense	60	
VAT		60
d) Creditor control account	120	
Suspense		120
e) Suspense	6,000	
Bank		6,000
f) Creditors control account	10	
Suspense		10
g) Discounts received	40	
Suspense		40
h) Insurance	10	
Suspense		10

Task 3

	£
Total from list of balances	76,780
Adjustment for a): add	400
Adjustment for b): less	(100)
Adjustment for c): less	(2,410)
Adjustment for d): add	90
Adjustment for e): less	(540)
Adjustment for f): less	(770)
Revised total to agree with debtors control account	73,450

PART B

Task 4

	£
Depreciation for vehicle sold 1 March 1999 ($^3/_{12} \times [18,000\ @20\%]$)	900
Depreciation for vehicle purchased 1 June 1999 ($^6/_{12} \times [10,000\ @20\%]$)	1,000
Depreciation for vehicle purchased 1 September 1999 ($^3/_{12} \times [12,000\ @20\%]$)	600
Depreciation for other vehicles owned during the year ([28,400 – 18,000] @20%)	2,080
	4,580

Task 5

(a)   £247,000 – 231,000 = £16,000 profit

(b)		£
	Capital b/f	164,230
	Profit for the year	16,000
	Drawings	(46,000)
	Capital balance as at November 1998	134,230

Task 6

(a)	Leased	
	3 months @£500	£1,500

(b)	Purchased	£
	Loss in use (£8,000 – 7,000)	1,000
	Interest on the overdraft ($8,000 \times 12\% \times {}^3/_{12}$)	240
		1,240

Task 7

a) $\dfrac{£240,000}{£200} = 1200$ members

	£
b) Cash received	230,000
Less prepayments	(10,000)
	220,000
Subscriptions for the year	240,000
Prepaid as at 31 December 1998	20,000

$\dfrac{20,000}{200} = 100$ members prepaid during 1998.

Task 8

MEMORANDUM				
To:	Phil Townsend		Ref:	Valuation of stock
From:	Accounting Technician		Date:	29 November 1999

The stock of ten Mica40z PCs is currently valued at £5,000 (10 × £500). This is valuation at cost.

Before we can sell, we would incur £100 of cost per machine and only be able to sell at £580. The net realisable value (NRV) is therefore £480 (£580 - £100).

Per SSAP 9, we must value stocks at the lower of cost and NRV.

This would be £4,800 (10 × £480).

If the Mica 40z PCs are to be scrapped or given away then we must write them off. We can only value them at cost if we will sell them for more than cost. If we cannot sell them at all then they have a NRV of zero. This is the prudence concept as laid out in SSAP 2.

SECTION 2

Task 1

	£
Money placed in new business bank account (50,000 – 40,000)	10,000
New machinery and equipment purchases	72,500
	———
Capital invested by Phil Townsend on 1 January 2000	82,500

Task 2

	£
Raw materials	180,000
Closing stock of raw materials	(15,600)
	164,400
Production wages	41,750
Prime cost	206,150

Task 3

	£
Prime cost (from **Task 2**)	206,150
Production supervisors' wages	22,000
Other production overheads	15,170
Depreciation of machinery and equipment (72,500 @10%)	7,250
	250,570
Less stock of work in progress	(10,170)
Total production cost of finished goods	240,400

Task 4

		£
Sales (220,000 @120%: see COS)		264,000
Cost of sales		
Opening stock	-	
Production cost of finished goods (from **Task 3**)	240,400	
Closing stock	(20,400)	
		(220,000)
Gross profit		44,000
Expenses		
Selling and distribution	38,800	
Loan interest (40,000 @8%)	3,200	
		(42,000)
Net profit		2,000

Task 5

	£	£
Opening balance (40,000 + 10,000)		50,000
Payments		
Raw materials	180,000	
Less creditors (180,000 × $^1/_{12}$)	(15,000)	
Production wages	41,750	
Production supervisor	22,000	
Production overheads	15,170	
Selling and distribution	38,800	
Interest on loan	3,200	
		(285,920)
Receipts		
Sales (from **Task 4**)	264,000	
Less debtors (264,000 × $^1/_{12}$)	(22,000)	
		242,000
Closing balance as at 31 December 2000		6,080

ANSWERS TO SAMPLE CENTRAL ASSESSMENT

ANSWERS TO THE SAMPLE CENTRAL ASSESSMENT

SECTION 1

Task 1

Extended Trial Balance at 30 April 1998

CREATIVE CATERING	Trial balance		Adjustments	
Account	Debit	Credit	Debit	Credit
	£	£	£	£
Sales		620,700		860
Purchases	410,650			
Purchases returns		390		
Salaries and wages	90,820			
Rent	16,300			1,300
Debtors control account	51,640			
Creditors control account		33,180		
Bad debts	6,650			
Provision for bad debts		3,100	518	
Motor vehicles (cost)	60,700			
Motor vehicles (prov for depreciation)		12,600		12,140
Equipment (cost)	24,200			
Equipment (prov for depreciation)		6,300		1,790
Drawings	28,500		5,000	
Cash	7,000			5,000
Bank	6,250			
Lighting and heating	2,100			
Insurance	760			
Advertising	3,470		2,750	
VAT (credit balance)		8,400		
Stock at 1 May 1997	5,660			
Motor expenses	4,680			
Bank deposit amount	20,000			
Bank interest received		700		700
Capital		54,010		
Polar Insurance Company			860	
Depreciation			13,930	
Closing stock (P&L)				5,340
Closing stock (B/S)			5,340	
Provision for bad debts (adjustment)				518
Deposit account interest owing			700	
Prepayments / Accruals			1,300	2,750
Subtotal	739,380	739,380	30,398	30,398
Profit for the year				
TOTAL	739,380	739,380	30,398	30,398

Task 2

	£	£
Balance at bank as per cash book (15 May)		5,800
Add unpresented cheques		
606842	120	
606843	440	
606844	260	
		820
		6,620
Less Credit already in cash book		320
Balance at bank as per bank statement		6,300

Task 3

Creative Catering
Bank Reconciliation as at 29 May 1998

	£	£
Balance at bank as per cash book		7,365
Add unpresented cheques		
606845	620	
606847	490	
606850	260	
606851	320	
606852	1,400	
		3,090
		10,455
Less Tennis Club credit not yet banked		1,810
Balance as per bank statement		8,645

SECTION 2

1

(a)

	£
Depreciation 6 months to 30 April 1996	1,236
Depreciation 12 months to 30 April 1997	2,472
Depreciation 12 months to 30 April 1998	2,472
Depreciation 1 month to 31 May 1998	206
Total depreciation	6,386
Book value (£12,360 – £6,386)	5,974

(b) Profit on disposal (£6,500 – £5,974)   526

2

	£
Subscriptions received	98,000
Less owing from previous year	1,500
	96,500
Less prepaid for following year	2,500
	94,000
Income for year - 380 members at £250 each	95,000
Owing	1,000

£1,000/£250 = 4 members have not paid

3

(a)

			£
Dr	Debtors control account		329
Cr	Sales		280
Cr	VAT		49
(b)	Dr	Hospitality	329
	Cr	Creditors control account	329

4   When the equipment is acquired.

5   (a)   No.

     (b)   The debtors control account balance should, as a control, match the total of the balances in the sales ledger. Errors such as missing entries or entries for wrong amounts in the ledger will be detected. In this case the entry has been made for the correct amount in the ledger and the total of the balances will therefore be unaffected.

6

MEMORANDUM	
To: Jane Sutton	Ref: Closing stock valuation
From:	Date:

I refer to our recent conversation regarding the £500 invoice for soft drinks that had not been entered into the books of the business. I have considered the matter further and now conclude that the profits for the year ended 30 April 1998 would have been affected by this omission. Although the invoice was not entered into the purchases account, the drinks were included in the valuation of the closing stock. The cost of goods sold would therefore have been reduced by £500, inflating the gross profit by that amount. The current reported profit is thus incorrect, income from sales not having been matched against the correct cost of goods sold expenditure as required by the accruals concept. Please let me know if you require further information.

SECTION 3

1

	£
Opening stock of baking materials	1,000
Baking materials purchased	84,000
	85,000
Closing stock of baking materials	3,000
Baking materials used	82,000
Baking production wages	44,000
Prime cost	126,000

2

Prime cost	126,000
Baking supervisory wages	25,000
Baking overheads	22,000
Depreciation bakery premises	2,000
Depreciation bakery equipment	5,000
Production cost	180,000

BPP
PUBLISHING

3

Cost of goods to shop	60,000
Profit on sales (100% mark-up)	60,000
Cost of goods to caterers and retailers	120,000
Profit on sales (50% mark-up)	60,000
Total gross profit	120,000

4

Purchases	84,000
Add Creditors 1 January 1997	6,000
	90,000
Less Creditors 31 December 1997	7,000
Paid to creditors	83,000

5

Credit sales	180,000
Add Debtors at 1 January 1997	12,000
	192,000
Less Receipts from debtors	179,500
Debtors at 31 December 1997	12,500

ORDER FORM

Any books from our AAT range can be ordered by telephoning 020-8740-2211. Alternatively, send this page to our address below, fax it to us on 020-8740-1184, or email us at **publishing@bpp.com.** Or look us up on our website: www.bpp.com

We aim to deliver to all UK addresses inside 5 working days; a signature will be required. Order to all EU addresses should be delivered within 6 working days. All other orders to overseas addresses should be delivered within 8 working days.

To: BPP Publishing Ltd, Aldine House, Aldine Place, London W12 8AW

Tel: 020-8740 2211   **Fax: 020-8740 1184**   **Email: publishing@bpp.com**

Mr / Ms (full name): _____

Daytime delivery address: _____

_____

Postcode: _____   Daytime Tel: _____

Please send me the following quantities of books.

	5/00 Interactive Text	8/00 DA Kit	8/00 CA Kit
FOUNDATION			
Unit 1 Recording Income and Receipts (7/00 Text)	☐	☐	
Unit 2 Making and Recording Payments (7/00 Text)	☐	☐	
Unit 3 Ledger Balances and Initial Trial Balance (7/00 Text)	☐	☐	
Unit 4 Supplying information for Management Control (6/00 Text)	☐	☐	
Unit 20 Working with Information Technology (8/00 Text)	☐		
Unit 22/23 Achieving Personal Effectiveness (7/00) Text	☐		
INTERMEDIATE			
Unit 5 Financial Records and Accounts	☐	☐	
Unit 6 Cost Information	☐	☐	
Unit 7 Reports and Returns	☐		
Unit 21 Using Information Technology	☐		
Unit 22: see below			
TECHNICIAN			☐
Unit 8/9 Core Managing Costs and Allocating Resources	☐	☐	
Unit 10 Core Managing Accounting Systems	☐	☐	☐
Unit 11 Option Financial Statements (Accounting Practice)	☐		
Unit 12 Option Financial Statements (Central Government)	☐	☐	
Unit 15 Option Cash Management and Credit Control	☐		
Unit 16 Option Evaluating Activities	☐		
Unit 17 Option Implementing Auditing Procedures	☐		
Unit 18 Option Business Tax FA00(8/00 Text)	☐		
Unit 19 Option Personal Tax FA00(8/00 Text)	☐		
TECHNICIAN 1999			
Unit 17 Option Business Tax Computations FA99 (8/99 Text & Kit)	☐	☐	
Unit 18 Option Personal Tax Computations FA99 (8/99 Text & Kit)	☐	☐	

TOTAL BOOKS ☐ + ☐ + ☐ = ☐

@ £9.95 each = £ ☐

Postage and packaging:
UK: £2.00 for each book to maximum of £10
Europe (inc ROI and Channel Islands): £4.00 for first book, £2.00 for each extra
Rest of the World: £20.00 for first book, £10 for each extra

P & P £ ☐

► Unit 22 Maintaining a Healthy Workplace Interactive Text (postage free) ☐ @ £3.95 £ ☐

GRAND TOTAL £ ☐

I enclose a cheque for £ _____ **(cheques to BPP Publishing Ltd) or charge to Mastercard/Visa/Switch**

Card number ☐☐☐☐ ☐☐☐☐ ☐☐☐☐ ☐☐☐☐ ☐☐☐☐

Start date _____ Expiry date _____ Issue no. (Switch only)___

Signature _____

REVIEW FORM & FREE PRIZE DRAW

All original review forms from the entire BPP range, completed with genuine comments, will be entered into one of two draws on 31 January 2001 and 31 July 2001. The names on the first four forms picked out on each occasion will be sent a cheque for £50.

Name: _____ Address: _____

_____

_____

How have you used this Central Assessment Kit?
(Tick one box only)

☐ Home study (book only)

☐ On a course: college _____

☐ With 'correspondence' package

☐ Other _____

Why did you decide to purchase this Central Assessment Kit? *(Tick one box only)*

☐ Have used BPP Texts in the past

☐ Recommendation by friend/colleague

☐ Recommendation by a lecturer at college

☐ Saw advertising

☐ Other _____

During the past six months do you recall seeing/receiving any of the following?
(Tick as many boxes as are relevant)

☐ Our advertisement in *Accounting Technician* magazine

☐ Our advertisement in *Pass*

☐ Our brochure with a letter through the post

Which (if any) aspects of our advertising do you find useful?
(Tick as many boxes as are relevant)

☐ Prices and publication dates of new editions

☐ Information on Interactive Text content

☐ Facility to order books off-the-page

☐ None of the above

Have you used the companion Interactive Text for this subject?   ☐ Yes   ☐ No

Your ratings, comments and suggestions would be appreciated on the following areas

	Very useful	Useful	Not useful
Introductory section (How to use this Central Assessment Kit etc)	☐	☐	☐
Practice Questions	☐	☐	☐
Practice Devolved Assessments	☐	☐	☐
Trial Run Devolved Assessments	☐	☐	☐
AAT Sample Simulation	☐	☐	☐
Central Assessment Style Questions	☐	☐	☐
December 1999 Central Assessment	☐	☐	☐
Content of Answers	☐	☐	☐
Layout of pages	☐	☐	☐
Structure of book and ease of use	☐	☐	☐

	Excellent	Good	Adequate	Poor
Overall opinion of this Kit	☐	☐	☐	☐

Do you intend to continue using BPP Assessment Kits/Interactive Texts/? ☐ Yes ☐ No

Please note any further comments and suggestions/errors on the reverse of this page.

Please return to: Nick Weller, BPP Publishing Ltd, FREEPOST, London, W12 8BR

REVIEW FORM & FREE PRIZE DRAW (continued)

Please note any further comments and suggestions/errors below

FREE PRIZE DRAW RULES

1   Closing date for 31 January 2001 draw is 31 December 2000. Closing date for 31 July 2001 draw is 30 June 2001.

2   Restricted to entries with UK and Eire addresses only. BPP employees, their families and business associates are excluded.

3   No purchase necessary. Entry forms are available upon request from BPP Publishing. No more than one entry per title, per person. Draw restricted to persons aged 16 and over.

4   Winners will be notified by post and receive their cheques not later than 6 weeks after the relevant draw date.

5   The decision of the promoter in all matters is final and binding. No correspondence will be entered into.